POP MUSIC

AND

THE PRESS

Edited by

Steve Jones

Temple University Press

PHILADELPHIA

Temple University Press, Philadelphia 19122
Copyright © 2002 by Temple University, except
    Chapter 3 copyright © 2002 Jeff Chang
Published 2002
Printed in the United States of America

Lines from the song "Day of the Dead" (page 251) by Lester Bangs © 1980 by Lester
Bangs. Used by permission of the estate of Lester Bangs.

∞ The paper used in this publication meets the requirements of
the American National Standard for Information Sciences—Permanence
of Paper for Printed Library Materials, ANSI Z39.48-1984

Library of Congress Cataloging-in-Publication Data

Pop music and the press / edited by Steve Jones.
    p.   cm. — (Sound matters)
    Includes bibliographical references (p.) and index.
    ISBN 1-56639-965-3 (cloth : alk. paper) — ISBN 1-56639-966-1 (pbk. : alk. paper)
    1. Musical criticism. 2. Popular music—History and criticism. 3. Mass media
and music. 4. Popular culture—History—20th century. I. Jones, Steve, 1961–   .
II. Series.
ML3880 .P67 2002
781.64'09—dc21

                                                    2001050819

POP MUSIC

AND THE PRESS

University Campus Barnsley

Telephone: 01226 216 885

Catalogue: **https://webopac.barnsley.ac.uk/**

Class No: ....7.8.1..6.4...J̶o̶N̶...........

This book is to be returned on or before the last date stamped below. Thank you!

Sound Matters

a series edited by Michael Jarrett

For Joel Rutstein and Mel Eberle—

keep on freein' the rock world.

> Doesn't all that listening
> Give you anything?
> —"Puzzle Boy," Area (*Fragments of the Morning,* 1990)

Contents

Acknowledgments

There are several origins of this collection of essays, but a particularly important one is the central role music journalism has played in its editor's life. Another is the realization that despite the central role the music press continues to play for music fans and musicians, little systematic study of popular-music criticism exists. Yet another derives from several conversations in the early 1990s with John Pauly about the New Journalism. His notion that the New Journalism has become a "literary canon," removed from its evolution and history, resonated with my sense that popular-music criticism had been disconnected from its evolution and history. Moreover, its history seemed in many ways entwined with that of the New Journalism. The conversations with Pauly led to the publication of an essay in 1992, from which I have borrowed liberally for chapter 1 in this collection—"Re-Viewing Rock Writing: Recurring Themes in Pop Music Criticism" (*American Journalism,* winter/summer: 87–107). The essay itself derived in part from still earlier conversations with Kevin Featherly, formerly a student at the University of Wisconsin–Eau Claire and now a journalist. He and I found, while he was enrolled in a course I taught there, that we had a mutual love of Lester Bangs's writing, and Featherly participated under my guidance in an early research project collecting examples of criticism. Both Pauly's and Featherly's contributions are evident in this collection, sometimes in the very words, other times in the concepts, and always in spirit.

A still earlier thread in the origins of this collection can be found in work I began in the mid-1980s with the assistance of Bob Reid, professor of journalism, and Cliff Christians, professor of communication, at the University of Illinois at Urbana-Champaign (UIUC). For a master's reporting project I became interested in the ethics of arts reviewing, specifically those related to music criticism and its relationship to the music industry. The trajectory of that work led to publication of an article in 1993 that examined the sometimes symbiotic, often sycophantic, relationships between music critics, record labels, and music periodicals—"Pop Music, Criticism, Advertising, and the Music Industry" (*Journal of Popular Music Studies* 5: 79–91). But the real beginnings of that work can be traced to the fall of 1979, when Steve Winner, a resident of the same dorm floor as I, noticed that I owned many records. Steve asked if I would be interested in writing for the school paper, the *Daily Illini*. That he said I would be paid for my work did little to help me overcome my lack of self-confidence at writing. But the promise of free records was sufficient motivation to make me believe I could learn to do it. Of course, by then I had long been reading rock criticism and had found friends with whom I could express my opinions about music, and whose opinions I could learn from—friends like Joel Rutstein, and later Mel Eberle and Steve Higgins. Subsequently, *Daily Illini* colleagues and editors, particularly Jon Ginoli, Ted Cox, Paul Budin, Jack Rundle, George Paaswell, Mandy Crane, and Andy Oleksiuk, and others at the various newspapers and magazines for which I wrote, Bill Knight, Rick Johnson, Jeff Tamarkin most notably, continued to teach me about writing. Eileen Geffin and Harry Chapin also helped to set me on a path toward writing about music.

Still another of the origins of this collection can be found in Larry Grossberg's "rock 'n' roll classes" at UIUC. No matter that his class was called Rhetoric and Popular Culture, those of us in the know were onto the mix of music, cultural theory, and debate unique to his courses. Were it not for his tutelage and his efforts to bring Dick Hebdige, Simon Frith, Stuart Hall, and others to Urbana, I am certain I would have made far less use of my interest in popular music beyond writing record and concert reviews. I also would not have had the benefit of the inspiration that Simon has continued to provide.

My interest in popular-music studies continues unabated. Ted Peterson, former dean of the College of Communication at UIUC, nurtured both my interest in writing criticism and my interest in learning more about the media industries, including the music industry. He also managed to broaden my musical horizon by regularly making cassette tapes for me of the jazz music to which he listened. Though he is no longer alive, I imagine him listening still.

If this has seemed like a roll call or name check, I am guilty of what I have encountered and sometimes perpetuated as critic and fan with great regularity, namely a music critic's listing of "influences" on a musician, band, song, or album. These lists help critics and fans make sense of the progression of music, and in a quite nonlinear (one might almost say hypertextual) way. We each build our histories of popular music, just as popular music builds (on and onto) our personal histories. One reason for weaving personal memories and thanks throughout this introduction is in part to exorcise old ghosts, in part to welcome new names, and in part to discharge some debts (like the thanks that I owe to David Sanjek, Mark Fenster, Thom Swiss, and Frank Kogan). Making connections between sounds and words links us, in turn, to the interpretive communities within which we exist. Sometimes the connections seem to solidify and for a time enmesh us in their structure. Other times we cannot quite seem to make them hold. Such is history. But the real point I want to make is that each musical and critical moment moves us further from history, like Walter Benjamin's angel who is blown backward into the future, or more pertinently (and tritely), like the record collector who can never really achieve "completeness."

Writing criticism and reading it means engaging in a conversation that twists and turns through numerous other conversations, and in my case an unexpected twist came when Ted Peterson introduced me to Joli Jensen in the mid-1980s. She was completing her Ph.D. in UIUC's Institute for Communications Research, studying the country music community and meaning making among country music fans, performers, and the industry within which it existed. (Jensen's work in popular-music studies, which can now be found in several journal articles, reached an apogee with the publication of her book *The Nashville Sound* in 1998 by Vanderbilt University Press/The Country Music Foundation.) Though I knew at that time very little about how to go about doing such work myself, I immediately knew that it was what I wanted, needed, to do. The wheels were set in motion toward engaging in academic conversation about popular music. It is a conversation that I have continued to listen to and participate in, thanks to Larry Grossberg, John Shepherd, Franco Fabbri, Sara Cohen, Roy Shuker, Anahid Kassabian, Peter Wicke, Reebee Garofalo, David Sanjek, Will Straw, and many others. The list could go on and on, and there are many members of the International Association for the Study of Popular Music to whom I am greatly indebted.

Many more debts were incurred during the several years of this book's making. Michael Jarrett, a fine music critic himself, was greatly encouraging during all phases of its life. I owe him a great debt for believing in its promise. I hope the promise has been realized, and if it has not been, the blame is entirely mine to bear. Janet M. Francendese, editor-in-chief of Temple University Press, has been encouraging and helpful throughout the book's development. Stanley Fish, dean of the College of Liberal Arts and Sciences at the University of Illinois at Chicago, and associate deans Larry Poston and Steve Weaver, were very supportive. Eric Gislason, vice chancellor for research at UIC, has been a kind and generous colleague, and I am grateful for his advice and friendship.

My colleagues in the Department of Communication at UIC have been helpful and understanding and quite tolerant of my obsession with music. Dace Kezbers and Mamie Gray, department staff, have been a joy to work with and provided much help and support. Christina Serradimigni, my research assistant, was all one could hope for when it came to tracking down information and citations, proofreading, and finding that last Starburst candy camouflaged in the bowl on the conference table. Her help with copy editing was invaluable too. Stephanie Kucker assisted in the early stages of research for the book. Chris Nelson has helped re-inject a passion for music criticism, for which I am very thankful. Roy Shuker's help with tracking down articles and information was most welcome. Thank you to Disco Dave Willingham and to Julie Markle. Judy deserves special thanks for scones and coffeecakes. The many musicians with whom I have worked and whose music I have had the good fortune of hearing, and the many music fans I have known, have been a great inspiration. I wish to thank Sam Rosenthal and Lisa Feuer for continuing to indulge my own music making, as does Trevert. Fred Milton—wow, you've been an inspiration! Joli Jensen's work on country music has re-invigorated my own interest in popular music—it is now your turn for another book about music, Joli. Larry Grossberg and Simon Frith have both been a tremendous inspiration in my work, and in my life. My mother and father had me learn piano at an early age, for which I am now grateful, just as they predicted each time I snuck off early from practicing. My musical choices are my own, and they should not take the blame for them. Without their help, though, I would not derive the great pleasure from music that I do.

The contributors to this book deserve special thanks. Many of them stuck with this project despite its tortuous and twisted course over the several years of its discussion and making. It is as much theirs as mine, except when it comes to its faults and peccadilloes.

Last, and most, thanks to Jodi White, who continues to be patient no matter how many times I repeat my arguments about why, even though there is so much great music to be heard, in the final analysis the Beatles are the greatest. I apologize for the many times I have played music, and will no doubt continue to play it, just a little bit too loudly.

POP MUSIC

AND THE PRESS

The Intro

*Popular Music, Media,
and the Written Word*

Steve Jones

When I began thinking about writing, collecting, and commissioning essays about music criticism, I wondered whether I might feel like Charlie Brown in *Merry Christmas, Charlie Brown!* When he puts a single ornament on the lonesome, fragile Christmas tree he finds, it falls over. Charlie Brown throws his hands up in the air and says, "Augh! I've killed it!" I wondered if making rock criticism an academic subject might do something of the same. But of course plenty of rock critics take their cues from academic work, so why not? And if Robert Christgau of the *Village Voice* is the "dean of rock critics," surely there is room for a professor, or perhaps even a full department, in the field.

It was among friends, colleagues, critics, and fellow students that the academic origins of my interest in popular music first took on clarity. However, from the conversations I had with them, it became clear that little existed in the way of systematic study of popular-music criticism as it has evolved since the 1960s in the press. Little understanding of its history exists among many popular-music critics either. Numerous academic studies of popular music are published each year, and there are several scholarly journals that serve as forums for popular-music scholars. Yet little has been published about popular-music criticism, in popular-music scholarship or in journalism and mass communication scholarship. Nor can

1

one find much context in the works of critics themselves. Roy Shuker noted the same in his book *Key Concepts in Popular Music*: "There has been little critical analysis of how these publications construct popular music and influence the reception of genres and performers" (1998, 195). That this is so is even more surprising given the list of print media in which one can find popular-music criticism. Shuker provides a comprehensive list: "Lifestyle magazines with major music coverage, music trade papers, and weekly and monthly consumer magazines devoted to popular music, or particular genres within [it]. In addition to these are privately published fanzines. . . . There is also a variety of book-length writing on popular music . . . [and] the 'quickie' publications aiming to cash in on the latest pop sensation" (195–96).

When one also considers the variety of Internet media, from newsgroups and chat rooms to web sites, in which one can find writing about popular music, the dearth of scholarship is still more surprising.

Journalism historians seem to have overlooked even the publications that popular-music critics wrote for, such as *Crawdaddy!*, *Creem*, *Musician*, *Spin*, and *Trouser Press* (to name the well-known ones), save for a handful of research articles on *Rolling Stone* magazine (the best history of *Rolling Stone* is still Draper 1990). But although histories of *Rolling Stone* offer glimpses into the publishing industry and the counterculture, popular-music criticism itself has largely been neglected as a site for academic study. Only Abe Peck's *Uncovering the Sixties* (1985), a history of the underground press in that decade, situates within the framework of cultural and political debate the rise of magazines that catered to a rock audience. Indeed, the editorial raison d'être of many underground periodicals (then and now) is to offer an audience published music criticism. Underground periodicals have been particularly tied to popular-music criticism, because such periodicals served (and continue to serve, by way of fanzines both online and print) as a kind of "farm league" for many journalists. Such periodicals remain the catalyst for many who subsequently choose reporting and editing in the mainstream or underground press as a career.

This collection of essays focuses on popular music since the 1950s, largely because it is from that point on that one begins to see jazz and pop criticism doing more than analyze music. That writing carried the seeds of a postwar U.S. cultural criticism based on the values, attitudes, and beliefs of the baby-boom generation. This criticism essentially recovered the aesthetic and cultural values of postwar youth and asserted the validity of their experience. Taking motion pictures, art, and music as their texts, critics helped blast a hole through the postwar social hardening of the 1950s—as well as through the journalistic conventions that the New Journalism came to question.

These essays focus on criticism of popular-music styles denoted by terms such as "rock," "rock and roll," "rap," "hip-hop," "rhythm 'n' blues," and "pop." Nevertheless, for the most part this book denotes those who write about these styles as, interchangeably, "rock critics" or "music critics." Before the music itself reaches a wide audience, such criticism is published almost exclusively in fanzines and the underground press, and only later does it appear in the mainstream press. In the 1950s and 1960s other journalistic space for criticism simply did not exist for those wishing to write about popular music. In turn, the underground press owes some of its life (and circulation) to its many pages of popular-music criticism.

Moreover, this collection almost exclusively considers English-language popular-music criticism. It focuses on its publication in the United States and the United Kingdom and for the most part excludes trade publications. It also excludes the "musician's magazines" that arose primarily in the 1980s oriented toward guitar players, keyboard players, and music technology, which Paul Théberge (1997) analyzed in his book *Any Sound You Can Imagine*. It will be important to examine the impact of English-language criticism in other countries. Bruce Johnson (1998) has begun such work in analyses of Australian jazz and its coverage in the press. As an example of how important such work might be, all one need do is turn to Jason Toynbee's 1993 article that examines the music press in Britain: "[Critic Charles Shaar] Murray was able to import highbrow methods [of criticism] because he found a language that was a credible complement to rock itself. This was partly a question of the judicious use of Americanisms which sounded both hip and hard-boiled; 'goddam' was a favourite. But it was also to do with a sentence structure out of Hemingway via the New Journalism, where irregular clusters of short sentences broke up much longer strings of subordinate clauses" (1993, 291). One reason for Murray's use of language is that in the 1970s, the U.K.'s *New Musical Express* weekly forged an agreement with U.S.-based *Creem* magazine to reprint articles, and at the time some of rock criticism's most notable writers (including Lester Bangs) were on *Creem's* staff (DeRogatis 2000b, 114).

Much important work remains to be done. As important as industrial and writerly relationships are, so is the influence of language, and thus examining the development of popular-music criticism in languages other than English should prove instructive. I hope that this collection can help serve as a foundation from which such work can proceed. While some of the contributors are themselves musicians and can provide some perspective from that vantage, a general overview of criticism from the musicians' perspective will also be of great interest, as will examination of criticism across a wide variety of musical styles and forms.

Further, rock critics regularly critique one another's work, and some do so in the pages of this book, but despite a spate of recent anthologies that collect a handful of critics' work, we know little with regard to their learning and knowledge about writing.

It is difficult, perhaps impossible, to assess directly the impact a critic has on sales of recordings and concert tickets. Shuker noted that "there is general agreement that rock critics don't exercise as much influence on consumers as, say, literary or drama critics" (1994, 93). One reason, as Shuker claimed, is that hearing music has greater impact than reading about it, and thus those who control airplay likely have greater influence on consumers. It may also be that the investments of time and money required for engagement with most literature and drama, and the concomitant lack of popular access and distribution (one rarely sees or hears, for instance, passages from *Death of a Salesman* mass mediated), create a greater interest in "preview" material consumers can use to guide their purchases. Some critics, most notably Robert Christgau, originator of the "consumer guide" approach to pop-music reviews, provide just such a service, and it is likely that there is greater consumer interest in it now than in the 1970s and 1980s, if only due to the increased variety and amount of music available in all media. An important future undertaking will be to examine the critical discourse in trade publications and to determine the differences and similarities to that discourse in consumer publications as a way to assess the degree to which music criticism is a gatekeeper (Shuker 1998, 199; Toynbee 1993, 290).

Critics' own understanding of their role in relation to consumers is important to assess, and it is related to the professionalization of the music critic (and in turn of the journalist). Lester Bangs gave us his version of what it takes to be a rock critic, fortunately reprinted in Jim DeRogatis's Bangs biography *Let It Blurt* (2000a), including a MadLibs-like template for an "original record review." DeRogatis gives us some insight into the professionalization of rock criticism when he writes about the rock critic conferences and associations and the music journalism awards, but most of all when he writes about Bangs's canonization and the history of *Creem*. It is important to remember that critics do unto one another as they do to others. They read and criticize (though rarely in print) one another and one another's writing and tastes in music, and most cling to a variety of elitist, though regularly shifting, beliefs, such as whether it is better to be a critic for a fanzine, magazine, or a newspaper.

In truth, we know very little about critics' own values beyond those that relate to music itself. What music critics and journalists believe their work to be bears scrutiny. In a 1990 article for the *Washington Journalism Review,* Jory Farr, popular-music critic at a daily newspaper in California, wrote:

Most of my weeks go by in a blur. When I'm not listening to the dozens of records and tapes that I get in the mail each week—everything from zouk and zydeco to samba and jazz—I'm setting up interviews, knocking out local entertainment stories, doing background research for larger pieces, arranging photo shoots or dealing with promoters. . . . I'm frequently exposed to music that's uncharted territory for me. And some weeks . . . I wonder if I haven't made a vocational mistake. Chronic fatigue and glamour just don't mix well.

I do get free tickets to the best shows (usually excellent seats) and free records and CDs. And whenever I'm feeling stressed, I remind myself that I'm not writing 10 inches on the new water board member, but on something I really love. Besides, as a columnist and critic I have a rare luxury in daily journalism: the freedom to write creatively.

Most of my colleagues agree, however, that their jobs are still the stuff of myth. Few readers—or even reporters—understand the rigors of the pop music critic's beat or its key role in American culture. (49–50)

Farr interviews several other music critics and the result is a most informative examination of the profession. Robert Wyatt and Geoffrey Hull conducted a survey of popular-music critics and their editors in the late 1980s and found that a

composite image of the "average" American music critic begins to emerge. That critic is, in all probability, a well-educated male in his 30s with about 10 years' experience covering music. He has at least a bachelor's degree with perhaps even some graduate work . . . his tastes do not change dramatically whether he works for a small daily in a rural area, a prestigious metropolitan newspaper or a slick national magazine. This composite critic also does not attribute high aesthetic and philosophical functions to music but understands its primary functions to include diversion, escape and companionship.

The music critic writes far more positive reviews than negative reviews. Perhaps this finding indicates that music critics, because of the popular nature of their chosen art form, are unaccustomed to employing stringent critical standards. Or perhaps this paucity of negative reviews is a reflection of the fact that . . . music critics have great discretion in choosing what to review. (1988, 20–21)

Wyatt and Hull discuss briefly the ethics of critics at newspapers in this survey and a 1990 article, but no studies exist that focus exclusively on the ethical dimension of popular-music criticism. Still, Farr's and Wyatt and Hull's efforts give us at least a glimpse into the wealth of information that can be gleaned from systematic study of popular-music critics and their profession.

Interestingly, these writers did not delve into the racial backgrounds of music critics. It is not until rap music leads to the development of publications devoted to its coverage (and to coverage of other African American musical forms) that black music critics begin to be widely heard and noticed. Criticism and reporting on jazz, R&B, soul, Motown, and numerous other genres established by black musicians or in which black musicians predominate was most often written by whites. And, as Holly Kruse, Brenda Johnson-Grau, and others in this book observe, women too have been excluded from the ranks of critics.

The demographic characteristics of music critics can provide insight. So can the ethics of popular-music criticism. Both are topics among many that can engage questions of the professionalization of criticism and connect it to analyses of popular-music criticism as industrial practice, with its own routines and expectations as a media industry embedded in another industry (the music business). As Shuker noted: "The music press and critics are not, at least directly, vertically integrated into the music industry. . . . A sense of distance is thereby maintained, while at the same time the need of the industry to constantly sell new images, styles, and product is met" (1998, 200).

However, as I found in a study of advertiser influence on music magazines (Jones 1993), *both* the music and publishing industries need one another and need to "sell new images, styles, and product." Very little research into their symbiotic relationship has been done. One of the best, and longest, studies of the popular-music press notes similarities between the popular-music industry and "practices in other industries more commonly called culture industries such as book publishing and film making" (Stratton 1982, 269). It is all the more imperative that we continue research in this vein for, as Shuker claimed, the music press is one of the few domains of media that has not been vertically integrated into the music industry and larger media industries.

In a sense, music criticism itself has become industrialized. At the level of content, Mark Evans, in a study of album reviews in Australian rock magazines, found that album reviews "are constituted by fundamental elements that can be individually identified . . . lyrical analysis, inter-artist comparison, artist background and musical analysis (1998, 49). At an institutional level, Mark Fenster noted well before he wrote the essay for this collection that "the music press has become conventionalized and based upon the same kinds of industrial structures" as the music industry (1989, 16). One writer even went so far as to claim that rock critics "are the bush league scouts for the process that turns music into money" (Lyons 1989, 27). Some critics have, in fact, gone on to work for record companies full-time, while others are on their payrolls only indirectly. In some ways, then, to understand popular-music criticism fully we need to delve well beyond the writing of it. Shuker noted that music magazines have "become part of a general magazine culture" but also spied an evolution away from covering music alone toward becoming "a guide to lifestyle, especially leisure consumption" (1994, 92). Just as popular music itself has penetrated virtually all media forms, the vehicles in which one finds popular-music criticism have brought added attention to the variety of media with which music fans engage. Shuker's analysis provides a particularly trenchant critique of the interplay of industry, consumerism, and nostalgia. But it is important not to underplay the significance of criticism itself, but to theorize the practice of popular-music criticism as creative work when it comes to writing it *and* to reading it.[1] The contributors to this collection occupy themselves with just such concerns.

Organization

Though this book does not reprint any critic's writing, it shares a few idiosyncrasies with a book that does, *The Penguin Book of Rock & Roll Writing* (Heylin 1992). Will you find mention of your favorite critic? Maybe, maybe not. Some of the "big names" appear, like Lester Bangs and Robert Christgau, but some are hard to find—among them, Dave Marsh, Jon Landau, Jon Savage, Joe Carducci, Richard Meltzer, Nick Tosches, and Jules Siegel. I'd like to believe they are in here between the lines, as are references to smaller magazines and fanzines like *Maximum Rock & Roll* and *OP*. All have made a contribution, whether it is a clearly visible one or not. The writers, articles, and publications named in the book are largely cited as examples and illustrations; the goal has not been to create a hall of fame (or museum, or "project").

The book is divided into three sections. The first examines the institutions and history of popular-music criticism. The essay Kevin Featherly and I wrote situates its practice in the United States within the social context and structure of the underground press in the 1960s and 1970s. Gestur Gudmundsson, Ulf Lindberg, Morten Michelsen, and Hans Weisethaunet draw on a broad range of humanist and sociological theories to illustrate and explain three turning points in popular-music criticism's development (discursive establishment, discursive transition, and diversification). The authors are an Icelandic sociologist, a Norwegian ethnomusicologist, a Swedish literature expert, and a Danish musicologist; they examine popular-music criticism in Nordic countries and provide a much-needed non-Anglo perspective on criticism. Jeff Chang historicizes and locates rap and hip-hop criticism in the larger media context, taking into account the role new media are playing in its development. The section's last essay, by Robert Ray, argues against the received wisdom that popular-music criticism adheres to an implicit legitimation of the music industry's commercial practices, noting that the most important rock critics have been attentive to the pitfalls of canonization and made constant efforts to acknowledge diverse artists and genres. Their standards are often openly subjective, and they have foregrounded the contingency of musical and aesthetic value long before it was fashionable among academic critics.

Mark Fenster's chapter opens the next section, one geared toward examining the discourses within and about popular-music criticism. Fenster places rock criticism within the institutional, economic, and ideological structures of the practices of contemporary rock music. His central argument is that critics and music journalism as a whole work within the dominating economic structures of the music industry and within the various cultural discourses of U.S. rock culture. Kembrew McLeod's essay examines the role of discourse in reproducing institutional social relations, with special attention to McLeod's own "dual citizenship" as music critic and academic author. Martin Cloonan's chapter traces the discursive history of the British press and its engagement with popular music. Of particular interest is Cloonan's illustration of the British press's shift from a position that opposed rock and roll to one that accommodates and appreciates it. Cloonan shows that criticism is increasingly incorporated into a broad range of contemporary periodicals (most notably in "lifestyle" magazines) and serves a wider audience than ever—mirroring the diffusion of popular music across media. Holly Kruse analyzes the ways popular-music criticism provides a discursive positioning by which music fans (and nonfans) situate themselves in relation to various genres, artists, and songs. The ubiquity of popular-music criticism, she argues, means that the ways in which it articulates gender can have a significant impact on how people are socialized into popular music. McLeod's examination of the discourses of authenticity in hip-hop criticism closes the section, underlining the tensions between fans, critics, and culture.

The book's third section consists of case studies of particular discursive formations in popular-music criticism. Thom Swiss examines the interplay of critical, fan, and artist discourses in the construction of Jewel as both a pop star and a poet. His essay illuminates the connections between multiple critical discourses and social structures and media, making it an excellent jumping-off point for others interested in unraveling the intertwining of popular music, criticism, mediation, authenticity, and representation. Joli Jensen's essay focuses on the coverage of country music in the mainstream press when SoundScan, the new retail scanning, reporting, and charting system, revealed that country music was outselling rock. It analyzes and elucidates the surprise, backpedaling, and attempts to "welcome" the popularity of country, even as it was being denigrated. Brenda Johnson-Grau shows us in her essay that the presence of women in popular music has been continual and constant. Yet, as she demonstrates, both the national and the music media portray the contributions of women as marginal and extraordinary, creating a notion that the presence of women in rock was unusual—that rock is an exclusively male preserve. Sharon Mazzarella and Timoth Matyjewicz provide a case study of the coverage of popular music in the press and focus on the media's use of the deaths of John Lennon, Jerry Garcia, Kurt Cobain, and Tupac Shakur to report on youth culture in addition to music.

Culture, Academia, and Journalism

Indeed, the links between popular music and youth that are forged in the places inhabited by musicians and young people are milled in the discursive spaces of popular-music criticism. Charles Hamm made an important connection between the two when he noted that rock journalism's focus "was on popular music as a manifestation of the culture of young people, . . . seen not as a malignancy requiring a cure but rather as a potential cure for a malignant society, with music occupying a central position in their culture" (1995, 22).

But an even more important connection, one Hamm only indirectly makes, is the one between academic critics and popular-music critics, between intellectuals and journalists. Though DeRogatis noted four "camps" of rock writers—academics, historians, gossips, and "unruly, contentious . . . Noise Boys" (2000, 89)—it is disingenuous of him to write that "two camps dominate rock criticism today: the two-thumbs-up consumer-guide careerists who treat rock 'n' roll as mere entertainment, and the academics who drain it of all the joy and fury" (xvi). Writers often have one foot in each camp, or migrate between the two. And what are we to make of critics who moonlight as musicians (and vice versa)? Lester Bangs himself occupied that territory, as do many others. Where might their camp be, and is the campfire still burning there?

It should not be surprising that youth culture is central to popular-music criticism, just as it should not be surprising that there is crossover between critics and musicians. All of these groups engage in critical discourse in one way or another. However, as Hamm points out, for academics youth culture was also central to "sociology in the decade following the end of World War II, when the study of youth behavior was a popular theme in that discipline" (1995, 21). The connections between academic critics and popular-music critics form a recurring theme throughout this book. Simon Frith has even claimed that "popular music is a solution, a ritualized resistance, not to the problems of being young and poor and proletarian but to the problems of being an intellectual"

(1992, 179). If Frith is even partly correct, then it should be no surprise that popular-music criticism, an expression and discourse surrounding and about popular music, will attract the attention of other intellectuals.

Angela McRobbie noted that by the early 1970s "there were a number of . . . forces which encouraged young journalists . . . to explore popular culture as a more general form: a recognition, for example, that pop music . . . could no longer be considered in isolation" (1988, xiii). Developments in several academic fields, such as sociology, communication, and media studies, at around the same time brought some scholarly attention to popular culture. By the 1980s it was not hard to see that in some cases McRobbie's assertion was twisted around by those who saw in popular music a microcosmic vantage from which to study youth culture. But what is most interesting is McRobbie's observation that "while pop journalism has moved towards a more serious mode, academic writing has, to some extent, shifted towards a lighter, more essayistic, style" (xvii). As I explained in an analysis of the controversy surrounding publication of an academic book about Madonna, journalists and academics now jointly occupy many discursive spaces (Jones 1997). Each group continues to hold its piece of ground, and sometimes the contestations make for interesting reading. But what is more significant than the struggles for symbolic turf is that each has found a public sphere, a "forum . . . where issues could be ventilated, speculations workshopped, where almost any opinion could gain a hearing," as Bruce Johnson noted in a history of Australian jazz publications (1998, 11).

That popular-music criticism continues to matter is evident simply from the 1998 publication of the "Rock Critical List," an anonymous rant about New York pop music critics and the *Village Voice*'s annual Pazz & Jop critics' poll, or the attack in 1998 on *Blaze* magazine editor-in-chief Jesse Washington for information revealed in a review of a rap record (and, it was speculated, for the review's lukewarm praise).[2] Thus, though there may be a limited supply of symbolic material over which competing interests may struggle (see chapter 1), the intensity of the struggle will tend to make the supply seem enormous (if not limitless); more importantly, struggle itself is a means by which such material is kept circulating and therefore in supply. The development of new media by way of the Internet, from the interpersonal to the mass (including the many combinations and permutations of those), has meant that what Johnson terms a "rippling out" of the influence of music criticism takes place within new spatial and temporal configurations.[3] Not only the Internet but also multimedia technologies are spawning new vehicles through which critical discourse takes place. *Launch* is a CD-R publication, for instance, and *Circuit* is published on DVD. Taking the concept initiated by the publishing of sheet music in periodicals and later by "flexi-discs" inserted into magazines, these media combine written criticism with musical examples, interviews, video footage, and entire songs. Most are hypertextual in design, and it is much too early to know the consequences such publications may have on popular-music criticism.

But it is not too early to note that new media will not likely drive music critics to extinction. They might create greater demand for music criticism, or they might be a proving ground for aspiring music critics. Look at the Usenet newsgroups, mailing lists, chat rooms, and web sites where the boundaries between fans and critics are blurred as never before. Rock critic Gina Arnold has gone so far as to write, in "Rock Lit Lite" in the *San Jose Metro* for 30 November 1999, that "nowadays, serious readers of rock lit tend to eschew the factual prose of *Rolling Stone* and the pretentious attitudinizing of *Spin*, preferring instead to troll for information about new music in the infinitely less literate areas of fanzines, the Internet or college radio" (1999, 23).

Yet in many cases, those areas are quite literate, and they may be where the function of music criticism as a public forum is being fulfilled, and we may be so early in the development of these forums that we have difficulty discerning their activities and roles. Kallioniemi noted that "the importance of interaction between writers and readers is gradually growing because of the introduction of internet-versions of most magazines" (1998, 25). According to Thomas Valovic:

> The ambiguity of roles found in the on-line environment . . . has puzzling implications for journalists. In an on-line venue, is a reporter a private citizen or a journalist?
>   There is a notion in Internet culture that "everyone on the Net is a reporter." Yet as reporters become more attuned to listening to their readers, a curious kind of role reversal is suggested: Reporters do the listening and readers do the reporting. (1995, 119–20)

The ambiguity about which Valovic writes may do more than puzzle us; it may be cause for concern, or even for anger. As Jim DeRogatis reported in "Hitting Some Low Notes" in the *Chicago Sun-Times,* 31 October 1999, such was the case after RCA Records launched a campaign to hype Christina Aguilera by hiring college students to populate newsgroups and chat rooms. The net.shills went so far as to encourage others online to request Aguilera's music on radio and MTV.

When Shuker noted the importance of the music press in melding music, style, and news to create fan communities, he added that "the ideological role of the rock press in constructing a sense of community and in maintaining a critical distance from the music companies had already become muted by the early 1980s (1994, 92; see also Mitchell and Shuker 1998). It is not clear from Shuker's analysis whether one should understand the formation of community from an industrial perspective (that relates it to the publishing and music industries' desire to create markets) or from a perspective rooted in literary criticism (that sees each act of reading criticism as creating an interpretive community). In some sense the music press provided an interactive environment for fans, insofar as readers could position themselves within the multiple discourses therein. But it is also important to consider the *integrative* aspect of engagement with the music press, the engagement in a common and regular practice (of going to the newsstand each week or month, or of subscribing and receiving a publication in the mail). Greater interaction is easily spotted in the new media; the multitude of chat rooms, newsgroups, listservs, and web pages attests to it. But its integrative aspect is more difficult to spot, though it should be of great interest, for it is more closely tied to the routines associated with popular-music consumption. It is a realm of activity quite closely articulated with fandom, with "collecting," and now with mp3 and other digital audio formats available online. The Napster mp3 file-sharing software, for instance, provides interfaces for uploading and downloading music *and* a bulletin board for discussion among users. Aspects of interaction themselves thus become integrated as the practices of popular-music fandom converge in and through new media and technology.

We cannot yet know how new media will serve to develop another generation of critics, nor what kind of critics it may develop; our notion of "critic" may need modifying. As it is, we know little about the development of critics in general. Despite one musician's utterance in the film *Almost Famous* that its protagonist was "never a person, he was a journalist," one of the great motivations of many critics is the desire to "build" a group of fans who see alike, because, as Lester Bangs's character puts it, "the only true currency in this bankrupt world is what you share with someone else who isn't cool." And one of the great frustrations is being unable to do so for any length of time, if ever.

My own story of how I came to be a music critic is probably rather typical (and just as typical is the way I eventually ceased being one). Few people set out on a career path toward music criticism. Fewer still are set on that path by parents, teachers, career counselors, job ads, or any of the myriad ways one typically finds a livelihood. Most become music critics due to a connection with music, be they musicians, students of music, scholars, or fans, and due to a concomitant and usually serendipitous connection to someone who can offer an outlet for their writing. Indeed, it seems as if many music critics do not realize they are music critics until they begin getting hate mail from disgruntled musicians and fans. None I am aware of has a degree in music criticism (though of course many do not have a journalism degree or a degree in music and have suffered no ill consequence as a result). Most "studied" music criticism by reading all of it they could get their hands on.

And yet, just a few weeks before I finished the final draft of this manuscript, a young undergraduate student stopped by my office to tell me that she wanted to become a music critic. I struggled only for a moment over whether her interest in music was a pure one, or whether she was just seeking glamour, access, and free records. But there is no such thing as "pure" rock criticism; there never was and never will be. Rock criticism is no more or less "pure" than the music it takes as its subject. My advice to her was to set to writing, with the thought that she can thereby gain the knowledge and skills for turning out publishable music criticism. Her interest, however, turned out to be in learning how to make a career of it, determining whether it was a way to make a living. Maybe, just maybe, popular-music criticism has reached the point at which its professionalization is complete. My hope, however, is that it also will continue to attempt "to make us see things differently," to borrow from Frith and Savage's critique of populism (1997, 16), for I could see in that student's eyes that if she was mercenary about anything, it was about having her voice heard in the debate about what music can mean in her, and our, life.

Notes

1. Unless one counts various radio and television talk shows or news shows on which critics may appear, or the "rate-a-record" phenomenon that seems to recur every dozen or so years on a music-oriented television program, there are few examples of critics taking to media other than print. A notable exception is *Sound Opinions* on WXRT-FM radio in Chicago. This weekly talk show, hosted by critics Jim DeRogatis of the Chicago *Sun-Times* and Greg Kot of the Chicago *Tribune*, often features conversations with other critics, reviews of concerts and albums, and interviews with musicians.

2. The "list" was e-mailed anonymously to several critics, commented on in the *Village Voice*, then published online in *Spin* at http://www.spin.com/poplife/koolthing/art%2D19990326%2Dkool/page2.html. Its pseudonymous author, JoJo Dancer, states: "So, in lieu of yet another over-analyzed, self-serving, year-end wankorama (that would be the Pazz & Jop; and it's Lauryn Hill best album, Aaliyah best single, Nuggets best reissue, if you need to care), we'd like to announce our first annual ROCK CRITICAL LIST, a self-serving circle jerk/séance on the grinding, but not irreversible, decline of POP MUSIC JOURNALISM."

3. The same is true, of course, of music. For an examination of the Internet's consequences for popular music see Jones 2000, where many of the issues set forth hold true for popular-music criticism and discourse.

References

Dancer, JoJo. (1998). Rock critical list. http://www.spin.com/poplife/koolthing/
art%2D19990326%2Dkoo1/page2.html. Accessed May 1999.
DeRogatis, Jim. (2000a). *Let it blurt*. New York: Broadway Books.
———. (2000b). Prisoner of punk. *Spin*, May, 108–16.
Draper, Robert. (1990). Rolling Stone *magazine: The uncensored history*. New York:
Doubleday.
Evans, Mark. (1998). "Quality" criticism: Music reviewing in Australian rock mag-
azines. *Perfect Beat* 3, 4: 38–50.
Farr, Jory. (1990). Rock, rock, rock till the broad daylight. *Washington Journalism
Review*, April, 48–52.
Fenster, Mark. (1989). What hot is. *Asymptote* 1, 1 (winter): 16–17.
Frith, Simon. (1992). The cultural study of popular music. In *Cultural studies,* ed.
Lawrence Grossberg, Cary Nelson, and Paula Treichler, 174–86. London:
Routledge.
Frith, Simon, and Jon Savage. (1997). Pearls and swine: Intellectuals and the
mass media. In *The clubcultures reader,* ed. Steve Redhead, Derek Wynn, and
Justin O'Connor, 7–17. Oxford: Blackwell.
Hamm, Charles. (1995). *Putting popular music in its place*. Cambridge: Cambridge
University Press.
Henry, Tricia. (1989). *Break all rules! Punk rock and the making of a style*. Ann Arbor:
UMI Research Press.
Heylin, Clinton. (1992). *Penguin book of rock and roll writing*. London: Viking.
Johnson, Bruce. (1998). Doctored jazz: Early Australian jazz journals. *Perfect Beat*
3, 4: 26–37.
Jones, Steve. (1993). Pop music, criticism, advertising, and the music industry.
Journal of Popular Music Studies 5: 79–91.
———. (1997). Reaping pop: The press, the scholar, and the consequences of
popular cultural studies. In *The clubcultures reader,* ed. Steve Redhead, Derek
Wynn, and Justin O'Connor, 204–16. Oxford: Blackwell.
———. (2000). Popular music and the Internet. *Popular Music* 19, 2: 217–30.
Kallioniemi, Kari. (1998). "Put the needle on the record and think of England":
Notions of Englishness in the post-war debate on British pop music. Ph.D.
diss., University of Turku, Finland.
Lyons, Benjamin. (1989). The critic or the egg. *Asymptote* 1, 3 (fall): 14–16, 26–27.
McRobbie, Angela. (1988). Introduction to *Zoot suits and second-hand dresses*, ed.
McRobbie, xi–xx. Boston: Unwin Hyman.
Mitchell, Tony, and Roy Shuker. (1998). Moral panics, national pride, and split
images: Music and the press in Aotearoa/New Zealand. *Perfect Beat* 3, 4: 51–67.
Peck, Abe. (1985). *Uncovering the sixties*. New York: Pantheon.
Shuker, Roy. (1994). *Understanding popular music*. London: Routledge.
———. (1998). *Key concepts in popular music*. London: Routledge.
Stratton, Jon. (1982). Between two worlds: Art and commercialism in the record
industry. *Sociological Review* 30, 1: 267–85.
Théberge, Paul. (1997). *Any sound you can imagine*. Hanover, N.H.: Wesleyan University Press.

Toynbee, Jason. (1993). Policing Bohemia, pinning up grunge: The music press and generic change in British pop and rock. *Popular Music* 12, 3: 289–300.

Valovic, Thomas S. (1995). Encounters on-line. *Media Studies Journal* 9, 2: 113–21.

Wyatt, Robert O., and Geoffrey P. Hull. (1988). The music critic in the American press: A nationwide survey of newspapers and magazines. Paper presented at the Association for Education in Journalism and Mass Communication convention, Portland, Ore.

———. (1990). The music critic in the American press: A nationwide survey of newspapers and magazines. *Mass Communication Review* 17, 3: 38–43.

INSTITUTIONS
AND HISTORY

Re-Viewing Rock Writing

Narratives of Popular Music Criticism

Steve Jones and Kevin Featherly

A s with most literary genres, one can in retrospect trace an evolution in popular-music criticism along a relatively linear path. And as with most such tracings, one quickly sees that the connections between writers, ideas, editors, publishers, subject matter, and readers make for little that is linear.

One way of assessing the evolution of popular music criticism has been to view it across the categories of media within which it has appeared. As Frank Hoffman notes, one can find writing about popular music in fanzines, underground journals, music trade magazines, serious music journals, newspapers, general interest magazines, and books (1981), and one can therefore classify music criticism according to the publications in which it has appeared. By this means of classification, for example, David Sanjek (n.d.) discusses the ideology of authenticity among rock music critics. Yet such categorization causes Sanjek to overanalyze the publications and underanalyze the criticism itself.

The approach in this essay is thus to analyze three intertwined themes in popular-music criticism—race, authenticity, and mass culture—one or more of which is likely to appear within the space of a single article, a paragraph, or occasionally even a heavily weighted sentence. Together they form the core issues with which popular-music critics have concerned themselves and, by corollary, have hoped are or will be of concern to readers.

We survey these dominant themes to understand the writing of critics whose styles seem to have left the strongest imprint on popular music and popular-music criticism, and thereby to trace the evolution of popular-music criticism. We do not propose to a build critics' hall of fame. The critics included—Nat Hentoff, Ralph Gleason, Robert Christgau, and Lester Bangs—are at the center of popular-music criticism in part because they are simply fine writers, and in part because the themes they have mined remain the themes of popular-music criticism. Many others have explored the same territory, but few have ranged as far as these four, and still fewer have crystallized the three themes with such force and impact on other critics.

These four critics also illustrate the trend in popular-music criticism from the late 1950s through the 1970s, a period that has influenced subsequent generations of critics. As Jason Toynbee noted in a survey of popular-music criticism in the United Kingdom, well into the 1980s criticism "remain[ed] remarkably close to the 1970s model" (1993, 296). The same is true of the United States. Perhaps the influence of *Rolling Stone*, the extent to which the most prominent critics wrote for it, and the extent to which many critics still aspire to write for it, has structured mainstream critics' style. It may have also determined what topics were off-limits; as Abe Peck notes, "*Rolling Stone* rarely muckraked about the music business, and didn't question its basic corporate structure" (1985, 168).

Just as likely, though, is that there are really not all that many ways to write about popular music. To put a twist on something Elvis Costello is rumored to have said, "writing about music is like dancing about architecture," and once around the block may well cover the territory. In "The Market of Symbolic Goods" Pierre Bourdieu noted that "[w]hen different producers confront each other, it is still in the name of their claims to orthodoxy, or, in Max Weber's terms, to the legitimate and monopolized use of a certain class of symbolic goods. . . . The more [a] field is capable of functioning as a field of competition for cultural legitimacy, the more individual production must be orientated toward the search for culturally pertinent features endowed with value in the field's own economy" (1985, 19).

To be simplistic, there are structural limits to the practice of popular-music criticism, and there may not be an endlessly renewable stock of symbolic capital for critics to use. Bourdieu's ideas about the means by which culture is legitimized are particularly true in the case of *Rolling Stone*, for it is the popular-music periodical that seeks most clearly to legitimate specific musics and musicians (in second place, perhaps, is *Maximum Rock 'n' Roll*). Of all periodicals, *Rolling Stone* has had the power to "consecrate" popular music in Bourdieu's terms.

Even among the four critics whose work is examined in this essay, one can see the desire to legitimate, destroy, shape, and savage. But though it is not difficult to discern similarities and differences among these four, it is as easy to see that their approaches to popular-music criticism are prototypical. Bourdieu's assertion that "conflicts disseminate the *consensus* within the *dissensus* which defines the field of cultural battle . . . inculcating an uncontested hierarchy of themes and problems worthy of discussion" (1985, 41) is evident in these critics' writing. What is most interesting is that, no matter the changes in music, the concerns of music critics writing for the popular press seem to focus on three recurring issues—race, authenticity, and mass culture—and it is Hentoff, Gleason, Christgau, and Bangs who seem to have "construct[ed] that intellectual space defined by a system of common references appearing so natural, so incontestable that they are never the object of conscious position-takings at all" (41). The reverence with which these four are regarded by a generation of critics who followed them is itself sufficient evidence of that construction, but it is in their writing that one can most clearly find the contours of the field they have shaped.

Race, Records, and Writing

"You see the discrimination and injustice in the music industry and you naturally gravitate toward [social criticism]," said Nat Hentoff, explaining why his writing shifted from music toward politics and cultural criticism. "Unless you're a totally aesthetic critic and that's a whole 'nother thing" (1990). If nothing else, the lyrical content of popular music itself forced critics to confront social issues and go beyond aesthetics to explore the ways in which meaning is made from popular music. Popular-music critics, as Patricia Bizzell has noted, have concerned themselves with "that part of human life which is constructed through shared language use, the life-in-language that connects us to various pasts, puts us in concert or conflict with contemporaries, and provides us with visions of collective futures" (1989, 229). That such collective envisioning should surface in this criticism is not surprising, since the music itself often seems to have a similar purpose. Popular music is considered to have a meaning beyond the aesthetic, and consideration of that meaning and its construction, constitution, and communication has occupied many critics.

Popular-music critics' examination of the urban music scene has led them to write about racism, urban decay, and moral decay. At first, critics addressed these issues within the context of popular song lyrics. Later, critics addressed them without prompting from lyrics. Since most music is recorded in and distributed from large cities, and since most "scenes" are labeled by the city in which they originate (the San Francisco Scene, the Liverpool-based Mersey Beat, the Minneapolis Sound, the Philly Sound), this connection seems natural. Many musical forms are tied to the inner city—in particular disco and rap music—and popular music incorporates elements of urban life (and vice versa).

One of the first popular-music critics to address race in his criticism was Ralph J. Gleason (1917–75). Though he was sometimes excitable, even giddy, his writing was usually stately, even slightly ponderous. His faith in the revolutionary promise held by rock and roll music, gleaned perhaps from his association with San Francisco's psychedelic avatars the Jefferson Airplane during the late 1960s, is legendary. To Gleason, at least late in his life, rock and roll was the revolution. Gleason passed that way of thinking on to his disciple, Jann Wenner, and to a generation by way of their joint project (later Wenner's alone), *Rolling Stone* magazine. The magazine continues to features Gleason's name at the bottom of its masthead, a tribute to his contribution to the *Rolling Stone* philosophy.

In 1960, Gleason was ready to move beyond the aesthetic criticism of jazz for which he was known. Racism provided the spark he needed to reinvent himself. In a "Perspectives" column in *Downbeat* magazine, he related his anger and frustration at the scaling down of the live San Francisco jazz scene by city authorities who feared rioting (there had been fighting in the crowds at several jazz and R&B shows). "What's behind this," Gleason wrote, "whether the people who make the decisions in such matters know it or not, is a fully functioning Jim Crow stereotype. . . . The fact that you can have a fight at a Guy Lombardo dance, the Harvest Moon Dance, or a football game between 22 Caucasians has nothing to do with it apparently. Some people can't think past their first impressions" (1960b). He goes on to partly blame schools and the education system, saying they do not encourage thinking and have made language "fuzzy" enough to allow words to mean many different things, apparently even that racism is okay, or that it is not even racism.

"We are in the midst of a gigantic social upheaval in which the Newport Jazz Festival riot, the southern lunch-counter sit-ins, Elijah Muhammad, and countless other things are part of the whole," Gleason wrote in that column. "Patience, tolerance and above all, compassion are needed everywhere. The protest inherent in jazz has always been protest for good, against evil. Let us not allow it to curdle into hate" (1960b).

Later that year, as the civil rights movement began to catch fire, many youths (as well as jazz musicians) saw themselves in a position to redirect the hatred of blacks. Gleason began to adopt a more socially aware standpoint. Music was the tonic, he seemed to be saying. "[The 1960 Monterey Jazz Festival] proved many things," he wrote, again for *Downbeat,* in an article that seems a turning point in his approach to criticism. "That a jazz festival devoted to music does not incite a riot; that American audiences can and will be patient, attentive, and sympathetic to the most exploratory of musical experiments; that, as in the words of Jon Hendricks sung by Lambert-Hendricks-Ross, 'everything started in the house of the Lord'" (1960a).

In this article, Gleason seems to realize that there is a cultural significance to the music of which he writes—the slave songs, African music, "sexually symbolic" blues—but he still concentrates on the performances, on music, focusing on the quality of the sounds and the power of their presence: "Communication was the key to both afternoon programs. It might be said that these two programs not only represented both sides of our society today but that they communicated directly to the audience with the same intensity with which the two sides of society burn. . . . But just as some can see the world of technology, of the Bomb, and of the giant shedding of skin of discrimination by black peoples of the world, with fascination and excitement and a kind of joy mixed with fear, so did this music communicate" (1960a)

Another critic who quickly realized the social significance of popular music and often wrote about the connections between jazz and race is Nat Hentoff (who after his career as a music critic became a prominent political journalist and columnist for the *Village Voice*). Less prone to out-on-a-limb blanket statements than Gleason, more thoroughly logical, and the younger of the two, Hentoff can, with Gleason, be rightfully considered an originator of popular-music criticism. Hentoff took a similar career path. Starting out as a music reviewer for such publications as *Downbeat* and the *Jazz Review,* he later contributed to *Playboy,* the *New Yorker, Commonweal,* the *Saturday Review,* and the *Reporter,* becoming in the process (like Gleason) as much a social critic as a music critic. Since the 1970s Hentoff has written little about popular music; instead he produces political analysis for the *Washington Post* and contributes regularly to such publications as the *Village Voice,* the *New Republic,* and the *Progressive.*

Hentoff's early writing demonstrates his social concern. He picked up early on the idea that jazz had much more to it than notes, charts, and scales, more than simple musical exploration. To Hentoff, jazz could also be about rebellion, but he always seemed to bring his writing back to the context of the music itself. Social concerns for Hentoff are a part of popular music, and his main concern is its authenticity.

As Gleason had in 1960, Hentoff began to write about racism in jazz. However, he was quicker than Gleason to turn to popular music as a vehicle for social commentary (and quicker to abandon it, too). In an article for *Commonweal* the connection becomes clear between the social commentary that brought him acclaim in his later career and his earlier writing on jazz and racism. "Being oneself, or trying to be, may mean being totally alone, and that prospect is for the most part unbearable. The overall context is somewhat similar to that in Southern cities where 'liberal' whites have become increasingly silent" (1960). Hentoff did not abandon writing about jazz in favor of rock at this early stage of his career, as Gleason did. His interest in the social issues surrounding jazz brought him more frequently to folk music than to rock and roll. His attention then, as later, focused on protest, regardless of the medium within which he found it. In 1965, for instance, one can find this in a review of the music of Miles Davis and John Coltrane: "Neither makes speeches on prejudice in their music, but their jazz speaks from a position of strength in their self-images as creators who do not have to—and will not—grin for the white man" (1965). Since jazz is the full expression of the man playing, Hentoff writes, it is clear that modern jazz is more grounded in protest than it ever has been.

The folk movement of the 1960s provided Hentoff with a fertile site for examining U.S. protest from the perspective of race. For instance, he wrote that urban white boys with admittedly good intentions are going to fail in their attempt to reproduce the rural black blues sound to which they have no cultural connection. It is impossible to recreate someone else's history, Hentoff says, so if they are to survive, artists must face the future more as themselves and create more of their own material. His focus is still on music, however, and on the expression of race via music.

By the late 1960s Hentoff had left popular-music criticism, but not before writing an article for *Parents* magazine that encapsulates his (perhaps essentialist) view of why popular music is important. Rock music, Hentoff tells the nation's parents, is a dialogue among young people. "It provides the quality of identification, what comes from knowing that your most urgent concerns and anxieties are understood by others who share them" (1969, 46). A central facet of rock music, the reason it seems to provide existential truths, Hentoff says, is because it is diversified culturally. "In a society increasingly divided by color and class, teenagers are able, at least through their music, to transcend those barriers."

Returning to a theme from his jazz criticism, Hentoff writes that such diversification had not always been present. There were clearer geographic and ethnic lines only fifteen years earlier. There was hillbilly music for southern whites, blues and jazz for blacks and some white aficionados, and Broadway and show tunes for most of the white youth. Elvis Presley and Bob Dylan helped change that, primarily because each was indebted to white and black artists. By 1969, Hentoff suggests, racial barriers were being torn down by the music.

Lester Bangs (1949–82) also believed in music as a bridge between races. Bangs, who has inspired many critics in the underground press since the 1970s, like Gleason and Hentoff was a fan of popular music. Unlike them, he began writing about rock and stuck with it, though he showed a taste for jazz and blues from time to time.

Bangs's articles, particularly those published during his tumultuous years as writer and editor at *Creem* magazine in the 1970s, were always an up-front challenge to his readers, to his editors, to his culture. At times he wrote to anger people, and he usually succeeded (Jann Wenner fired him from the staff of *Rolling Stone* in 1971 for being disrespectful to musicians).

In his first published piece, a review for *Rolling Stone* of the MC5's debut album *Kick out the Jams,* Bangs sounded somewhat like Gleason or Hentoff, and his later writing harked back to the blues as an indicator of a "true" roots heritage. As with Hentoff, it was always the music that counted most; but revolution counted too, and the MC5 were judged not only by their music but also by their political stance. Bangs found them lacking on both counts. There were hints of the coming Bangs bombast, the style that first took form in his review of the Count Five's *Carburetor Dung:* "I suppose the best way to characterize the album would be to call it murky. Some of the lyrics were intelligible, such as these, from 'The Hermit's Prayer': 'Sunk funk dunk Dog God the goosie Gladstone prod old maids de back seat sprung Louisiana sundown junk an' bunk an' sunken treasures / But oh muh drunken hogbogs / I theenk I smell a skunk.' Lyrics such as those don't come every day, and even if their instrumental backup sounded vaguely like a car stuck in the mud and spinning its wheels, it cannot be denied that the song had a certain value as a prototype slab of gully-bottom rock 'n' roll" (1971a, 63).

Like Gleason, Bangs could be excitable and giddy; he too had great faith in the revolutionary promise of popular music, but as personal fulfillment and transcendence rather than as social revolution. Bangs was as troubled by racism as by the sheer nihilism of the rock generation he had grown up with, which expressed itself in punk rock. In a 1979 *Village Voice* article titled "The White Noise Supremacists," Bangs scolded the New York punk scene for its racism: "You don't have to try at all to be a racist. It's a little coiled clot of venom lurking there in all of us, white and black, goy and Jew, ready to strike out when we feel embattled, belittled, brutalized. . . . But there's a difference between hate and a little . . . gob at authority: swastikas in punk are basically another way for kids to get a rise out of their parents and maybe the press, both of whom deserve the irritation. . . . Maybe. Except that after a while this casual, even ironic embrace of the totems of bigotry crosses over into the real poison" (1987, 275).

Unlike other popular-music critics, Bangs was self-reflexive in the extreme, and this is what largely sets him square in the ranks of the New Journalists. For example, in the same 1979 *Voice* article, he wrote that "in Detroit I thought absolutely nothing of going to parties with people like David Ruffin and Bobby Womack where I'd get drunk, maul the women, and improvise blues songs along the lines of "Sho' wish ah wuz a nigger . . . ," and of course they all laughed. It took years before I realized what an asshole I'd been" (1987, 276).

But Bangs is less interested in the details than in larger cultural patterns:

> All I knew was that when you added all this sort of stuff up you realized a line had been crossed by certain people we thought we knew, even believed in, while we weren't looking. Either that or they were always across that line and we never bothered to look until we tripped over it. And sometimes you even find that you yourself have drifted across that line. . . . Most people think the whole subject of racism is boring, and anybody looking for somebody to stomp is gonna find them irrespective of magazine articles. Because nothing could make the rage of the underclass greater than it is already, and nothing short of a hydrogen bomb on their own heads or a sudden brutal bigoted slap in the face will make almost anybody think about anybody else's problems but their own. And that's where you cross over the line. (1987, 280, 282)

Bangs's ire flared less over individual acts of racism and nihilism than over the big social picture he perceived, the center of which was occupied by popular music: "Since rock 'n' roll is bound to stay in your life you would hope to see it reach some point where it might not add to the cruelty and exploitation already in the world" (1987, 282). As a result, his writing often included sweeping, sad, and bittersweet speculation about the baby-boom generation, such as this in a piece written just after Elvis Presley's death: "If love is truly going out of fashion forever, which I do not believe, then along with our nurtured indifference to each other will be an even more contemptuous indifference to each other's objects of reverence" (216).

What is conspicuously absent from Bangs's writing is the inherent sense of optimism that suffused popular-music criticism. Gleason and Hentoff, for instance, did not so much champion popular music as voice their faith in it as a force for positive social change. They were not convinced that popular music would end racism, but they did seem to believe that popular music would bring it to a swifter conclusion among youth. In Bangs's writing, such faith is present but far from certain, and it is a marker of change in popular music and the popular music audience, a change playing itself out still in the critical discourse concerning rap music, racism, and violence. Today's broken, mass-mediated conversations between generations that find more disagreement than harmony in the popular music to which they cling exemplify Bangs's conviction: Popular music can bring people together . . . but it is just too late.

Reaping the Counterculture: Criticism, Mass Culture, and Commercialization

That mass media and mass culture remain prevalent topics in pop-music criticism is a commentary on pop culture itself—the aspirations and self-projecting fantasies of those within that culture, the dissolution of that culture, and in some cases a blueprint for the improvement and preservation of that culture. Such commentary makes up a vast amount of Robert Christgau's work, as it did Bangs's and Gleason's.[1]

Christgau is one of the few contemporary rock critics who can boast of a career traversing popular music since the mid-1960s and of a career as a rock critic without *Rolling Stone* as its springboard. He first appeared on the scene as a columnist for *Esquire* in 1967. He has called himself "the dean of rock critics," and while writers like Greil Marcus, R. Serge Denisoff, and Wilfred Mellers have displayed a more classic academic tone, Christgau is, if not the dean, at least the senior professor of the popular critics. He may have been the first deliberately to form a theory about the job of the pop music critic in society, and his vision certainly has helped define the mainstream approach to popular-music criticism as it now exists. Rock is art, Christgau says, nothing less, nothing more. And it is a powerful social force, magnified by its place in mass media.

Christgau's writing reflects a remarkably unified vision of popular music and popular-music criticism, even if one can also discern a tendency to repeat things that have already been said. His intentions seem the same today in his "Consumer Guide" columns for the *Village Voice* as they were in his earliest "Secular Music" columns for *Esquire.*

Elements that informed one of Christgau's earliest *Esquire* columns, a review of folk singer Phil Ochs, echo in his writing today: a demanding sense of what makes music musical (a standard missing among some critics, notably Lester Bangs), a sense of political certainty, a sense of where pop music should be and what it should be saying to the culture or subculture it addresses. Unlike Jann Wenner, Gleason, and others who gathered under *Rolling Stone*'s masthead, Christgau rarely reeled with giddiness over the revolutionary promise of rock music. "Good intentions," he wrote, "are never good enough" (1969, 19), and revolutionary promise had little influence on his musical taste.

After five years as a rock critic, Christgau collected his writing in a book, *Any Old Way You Choose It,* in which he outlined his theory of criticism. He talks of formulating this theory as a college student, first impressed with the idea of rock as an "art form" (or "antiart," as he also terms it) after seeing a painting of a nude woman into which a radio had been installed. The radio was tuned to a pop music station. He declared an early penchant for jazz and literature, amplified by Motown and Phil Spector recordings (which inspired him to compile charts, precursors to his "Consumer Guide," a regular feature in the *Voice*). When he heard the Beatles, he says, he began to view the music through the "secular theology of new-critical literary analysis" he was studying: "I certainly didn't reject all art, and I didn't exactly decide that what is called high art is bullshit—I still don't believe that. But I did come to understand that popular art is not inferior to high art, and achieved a vitality of both integrity and outreach that high art had unfortunately abandoned" (1973, 3).

In *Any Old Way You Choose It*, he dismisses much of his period with *Esquire* as one of "Hooray Little Richard, boo Jefferson Airplane," a position quite contrary to the one West Coast critics (especially Gleason) asserted. But he softened and learned to like the hippies: "Most important, they like mass culture: What was then called rock-popular-music created by the counterculture—embodied my own personal contradictions" (1973, 6). His impulses were part pop-culture theorist and part bohemian, and these fused in his politics, he said. Both approaches were pragmatic, suggesting complementary modes of self-preservation. "Pop is really a system for beating the system, both perceptually, by aesthetic reinterpretation, and physically, by selective consumption. And bohemianism has always sought to shed the system's outworn, wasteful usages and uncover the true self." Both, he wrote, are too insular on their own; he rejected the elitism of the pop and the bohemian and claimed to have melded the two into a sensibility:

> I always resisted the term "criticism" to describe secular music—I preferred "amateur sociology" or "journalism" or just "writing," because the idea of criticism had been deracinated for me in college. As practiced by academics, it leeched life from works that had to survive, if they were to survive at all, not in some specimen bottle but in the commerce of the world, and it separated the critic—or, anyway, the critic's student—from the pleasure that has always been the secret of art. . . . My understanding was that criticism should invoke total aesthetic response. . . . The richest and most useful kind of criticism respected the work as it was actually perceived, by people in general. . . . Any critic who wrote about the music as if he/she were no longer a fan—or who was no longer a fan—was shirking all the fun. (7–8)

Christgau here not only tackles the issues between high culture and mass culture but also addresses the critical discourse regarding those issues, a remarkable thing for a critic in a musical genre that was less than ten years old.

Toward the end of the sixties, Christgau took to keeping one eye on the records being released and the other on the record companies releasing them, and in time his writing showed a savvy understanding of the music industry. Like Gleason, Christgau bemoaned the industrialization of rock and roll. It had, he believed, spread widely as a commercial force but thinly as an art form, and though he blamed the music industry he mostly blamed the popular-music audience for its unwillingness to make its own aesthetic choices. This is an interesting and somewhat ironic perspective for the author of the "Consumer Guide," which, it could be argued, itself has led to the industrialization of popular music—or at least to the industrialization of popular-music criticism, as many publications (particularly ones online, even though space for lengthier reviews is not an economic issue) have adopted Christgau's one-paragraph review style and grading system.

Hentoff, too, turned an eye to the music industry. In *Commonweal* he writes of being able to overcome some of his derision as a jazz fan for the simplicity of teen-aged rock and roll music, saying that there are adult reasons for the mediocrity of most rock and roll (1960). Although he quotes a claim by ASCAP (the American Association of Authors, Composers, and Publishers) that music owes its decline to the infestation of the young by rock and roll, he maintains that ASCAP's concern is less aesthetically than financially based, since its upstart competitor, BMI (Broadcast Music, Inc.), had signed the most rock acts, at considerable profit. Payola seemed to fill out the equation. Rock and roll was being selected and distributed on the basis of publishers' greed.

Gleason turned fifty at the height of the summer of love. He was too old to be accepted into the now generation but young enough to feel part of it anyway, and he had begun to ponder the impact of rock music on U.S. mass culture. He had seen jazz give voice to the frustrations of urban blacks, and he was now aware of rock music giving voice to the frustrations of a much larger audience, American youth. With many other critics, Gleason at first saw the whole "Beatles-Sgt. Pepper-Airplane-Dead-hippy" movement as an unbelievable utopia under construction. A generation was in motion, and rock music had propelled it.

It was exactly as Plato had predicted, Gleason wrote. "Music, if Plato was right, might save us yet. Certainly no hippie, no folk singer, no long-haired guitar-playing rock musician is going to fry us all with napalm or blow us up with the bomb. This would be a better country with Zally [Yanovski, a member of the Lovin' Spoonful] as president, to say nothing of the thousands of others" (1968a, 29). For Gleason, the communities that rock fostered mattered most, ones tenuously tied together by a variety of constructs: folk music, art, politics. As Simon Frith claims about rock music's shift in the 1960s, "Music is no longer commenting on a community but creating it, offering a sense of inclusion not just to the musicians, bohemian style, but also to the audiences, to all those people hip enough to make the necessary commitment to the music, to assert that it matters" (1981, 88). Gleason said the same: "I don't think music has lit up the world, so to speak," he wrote for *Rolling Stone* in April 1968. "But I do think the new music has established a kind of 'Stranger in a Strange Land' head community, vibes in concert, thoughts and ideas and concepts changing together" (1968a, 28). He predicted that 1968 might be the year the counterculture would find out whether deviants in society might be accepted or squashed.

By December 1968, there were many clues about the direction in which the counterculture would travel. Assassinations, the party conventions, the election of Richard Nixon as president, escalation in Vietnam to 500,000 troops, drug busts of the Rolling Stones and Lovin' Spoonful, and a dissipation of spirit in the underground community were among the hints. Gleason was still committed to the idea of a youth rebellion, but he now complained it was being sapped by Madison Avenue ads that could take the words "world revolution" and make them a pun on the revolving door of a Sheraton Hotel, sell Nehru shirts with the slogan "Meditate in '68," and make radio commercials that sounded like a drug pusher peddling the finest Acapulco gold. Columbia Records launched an advertising campaign whose slogan was "The Man Can't Bust Our Music." Gleason was not pleased: "Neither Columbia Records nor any other entrenched privilege group is going to nurture any power which will obviously destroy it. The key word is obviously. As long as any point of view or doctrine is not considered a threat, it will be expressed and even encouraged because it proves the deification of the system was worthwhile" (1968b, 34).

Having left jazz, Gleason now saw the co-opting of the counterculture occurring before his eyes, and he predicted the total blurring of the line between rock music and commercialism. He had helped draw that line in the 1960s while writing about the San Francisco music scene. The greatest danger to the counterculture, and to youth rebellion, he had said, is the ability of the established society to co-opt its leading elements and ideas. That it had not happened yet was no protection against that danger, he felt. "They haven't figured out yet how to utilize all this power that's floating around, but you can believe that somewhere somebody is working on it. In fact, you'd better believe it" (1968b, 34). One can imagine how Gleason would have reacted to the similar implosion of the punk movement in the United Kingdom from the co-optation it sought to overcome.

By March 1969, Gleason had constructed a theory of exactly how music works on its audience, and how music might be used as a cultural tool. He quotes Herbert Marcuse to claim that public opinion is made by

the media of mass communication: "If you cannot buy equal and adequate time, how are you supposed to change public opinion in the monopolist way?" (1969, 19). By then he had moved almost completely away from his earlier traditional music criticism, based on reviews of performances, to social and cultural criticism.

Much of his writing in this period begins to echo that of media critics. Gleason wrote about understanding what makes news and how to get the news out to the media. He takes on issues of epistemology and the social construction of reality in popular culture. "When you accept 'Desolation Row' and 'Tom Thumb's Blues' along with 'Mr. Tambourine Man' and 'Rolling Stone' and the rest, you are accepting a definition of the world around you" (1969, 22). The wildness of some of his theories can make one wonder about his sanity, as, for instance, when he claims that Dylan and the Beatles had started "programs" to indoctrinate youth that will begin when the time is right.

For these and other critics, the co-optation of popular music was to be guarded against, yet none wrote about the connections between commercialization and the underground press. While seeking to preserve popular music's positive spirit, as with their writing about racism, popular-music critics articulated their thoughts within a mass medium, just as the music articulated itself in a bundle of media texts: records, films, radio, books, magazines. Popular-music fans, musicians, and producers have forever sought to retain (or create) that positive spirit in the name of authenticity or credibility. Only Christgau managed to extricate himself from the morass of glib pronunciations about rock's demise, in an essay on the Rolling Stones: "Only popular culture could have rendered art accessible—in the excitement and inspiration (and self-congratulation) of its perception and the self-realization (or fantasy) of its creation —not just to well-raised well-offs but to the broad range of less statusy war babies who in fact made the hippie movement the relatively cross-class phenomenon it was. And for all these kids, popular culture meant rock and roll, the art form created by and for their hedonistic consumption" (1980, 196).

License and Essence: Criticism and Authenticity

Authenticity is probably simultaneously the most invisible and most opaque of the concerns that occupy popular-music critics, yet it is referred to or implied in almost all popular-music criticism. It is also the most frequently debated topic, and one that brings popular music's inherent elitism to the fore. Since the job of the music critic is, fundamentally, to convince readers that particular music is good or bad—"the second commandment," Deena Weinstein noted, "is to elicit and dutifully quote musicians' proclamations of their artistic integrity" (1999, 57)—and since standards are difficult to come by in popular music, critics often refer to authenticity as a measure of aesthetic soundness, to bolster their opinion. In numerous ways, critics claim that music is either "authentic" or "inauthentic." Some contradict themselves.

David Sanjek (1991) defines authenticity as central to the ideology of rock music, "the degree to which a musician is able to articulate the thoughts and desires of an audience and not pander to the 'mainstream' by diluting their sound or their message." Music critics seem to use a similar definition. Frith argues that the importance of the music press is "not commercial . . . but ideological. Fanzines, fanzine writers (and the important critics in the mass music papers share the fanzine stance) are the source of the arguments about what rock means, arguments not only about art and commerce, but also about art and audience" (1981, 77). Popular-music criticism can therefore be understood as meaning making, a way of continuing the discourse of popular music on a nonmusical plane.

As do most critics who are also fans, Nat Hentoff started out with a sense that he had to protect the authenticity and validity of the music he reviewed. In a *Saturday Review* article in 1956, he scolds the jazz audience for not being more responsive to jazz history, for allowing older jazz musicians such as Coleman Hawkins, Jack Teagarden, and Cootie Williams to become dispossessed as their styles fell out of favor. Many were having trouble even securing club dates. "If jazz is indeed an 'art form,' a fair majority of its practitioners and supporters ought by now to be expected to possess—and listen according to—an informed sense of the history of this young musical language" (1956, 30). As things stood, Hentoff wrote, there was little room for any jazz player who had reached forty or forty-five years of age.

The best of the modern jazz musicians—Miles Davis, John Lewis, Tony Scott, Charlie Mingus—have a good sense of what has come before, Hentoff writes, "but had there been more modernists fully aware of from whence they swung, it's possible that the quality of some of the present-day experimental jazz might have been of higher quality with longer likelihood of fruitable durability" (1956, 30). Like many popular-music critics, Hentoff claims that a "return to the roots" signifies authenticity. History, in other words, provides a context without which one cannot claim to be authentic.

And yet in a 1967 essay on folk music, Hentoff urged young musicians not to rely on history too much, to compose and perform more of their own material as a way to get in touch with their own history. "For the city young, in sum, 'ethnic authenticity'—as that term refers to someone else's past of whatever color or region—is the route to absurdity" (1967,

327). Hentoff claimed that the mass media had for the most part destroyed the possibility of "ethnic authenticity," even for rural youths, who would now hear Marvin Gaye on the radio and not Mance Lipscomb on their porches. "Influences will, of course, continue, but the quest for authenticity must be pursued from within," he wrote. He extended this claim to encompass black youth as well, stating that as blacks adapt the roots of the music of their culturally native Africa, they will no longer be, technically speaking, culturally authentic. He pronounces that they will be, however, personally authentic. Hentoff's turn from historical authenticity based largely on ethnicity and "roots" to personal authenticity and self-expression is thus clearly documented and delineated in one essay. It is as if, in the folk music movement, Hentoff determined that the ease of cultural assimilation provided by the mass media renders historical authenticity impossible.[2]

Given the frequency and intensity with which he had written about authenticity in the past, Hentoff was forced to reconceive authenticity as a form of self-expression. He returns to the theme of his 1960 *Commonweal* article: Rock, he says, is fundamentally a release of feelings—expressing the poignant loneliness felt at times by all adolescents and their fear of becoming as emotionally gray as they perceive their parents to be. Hentoff adds a final note: Rock is also big business and will lose some of its credibility as its market expands, and as it becomes politically co-opted. Here he introduces a point that within two years would in the hands of other critics (and fans) become a key issue in the debate on authenticity in popular music.

Christgau, too, showed a propensity toward using popular music's history to measure its contemporary authenticity. In 1969 Christgau wrote a feature for *Stereo Review* titled "A Short and Happy History of Rock." Rock had become "canonized" by the mass media after the Beatles' "Sgt. Pepper" album, he argued, "making it the hottest item since the Lindbergh kidnapping" (1969, 80). In the article Christgau reveals a prejudice for the rock and roll of the 1950s, detailing the criteria the music must meet to pass the "Christgau test." But first he tries to explain how rock ever got commercially successful in the first place: "The success of rock and roll was as much a rejection of contemporary popular music as it was an affirmation of the blues and the country-and-western music in which rock is rooted. The vitality of rock and roll . . . was the vitality of an oppressed subculture—all right, not that of urban blacks or hillbillies, but of the young, particularly the white young."

Christgau echoes Hentoff's claims about rock music's ability to cross racial barriers and refers to rock's "roots" in much the same way that Hentoff referred to authenticity. More importantly, he claims that rock's success is based on musical values, not political ones. Though he acknowledges the relation between social status, subculture, and rock's "vitality," he keeps musical and political issues separate.

For Lester Bangs, authenticity was tied to fandom, and Bangs was, simply, a fan. As he once claimed, "My most memorable childhood fantasy was to have a mansion with catacombs underneath containing, alphabetized in endless winding dimly lit musty rows, every album ever released" (1987, xi). What better evidence of fandom than the desire to be the ultimate collector?

For Lester Bangs, gritty, grungy, gully-bottom rock and roll was the core of all rock and roll, the brutally honest, vulgar, and savage heart of his culture, one of the last brilliantly gleaming torches that culture had bothered to keep lit in its ascent toward extermination. Unlike Jann Wenner, who seemed to believe the torch would keep burning with an eternal flame fueled by the "classic rock" canon, Bangs struggled to discover new music that would keep the torch alight. As Christgau noted in Bangs's *Village Voice* obit, on 11 May 1982, Bangs kept "alive the dream of insurrectionary rock and roll as *Rolling Stone* turned to auteur theory and trade journalism," words that say as much about Christgau as about Bangs but sum up the direction that Bangs took upon leaving *Rolling Stone.* They also say much about the direction popular-music criticism took in the mainstream media in the 1980s and later, when it became a staple of entertainment reporting.

Given his interest in finding new rock music, it is not surprising that Bangs often wrote about punk rock (he is commonly credited with coining the label). He kept a close ear on New York's punk scene in the 1970s and traveled to England to view British punk firsthand. Bangs espoused a punk aesthetic long before it came to be associated with safety pins, and that aesthetic more than any other informed his writing. Indeed, it formed the core of his concept of authenticity; inept, grungy rock was the only true rock and roll:

> "It wasn't until much later, drowning in the kitschvats of Elton John and James Taylor that I finally came to realize that grossness was the truest criterion for rock 'n' roll, the cruder the clang and grind the more fun and longer listened-to the album'd be. By that time I would just about've knocked out an incisor, shaved my head or made nearly any sacrifice to acquire even one more album of this type of in-clanging and hyena-hooting raunch. By then it was too late" (1971a, 63).

Bangs's main concern was always to keep the music aesthetically authentic, politics be damned, because, if the music became fake, there would be nothing left to grasp at to stem the tide of artificiality and hopelessness, of the existential nihilism he believed was already smothering his society. If his ideas of what made music authentic were extreme

and unapproachable, he still defended them with the passion and elo-
quence of a writer one would never think of finding in the pulp pages
of an underground fanzine. For instance, in 1979 in a fanzine called
Stranded he wrote:

> [Van Morrison's] "Astral Weeks" would be the subject of this piece—i.e.,
> the rock record with the most significance in my life so far—no matter how
> I'd been feeling when it came out (Fall 1968). But in the condition I was
> in, it assumed at the time the quality of a beacon, a light on the far shores
> of the murk; what's more, it was proof that there was something left to ex-
> press besides nihilism and destruction. . . . It sounded like the man who
> made "Astral Weeks" was in terrible pain, pain that most of Van Morrison's
> previous works had only suggested; but like the later albums by the Velvet
> Underground, there was a redemptive element in the blackness, ultimate
> compassion for the suffering of others, and a swath of pure beauty and
> mystical awe that cut right through the heart of the work. (1987, 20)

Bangs scoured records for transcendence, for anything that raised
music (and thus Bangs) beyond everydayness. In his writing, self-reflex-
iveness counts. Self-parody counts as well, and self-knowledge most of
all. He displayed all three, chronologically, as his style developed. More
than any other popular-music critic, Bangs summoned authenticity from
within himself. Like Norman Denzin's ideal interpretive interactionist,
Bangs "moves outward . . . from [his] personal biography to those social
settings where other persons experiencing the same personal trouble
come together" (1989, 126). For Bangs, those settings were most often
found in the presence of music and not in the presence of people. His
writing resonated not because of any claims he made for the authenticity of the music he wrote about, but because of the authenticity he
evoked by interacting with experiences familiar to the popular-music audience. To claim that Bangs was consciously practicing interpretive interactionism is absurd, but not pointless; he achieved what most scholars
and critics alike seek, to understand "how this historical moment univer-
salizes itself in the lives of interacting individuals" (139). Bangs also
clearly demarcates the shift away from what Weinstein has termed "exog-
enous" authenticity—the kind espoused by Hentoff, "music 'borrowed'
from authentic sources" (Weinstein 1999, 58) being the best example—
and toward "obedience to one's own muse" (59). That shift has pos-
sessed popular music since the 1960s, no matter how hard Bangs tried to
exorcise it.

Conclusion

Race, commercialization, and authenticity together illuminate the problems with which popular music and its audience have grappled. What

sets popular-music criticism apart from most all other forms of opinion writing is its tendency from its earliest postwar days to venture beyond the particular work being criticized. Popular-music criticism served as a springboard for social discourse on many levels.

It is also the springboard for what Bourdieu termed the determination "of relationships of symbolic domination; that is, [it] constitute[s] the means for obtaining or safe-guarding the monopoly of the legitimate mode of practicing a[n] . . . activity" (1985, 42). Intertwined with fan discourse, popular-music criticism had, in the 1960s and 1970s, a national audience in the United States that other music media would not reach until the advent of MTV. To a great degree, the popular-music criticism of that era shaped a national consciousness, aesthetic, and symbolic system that put in motion a dynamics of cultural consecration.

That motive force is best understood in the context of the underground press, with which the history of popular-music criticism is inextricably intertwined. Frith claims that "underground papers were important as the source of what became the dominant ideology of rock" (1981, 169). Underground papers were also the forum within which popular-music critics could work, not only because editors selected them but also because those publications delivered—and needed—an audience eager to read their writing. Few of the more prominent music magazines (*Rolling Stone, Creem, Musician,* for example) departed from the formula followed by other media fan magazines. As Frith notes, "Music papers and record companies work together not because the papers are 'controlled' by the companies' advertising, but because their general images of the world, their general interpretations of rock, are much the same" (173). The connection between the music industry and the music press is compelling. But the same connection does not necessarily hold between the music industry and music critics. One could rework Frith's statement about music papers and record companies and claim that music critics and the underground press had a similar "general image of the world." It is that image that the critics maintained, long after the publications for which they wrote ceased to exist or matter (Jones 1993).

The "general image" created by music critics illustrates not only Bourdieu's theories of cultural production and legitimation but also the discourse about media and modernity that Joli Jensen analyzes in *Redeeming Modernity.* The "tensions and contradictions" that she identifies are present in popular-music criticism as well, and they give that criticism its poignancy. According to Jensen, the recurring themes of the modern discourse about media are "seduction, transgression, pollution and doom" (1991, 161). These themes are found in popular-music criticism, too, from groping for an end to racism and decrying the pollution of "pure" music by commerce, to searching for redemption and transcendence in "authentic" rock and roll. The cultural arguments Jensen examines—essential worth, the lowest common denominator, egalitarian elitism, contamination, blurred boundaries, the pure and the polluting—are at once present in popular-music criticism and in the critics. Not only do critics reflect on these "tensions and contradictions" in their writing, but also they reveal their own belief in popular music and in youth. Consequently, it is another arena within which Jensen's aptly named "modernity story" (59) might be told. Popular-music criticism reveals a sense that a promise of social development based on progressive ideals has been betrayed.

A telling story is the one Abe Peck relates about Gleason's review of the Beatles' "Revolution," in which the critic noted the Beatles' own reticence about revolution. The underground press, particularly the *Barb*, went on the attack and accused Gleason of having "bad politics," then proceeded to discuss the music and leave aside the politics (1985, 168). Another telling story Peck tells is about Cameron Crowe. While writing for the underground *San Diego Door*, Crowe noted that he "was made to feel that [he] was doing scrap work for the Movement. . . . Plus someone in the collective was stealing the best records." When Crowe found that in his review of Carole King her name was misspelled "Cosol Kirg," the paper's editors replied, "Oh, dude, c'mon. It's *just* a record review" (281). Crowe went on to write for *Rolling Stone*. The "tensions and contradictions" between music and the counterculture eventually became too much, as Peck notes, culminating at Woodstock when the Who's Pete Townshend bumps Abbie Hoffman offstage: "The honeymoon was over between the rock elite and the politicized counterculture . . . promoters would make their million selling the rights for a movie that deliberately excised signs of radical politics" (180).

These same "tensions and contradictions" gave rise to the New Journalism, too. David Eason argues that the New Journalism emerged from "cultural criticism focused on how the self might find its bearing in a society characterized by a breakdown in consensus about manners and morals and by the permeation of everyday life by a mass-produced image-world" (1990, 191). Perhaps popular-music criticism seemed to have divorced itself from politics, but the writing of the four critics examined here shows that it had only shifted strategies. Eason describes two approaches—realism and modernism—by which New Journalists responded to that "breakdown in consensus": "Both . . . reflect an absorption in aesthetic concerns. . . . In realist reports, the dominant function of the narrative is to reveal an interpretation; in modernist reports it is to show how an interpretation is constructed" (199). Popular-music criticism has attempted both strategies, sometimes in the same article. It has also stretched journalistic conventions, as did the New Journalism, in ways that foregrounded meaning making. In terms of its importance to popular music, criticism is one of those areas Grossberg identified in which "rock and roll organizes, not the meanings we give to the world, but the ways we are able to invest and locate energy, importance, even ourselves, in those meanings" (1992, 160). The politics became personal, but no less powerful.

As a literary form, popular-music criticism grew up side by side, often page to page, with the New Journalism. Roy Shuker noted that even U.K. music magazines like *New Musical Express* were using "'new journalist' prose" in the 1970s (1994, 87). However, even as popular-music criticism mirrored and intertwined with the New Journalism, as John Pauly observed about the latter's becoming a "literary canon," the former also moved away from its evolution and history. Pauly noted that the New Journalism "affirmed a generational identity . . . [and] also articulated a cultural identity" (1990, 119). Popular-music critics were writing about both generational and cultural identity well before the phrase "New Journalism" came into popular use. Popular music itself is precisely about such affirmation, even if, as evidence, it is easiest now to point to the music's use in advertising targeted to the very generations the critics examined in this essay believed it might help achieve transcendence.

Popular-music criticism was from the start concerned with the struggle over meaning. It is useful to think about Michael Jarrett's description of jazz criticism: "Writing about jazz functioned within two aesthetic economies that, while distinct, even competitive, were founded on the image of jazz as a simulacrum. One group . . . pointed to the dependence of jazz on European harmony and form. . . . Another group, however, represented the musical and cultural value of jazz as inversely proportional to its adherence to established musical standards" (1992, 189).

The lesson Jarrett teaches is that "jazz functions as a sign; . . . it enters discourse (in Lacanian terms, moves from the *Imaginary* to the *Symbolic* Realm) as a projection or objectification of warring systems of representation" (1992, 193). The struggle has continued—but it is clearer now than ever that there are many systems of representation. Whether popular-music criticism continues to wield discursive power—there are those, like Gina Arnold (1999), who claim it has become altogether powerless—will depend on not only pop or the press, but also how much those who wish to express themselves believe it worth the struggle.

Notes

1. Though not included in this essay, Greil Marcus's writing is particularly relevant in comparison to Christgau's. Both critics achieve many of the same ends,

though they begin in different places. Christgau's emphasis remains rooted in music, Marcus's in sociology. For a representative sample, see Marcus 1989.

2. One wonders what Hentoff would think of contemporary "world music," given that at one point he urged pop musicians to look to international and indigenous music. Would he find world music's authenticity dubious and its pervasiveness further complicating matters of historical authenticity that he noted are difficult to preserve?

References

Arnold, Gina. (1999). Rock lit lite. *San Jose Metro*, 30 November, 23–26.

Bangs, Lester. (1971a). Psychotic reactions and carburetor dung. *Creem*, December, 63.

———. (1971b). Lick my decals off/Captain Beefheart. *Creem*, March, 76.

———. (1987). *Psychotic reactions and carburetor dung*. New York: Knopf.

Bizzell, Patricia. (1989). Cultural criticism: A social approach to studying writing. *Rhetoric Review* 7: 211–38.

Bourdieu, Pierre. (1985). The market of symbolic goods. *Poetics* 14: 13–44.

Christgau, Robert. (1968). Secular music. *Esquire*, May, 19.

———. (1969). A short and happy history of rock. *Stereo Review*, March, 80.

———. (1973). *Any old way you choose it*. Baltimore: Penguin Books.

———. (1980). The Rolling Stones. In *The Rolling Stone illustrated history of rock 'n' roll*, ed. James Miller, 190–200. New York: Random House/Rolling Stone Press.

Denzin, Norman K. (1989). *Interpretive interactionism*. Newbury Park, Calif.: Sage.

Eason, David. (1990). The new journalism and the image world. In *Literary journalism in the twentieth century*, ed. Norman Sims, 110–29. New York: Oxford University Press.

Frith, Simon. (1981). *Sound effects*. New York: Pantheon.

Gleason, Ralph J. (1960a). Monterey: The afternoons. *Downbeat*, 10 November, 18.

———. (1960b). Perspectives. *Downbeat*, 15 September, 38.

———. (1968a). The final paroxysm of fear. *Rolling Stone*, 6 April, 28–29.

———. (1968b). So revolution is commercial. *Rolling Stone*, 1 December, 19, 34.

———. (1969). Songs would do more than books. *Rolling Stone*, 1 March, 19–22.

Grossberg, Lawrence. (1992). Rock and roll in search of an audience. In *Popular music and communication*, ed. James Lull, 152–75. Newbury Park, Calif.: Sage.

Hentoff, Nat. (1956). New audiences and old jazzmen. *Saturday Review*, 15 September, 30.

———. (1960). They are playing our song. *Commonweal*, 6 May, 145.

———. (1965). Jazz and race. *Commonweal*, 8 January, 144.

———. (1967). The future of the folk renascence. In *The American folk scene: Dimensions of the folksong revival*, ed. David A. DeTurk and A. Poulin Jr, 326–31. New York: Dell.

———. (1969). What pop means to kids. *Parents*, May, 46.

———. (1990). Conversation with the author, 26 September. Tulsa, Oklahoma.

Hoffman, Frank. (1981). *The literature of rock, 1954–1978.* Metuchen, N.J.: Scarecrow.

Jarrett, J. Michael. (1992). On jazzology: A rapsody. *Black Sacred Music: A Journal of Theomusicology* 6, 2: 177–200.

Jensen, Joli. (1991). *Redeeming modernity.* Newbury Park, Calif.: Sage.

Jones, Steven. (1993). Pop music, criticism, advertising and the music industry, *Journal of Popular Music Studies* 5: 79–91.

Marcus, Greil. (1989). *Lipstick traces.* Cambridge: Harvard University Press.

Pauly, John. (1990). The politics of the new journalism. In *Literary journalism in the twentieth century,* ed. Norman Sims, 110–29. New York: Oxford University Press.

Peck, Abe. (1985). *Uncovering the sixties.* New York: Pantheon.

Sanjek, David. (1991). Pleasure and principles: Issues of authenticity in the analysis of rock 'n' roll. Manuscript.

Shuker, Roy. (1994). *Understanding popular music.* London: Routledge.

Toynbee, Jason. (1993). Policing Bohemia, pinning up grunge: The music press and generic change in British pop and rock. *Popular Music* 12, 3: 289–300.

Weinstein, Deena. (1999). Art versus commerce: Deconstructing a (useful) romantic illusion. In *Stars don't stand still in the sky,* ed. Karen Kelly and Evelyn McDonnell, 57–68. New York: New York University Press.

2

Brit Crit

Turning Points in British
Rock Criticism, 1960–1990

Gestur Gudmundsson, Ulf Lindberg,
Morten Michelsen, and Hans Weisethaunet

ntil the mid-sixties, writing on rock music still amounted to little more than news and gossip. The music press was serving the record industry, going for what sold or might sell to teenagers, and there was nothing very remarkable about that. But as growing audiences of middle-class kids and a heavy input of art ideology began to invest sixties rock with ambitions surpassed so far only by jazz, the phenomenon demanded more serious attention, which was provided by a number of young, predominantly male, white U.S. critics and specialist magazines. Thus the period 1964–69 marks the genesis of rock criticism proper. At the beginning of the 1970s, the confluence of several sources also produced a full-fledged criticism in the United Kingdom. In the perspective established here, this registers a decisive turning point in the development of British rock criticism.[1] Two more were to follow. One began with the advent of punk in 1976 and ended in the early 1980s with New Pop's celebration of style for its own sake. Yet another, which marked a diversification of the market and the polarization of consumer guidance and advanced criticism, occurred in the mid-1980s.

The concept of turning points structures this overview of some thirty years of British rock criticism. These turning points also provide sites from which to view its development. On

41

a general level, the high-low divide in culture that postmodernism boasts of erasing offers one such perspective: The emergence of serious rock criticism challenged this divide. More specifically, our study draws on the cultural sociology of Pierre Bourdieu and in particular on his field theory. In Pierre Bourdieu's terms, our object, situated at the intersection of the fields of rock and journalism, is the semi-autonomous field of rock journalism populated by publishers, magazines, editors, writers, readers, artists, record companies, and so on. Here, our main interest is the role of prominent writers and magazines.

At times the battles in this field have reached a particular intensity, often in connection with paradigmatic musical shifts. These peaks constitute turning points, or shifts on a number of levels: in internal aesthetic standards (e.g., artificiality vs. authenticity), in references to external model systems (e.g., literature vs. theory), in writing styles, and in the circulation and profiling of magazines. Departing from the argument of Motti Regev (1994), we contend that the construction of the field of rock music has been a process of legitimation, for which rock criticism is largely responsible. This ongoing process has caused a drastic rise in the cultural status of key artists in the field. If few people would claim that all rock (whatever that word means today) is art, most would agree that some certainly is.

Some Theoretical Perspectives

Bourdieu's most-read work, *Distinction: A Social Critique of the Judgement of Taste* (1984), is a radical riposte to Kant, who considered taste judgments universally valid. For Bourdieu, taste serves social distinction; it is a means whereby a social group (the "cultural bourgeoisie") wields its power. This power is expressed in the recognition of a "legitimate" culture that sets itself apart from "legitimable" and "illegitimate" cultural forms. Bourdieu thus assumes the existence of a cultural center whose backbone is the educational system, but at the same time he acknowledges a cultural field dynamic that allows for up- and downmarket movements. Such changes, however, presuppose that agents have access to Kant's "pure aesthetic" disposition, which, in Dick Hebdige's words, "perceives as art that which it nominates as art" (1987, 58). The ongoing aestheticization of everyday life seems to imply that the pure aesthetic disposition, once the privilege of the "cultural bourgeoisie," has become more widely accessible.

In late modernity, several forms of low culture have proved to be legitimable. Film, photography, science fiction, jazz, and rock music have all moved upmarket and become more or less accepted as legitimate culture, as music producers and critics have applied high- and folk-art parameters to low art. Simon Frith and Howard Horne (1987) have stressed the impact on British musicians of art ideology as mediated by art schools, while Regev focuses on the parallel effect of U.S. critics' move to art discourse beginning in the mid-sixties.[2] In underground publications, specialist periodicals, and, above all, a number of books, these writings by critics—roughly the age of the artists and involved in the same lifestyle experiments—became extremely influential: "In the way they categorize entries (in encyclopedias) and divide chapters, in their choice of musicians and topics worthy of lengthy articles, in their taken-for-granted periodizations, in the adjectives they use, in their ranking of records in terms of quality—these books (and others) contain, and therefore construct, the accepted truths about rock music up to 1980" (Regev 1994, 91).

However, the genesis of rock criticism draws on British as well as U.S. sources, on film criticism as well as jazz criticism, on folk art as well as high art, and on the Frankfurt school as well as the journalism of Tom Wolfe and Hunter S. Thompson. Rock criticism is a typical child of the sixties' generation gap, behind which Bourdieu in *Distinction* discerns the agency of the so-called new intellectuals, largely autodidacts specializing in "legitimate" cultural capital. In the sixties the rise of this "petit-bourgeois" fraction bred a cultural egalitarianism that became particularly visible in the aesthetic field, where neo-avant-gardist experimentation, pop culture, and political revolt were opening dialogues, clashing and flowing together, and marked an era of happenings, camp, pop art, and countercultural utopianism. In this turbulent climate, rock critics became what Robert Christgau has called "prepostmodern multieverythingists" (1998, 2) who positioned themselves somewhere between the aesthetic neo-avantgardism of Susan Sontag, arguing that culture and politics were inextricably linked, and Tom Wolfe's populist celebration of the purchasing power of common people, insisting on transcendence—the spiritual significance of sensuous experience (cf. Aronowitz 1993, Chapter 6).

It seems fair to regard Christgau and his colleagues as forerunners of postmodernism, at least with respect to the jumbling of high and low cultural codes. Yet, one should not overrate postmodernism's leveling effects. As Brian McHale has observed, the thought that the distinction between high and low culture has had its day is one of the most vivacious myths of postmodernist culture and criticism—"one that postmodernist writers themselves . . . seem to find irresistibly attractive" (1992, 225). That nobody knows what is "high" or "low" has by no means put a stop to thinking of culture in hierarchical terms. Still, it seems that yesterday's "Great Divide" (Huyssen 1986) now lies somewhere *within* popular culture.

Further, postmodernist ideology tends to regard modernism as a high-cultural straitjacket that postmodernism abolished. But modernism never was a monolith. While the high modernism of Adorno and others advocated "pure" art, the various strands of twentieth-century avant-gardism certainly did not. From a historical perspective, it is difficult to maintain that an iron curtain ever separated modern culture into high and low. Instead, the rationalizing, disciplining, and civilizing processes launched in early modernity and described by Habermas, Foucault, and Elias have been quite unsuccessful in shutting out low subject matter as well as low discursive forms from legitimate culture. This failure is mirrored by the introduction of a series of categories into aesthetic theory from the eighteenth century on, ranging from the sublime (Burke, Kant), the interesting (Diderot), the grotesque (as revised by Hugo), and the "modern beautiful" (Baudelaire) to the shock aesthetics of the historical avant-garde, camp, and pop art.

Cultural recognition in Bourdieu's theory depends on the ability of a cultural form to achieve a certain autonomy—a relative freedom from the interests of the power bloc and a dependence instead on an aesthetic sphere governed by its own laws. Not until then is a field established. Donald Broady offers a "minimum" definition of a social field as "a system of relations between positions occupied by specialized agents and institutions engaged in a battle on something they have in common" (1990, 270, our translation), above all the belief that such battles matter. Cultural fields are structured by a primary opposition of aesthetics and economy, of small-scale and large-scale production. At the "autonomous" or "pure" pole, the producers seek recognition from a public largely consisting of colleagues and critics that paves the way for artist-critic alliances. At the "heteronomous" or "commercial" pole, the producers aim for public success. A secondary opposition at the autonomous pole pits the old against the new, as established, orthodox producers battle the heterodoxy of the next generation. In a well-developed cultural field, where the exclusive logic of the "pure" standards celebrated at the autonomous pole tends to subdue those at the opposite pole, public success may even awake suspicion. In the rock field, these oppositions have generated similar struggles, but there is also a certain understanding of their value that makes the view of popular success ambiguous. This explains why authenticity became such a focal concept for the early critics. Taken for granted in the established fields of cultural production, authenticity was needed to explain why rock mattered more than other forms of popular music.

A cultural field produces not only artifacts, but also genres, schools, standards, and even the producers themselves, their habitus and the lifestyles cultivated in professional coteries.[3] All this takes time to develop. A field constitutes itself slowly, by successive specialization, until it possesses its own rules, a clergy endowed with sufficient capital, and admission criteria. Thus, in Bourdieu's account, it took several decades and a great amount of labor to move from Kantian aesthetics via the doctrine of *l'art pour l'art* to the final establishment, in the 1880s, of the literary and artistic fields in France—a process he outlines in *The Rules of Art* (1996). Further, a field's autonomy is always relative. It may be strong, as in the case of mathematics, where the producers' sole customers are their competitors, or it may be fatally weak, as Bourdieu (1998) thinks is the case with the field of journalism.[4]

In the case of rock, one might talk of a rather successful legitimation process. The embryonic rock field has acquired at least semi-autonomous status. This means that one may distinguish in it more-or-less authorized standards, arbiters of taste, investments (in styles and artists), symbolic gains (recognition as artists or critics), educational institutions, attempts at canon formation, and the like. It is telling that the last twenty years or so have witnessed something of an explosion of academic writings on rock, in several disciplines. Rock musicians have even received public funding (Björk won the prestigious Nordic Music Prize in 1997). But the field is also characterized by low admission thresholds, a weak consecrating power (for a broad cultural legitimacy it is dependent on the acceptance of the clergies of other fields), and a dominant commercial pole. So is the field of rock journalism, whose status only periodically, and with a few writers, has risen to that of cultural journalism.

The Genesis of British Rock Criticism

"Lo these many times have I heard bad records, [but] for sheer repulsiveness coupled with the monotony of incoherence, Hound Dog hit a new low in my experience," wrote Steve Race in his review of Elvis Presley's new single in *Melody Maker* (*MM*) on 10 October 1956 (qtd. in Chambers 1985, 30).

Launched by music publisher Lawrence Wright in 1926, *MM* evolved as a trade paper and the major paper that featured jazz and popular music criticism in Britain. Yet the emergence of rock 'n' roll was viewed as a threat to "good taste" and "integrity," and as "the antithesis of all that jazz has been striving for over the years," Race wrote in *MM* (5 May 1956, 8).

Only after 1964—that is, after the breakthrough of the Beatles and the advent of what would later be termed "progressive rock"—did writers start treating pop and rock music seriously. Slowly, a criticism of rock (then labeled "beat") evolved that differed from contemporary fan discourse. Its central agents were a new generation of writers at *MM*, most notably Chris Welch and Ray Coleman. As a paper that catered to the relatively new category of postwar "teenagers," *MM*'s rival weekly (launched in 1952), *New Musical Express* (*NME*), was from the outset much more oriented toward pop and had by the mid-sixties far surpassed *MM* in circulation.[5] Nonetheless, it was *MM*'s more serious attitude, determined by traditional journalistic practices and by jazz criticism, that helped it pave the way for a more autonomous rock criticism. Central to Chris Welch's agenda was the idea of "treating rock just as seriously as jazz," he told Hans Weisethaunet in a phone interview in London on 9 December 1998. Simultaneously, Ray Coleman's lengthy interviews and articles on the Beatles from 1963 on contributed to a deliberate shift in *MM*'s focus from jazz to the new beat.

The main shift in the discourse was the emergence of a new set of criteria for rock criticism. For Welch, standards of skill and creative musicianship were as important in rock as in jazz. Yet the criteria for what makes good music were not the same as in jazz or earlier popular styles. For instance, as Coleman wrote in *MM*, Jagger has "passion" and "drive" as opposed to "swing": "His singing is impolite. It has passion. . . . They [the Rolling Stones] don't swing much, but they drive and they generate" (*MM*, May 23, 1964:9). Thus, rock criticism gradually evolved and made itself independent of the criteria hewed to by the older generation of critics, who continued to characterize the new music as "rubbish."

The role of the critic in the creation of artistic images and lasting myths often seems neglected. Depicting the Rolling Stones in early 1964 as, among other things, "the group parents hate" (*MM*, 7 March, 9) and as "the guys you don't want your sister to hang out with" (*MM*, 14 March, 8), Ray Coleman seemed ahead of the Stones themselves, if not manager Andrew Loog Oldham, in this respect. As Mick Jagger complained: "The first thing I knew about images was when *MM* started asking us questions and there was a big thing in your paper about it" (*MM*, 7 March 1964, 9). In *MM*, Keith Richards comments: "We think a lot of this 'rebel' thing has been brought up by people thinking too much about it. People like you come up to us and say 'are you rebels?' The answer is no" (8 February 1964, 11). Of great impact on the construction of such images were the close ties that existed between certain writers, artists, and managers. (Ray Coleman, for instance, worked in close association both with Brian Epstein and Andrew Loog Oldham.)

The interactions between musical events and the critics reporting on them in Britain and the United States are more complex than is often recognized. The launch of *Crawdaddy!* in 1966 in the United States, for example, is often cited as marking the birth of rock criticism (see Heylin 1992, xi). Yet the magazine's founder, Paul Williams, commonly reckoned as the first "rock critic," looked to England for material and even included a quote from the British magazine *Music Echo* on the cover of the first mimeographed issue of *Crawdaddy!* in February 1966.[6]

Four main areas of influence seem seminal to the genesis of rock criticism in this early period. The first is popular culture. In the wake of the growth of the U.S. film industry, numerous magazines and papers were catering to a young audience, escalating the impact of what might be termed fan culture. Moreover, U.S. trade papers like *Billboard* (founded in 1894), *Cash Box, Variety,* and *Record World* were influential insofar as they focused extensively on popular music, if only from the point of view of an act's sales potential. The influence of a second area, jazz criticism, was significant both in Britain and in the United States. Yet, in England and in particular in *MM*, jazz as early as the twenties was viewed from a position geographically and critically more distant than in the United States. Jazz criticism in Britain involved a different, more exotic conceptualization of the other, the African American originators of jazz. Various revival strands came to embrace conceptions of tradition and authenticity that were also to impact rock criticism.

A third area of influence seminal to the birth of rock criticism concerned notions of folk authenticity. Whereas British jazz criticism was specifically concerned with competence and quality and to some extent influenced by high-art values and classical music criticism, folklore discourse was less political than in the United States. In this discourse, jazz conceptions of musicianship and skill (heightened with the emergence of be-bop in the 1940s) were contrasted by metaphors referring to expression, such as "lived experience" and "feeling." British blues enthusiasts, among them Alexis Korner, had an impact on mediating these concepts and initiating the R&B revival in London from the late 1950s throughout the 1960s. Korner also wrote for *MM* by the late 1950s, and so did U.S. scholar Alan Lomax, an ideological progenitor who approached the blues as an "authentic" folklore tradition (see, e.g., *MM,* 20 February 1954, 13).

The fourth strand in the genesis of rock criticism was the British youth subcultures that brought with them new ideas of Britishness. The subcultural youth "rebellion" that surfaced with the teddy boys in the early 1950s already bore the double imprints of U.S. popular culture and British class society. As Chambers (1985) points out, the cross-Atlantic cultural traffic grew because of media expansion (radio, records, film, and later television) and in the 1960s transformed ideas of what it was to be British and of British style. It was not only a question of slogans like "Swinging London" and "Mersey-beat." In the field of criticism from 1964 to 1965 a discourse emerged that constructed a specific British authenticity, as opposed to the U.S. folk authenticity British rock had first copied. Writers such as Coleman and Welch gradually concluded that it was possible to be "authentic" even if one were British, anticipating some of the more explicit strategies of "artificiality" that would be played out in the discourse of the 1970s. While bands such as the Beatles and the Rolling Stones began by imitating and copying their U.S. mentors, they gradually imprinted their music with their personal stamp, until finally they turned to original material.

The most important tendency in this formative period (1964–69) was the emergence of a discourse in which popularity and sales numbers no longer were decisive factors for critical acclaim. As in jazz criticism, the contours of an autonomous pole emerged that opposed what was considered commercial, and the quest for authenticity became the central issue around which this discourse emerged.

To begin with, the question of authenticity was one of origin; 1950s visitors to England such as Big Bill Broonzy, Sonny Terry, and Brownie McGee were therefore considered authentic artists. But with the skiffle boom, and later with the R&B revival scene in London, the crucial question became, "What is real R&B?"[7] A turning point seemed to occur when Muddy Waters called the Rolling Stones "my boys" (*MM*, 23 May 1964, 9), which at least implied a degree of fatherly acceptance. As the Stones moved on to their own material and Jagger quite deliberately took on a Cockney accent, the hegemonic discourse on blues authenticity was challenged. As Chris Welch wrote, the new take on "authenticity" was one of "blues in a Cockney accent. . . . Strong accents seem to be a vital factor in the production of authentic blues voices. Not fruity Oxford tones or distilled essence of BBC, but the cheerful, gruff sounds of Islington and Newcastle" (*MM*, 10 July 1965, 7).

The term "authenticity" frequently appeared in journals, and many artists were acclaimed for their "authentic" Britishness, such as the Who and not least the Kinks. But Welch found the main authentic voice on the British scene in 1966 to be seventeen-year-old Stevie Winwood's, "utterly devoid of pretension" and delivered "with compelling authority" (*MM*, 8 January 1966, 3).

Welch connected much of the "fun" of being a writer with the opportunity to be with "the boys." A more narrative and documentary journalistic style developed, in which reporters make themselves present in the events depicted. Another central agent in the burgeoning field of rock criticism was Nik Cohn, who by the late 1960s had become the first writer to carry this perspective of "presence" and "rock 'n' roll attitude" more deliberately into the writing style itself. Starting off as a writer for the *Observer,* the *Sunday Times,* and *Queen Magazine,* Cohn gave a blunt and interpretive historical account of the rock style in his book *Pop From the*

Beginning, issued in 1969 (Cohn 1996). Unlike writers like Welch and Coleman, Cohn did not care whom he offended. As he admits in his introduction to the 1996 edition of the book, accuracy was not of prime importance; he was after guts, flash, energy, and speed. From the very moment that, aged eleven, he had heard Little Richard sing "Tutti Frutti" from a coffee-bar jukebox in his hometown of Derry in Northern Ireland, rock was about "sex, and danger, and secret magic" (2), and most of its spell "came from its beat" (11).

Short sentences and direct, powerful language convey Cohn's belief that writing should "drive" just like the music. He was the first rock writer to make wham-bang characterizations like "Bill Haley was large and chubby and baby-faced" (1996, 18), and to judge authenticity by bodily aspects of the rock performance: "Little Richard was the real thing. Bill Haley wasn't. Haley kept grinning but he sounded limp by comparison, looked downright foolish" (20).

Cohn also constructed some vital myths of rock listening. With him, for the first time, the reception aspect becomes rock criticism's most important aspect. He did not particularly care about the intentions of artists, producers, record promoters, other writers, or the public in general. To Cohn, rock music is part of a subjective dream world; it exists solely for the sake of the listener. Rock is a dream, a heaven, an imagined community of lonely boys with subversive attitudes. Life itself is all about listening to records. Cohn was perhaps also the first writer to derive rock's "meaning" from a larger historical context, tying the effect of artists on various publics to differences produced by the ethos of place, subculture, social background, and so on. Southern rock was hard rock; northern rock was high school (1996, 52).

Other central writers of this period included Derek Jewell, who began working as a jazz and popular-music critic for the *Sunday Times* in 1963, and Hunter Davies, whose rich and detailed biography of the Beatles, published in 1968, still represents a cornerstone of Beatles literature. Another major contribution to the early history of rock criticism was William Mann's path-breaking review, which on 27 December 1963 for the first time put a pop/rock group, the Beatles, in the arts pages of *The London Daily Times.*

Several writers tried in this period to elevate rock to the realm of art. At *MM*, Nik Jones by the mid-1960s perhaps better than anyone represented the new generation of young rock critics. Some artists, like Pete Townshend of the Who, had already become self-conscious about art influences. In his writing, Jones unfolded such ideas, as in his portrait of the Who titled "Look out Dylan, Dolphy, Debussy, and Diddley." In many ways, the article illustrates the naiveté of the period: "Pete Townshend, the tall lean mind behind most of the Who's musical madness has been absorbing 'sounds' for a long while. They range from Dylan, Debussy, Dolphy and Diddley. The deciding factor is that at last he's got beyond absorption. Not only does he dig the music, he completely understands it all, as well" (*MM*, 10 September 1966, 9).

The U.S. Connection, The First Turning Point

In the United States, popular music discourse from the 1920s to the 1960s was structured differently than in Britain. There was a clear though small autonomous pole, divided between two aesthetic conceptions of the authentic other: The first romanticized blues and folk singers as the voices of the oppressed (Lomax, Guthrie), while the second associated jazz, especially be-bop and hipsterism, with the free spirit of the African American (Kerouac, Mailer). Compared to Britain and Europe, segments at the heterogenous pole also enjoyed far more recognition, glamour and commodification being more accepted in the U.S. consumer society. At the same time, popular culture was marked by conspicuous vertical distinctions that marginalized southern white trash as well as the black population. The first generation of rock 'n' rollers helped make some features of these marginalized cultures acceptable. The subversiveness of Elvis Presley, Chuck Berry, Jerry Lee Lewis, and other innovators was always ambiguous: At the same time as they crossed the borders of race and sexuality and even hinted at liaisons with the devil, they signaled their primary aims as high life and a pink Cadillac.

Around 1964 and 1965, the Beatles, the Rolling Stones, and Bob Dylan evoked the autonomous pole in a near-unambiguous way and thus introduced a new legitimation strategy. They took the black and folk roots of their music seriously while claiming recognition as individual creators. The media did not know how to treat these popular-music artists. While blues and folk aficionados wrote off British R&B as a commercial rip-off and the electrified Dylan as a traitor, other critics tried to apply classical music criteria to the Beatles and discuss Dylan's lyrics as poetry. But there were also young intellectual fans more at home with the border crossing of the 1960s. Convinced that these artists were onto something new that mattered more than traditional art forms, and inspired to some extent by British predecessors like Nik Cohn, they tried to express their belief in words. Like their British colleagues, they found models in jazz or avant-garde art writing, but even more in the film criticism of writers such as Pauline Kael and in New Journalism's fondness for the extraordinary in ordinary life.[8] There was a far larger public in the United States than in England for serious rock writing. More than a third of American youth was going to college, most of them without family roots in upper-class culture, while upward mobility in Europe meant white-collar jobs for blue-collar kids, and the surest route to the intellectual world was through art school, not academia.

Serious writing on rock emerged in the United States around 1965 in the more hip parts of the established press and in the underground press. The launching of Paul Williams's *Crawdaddy!* in 1966 was followed by the founding of the more professional *Rolling Stone* within a year and then by *Creem*. Within three years *Rolling Stone* boasted a circulation of 250,000, although *Rolling Stone* chronicler Robert Draper puts the figure much lower (1991, 184).

During the first years of rock criticism, writers experimented with various styles and interpretative strategies, but by the end of the 1960s certain aesthetic standards had become relatively established. The basic demand was that the music should "kick butt," but the highest praise was often reserved for works and artists that could be considered "important" as well. The formulation of explicit standards can be ascribed largely to one man, Jon Landau, who started writing for *Crawdaddy!* but in 1967 moved to *Rolling Stone*, where he edited the review section for a number of years. Landau (1972) advocated clear criteria of artistic authenticity that mixed the auteur perspective of film criticism with the folk and blues emphasis on roots. His cool-headed, self-confident approach, informed by his college education and his experience playing and recording rock, focused on the record as a work of art that reflected both the concrete setting of the production and the wider cultural context.

Landau invented his criteria in a hurry, under the pressure of delivering reviews before deadline. Other writers also took what they had gathered for cooincidence. Robert Christgau (1973) was one of many who could apply academic tools to rock; at the same time, he emphasized that rock surpassed such criteria. Later, Christgau found his strongest asset as a critic to be the taste he had internalized listening intensively to rock for years and living as a critical member on the margins of the counterculture community, he told Ulf Lindberg in an interview in New York City on 22 May 1998. Greil Marcus was less troubled by his academic training in American studies. He started to dig out the deep roots of rock in U.S. culture (1975), an approach that he later transferred to the relation between punk and utopian strands in European history (1990). Within this male camaraderie of "new intellectuals," a woman, Ellen Willis (1992), often displayed the sharpest insights into the foggy mystique of middle-class men like Dylan or Lou Reed. In some cases, writing on rock seemed a way of developing New Journalism. Christgau came into rock criticism as a New Journalist of some reputation, but among the many wanna-bes of the U.S. rock magazines, Lester Bangs (1988) was the one who used a wild gonzo-influenced style to cut deepest into the meaning and the context of contemporary rock.

In England, pop had been, in Iain Chambers's words, "a central symbol of fashionable, metropolitan, British culture" between 1963 and 1965 (1985, 57). Once the hegemony in popular music had been brought back to the United States, it was not long before American counterculture, New Journalism, and rock criticism started feeding into a British music journalism that by then showed visible signs of stagnation. There arose an indigenous underground press, spearheaded by *IT* and *Oz*, that was passionately devoted to provocation, alternative living, and revolution in a broad sense. Stressed were subjects like sexual liberation, drugs, the Vietnam War, black power, and police brutality (Neville 1971, 122–23). Music was considered a vital part of the movement and extensively covered. As Jeff Nuttall observed in 1968, popular music's crossing the border between high and low culture and art and everyday life was commonly seen as an important step in the development of a new subversive sensibility. Yet, the attention given to music seldom surpassed this instrumental function.

With the demise of the counterculture around 1970, a host of young writers were recruited from *Oz* and its like by the established music weeklies and the fresh *Sounds* as a response to the new rock audience's demand for hip and intelligent commentary. *MM* launched itself as "the thinking fan's paper." *NME* went through a revolution in the years 1972–73 after a period of falling sales, was back on top with a circulation of 200,000 by 1974, and entered its heyday. It gained a reputation as a writers' paper; in the early 1970s "everyone had their copy of Tom Wolfe's *New Journalism* collection, and U.S. writers like Lester Bangs were avidly read," according to editor Neil Spencer (1991, x). Bangs was even hired to write a column for a number of years, and most of the cream of U.K. rock journalists—Nick Kent, Charles Shaar Murray, Ian MacDonald, Paul Morley, Ian Penman, Julie Burchill, and Tony Parsons—contributed more or less regularly. So did photographers like Penny Smith and, later, Anton Corbijn. Further, at a time when rock journalists were treated like stars (see Jones 1996, 6–7), *NME* cultivated an irreverent stance, mirrored in its layout, toward musicians and representatives of the record industry. This approach helped critics maintain their independence in the eyes of *NME*'s readers—upwardly mobile and middle-class young men alienated from the established British culture. The magazine tended toward what Simon Frith calls "a sociological response to rock, valuing music for its effects on an audience rather than for its creators' intentions or skills" (1981, 172).

Of the *NME* writers, Charles Shaar Murray and Nick Kent were recruited from the underground press in 1972, where they had picked up their (basically counterculture) standards as well as their erratic, self-conscious writing styles. Murray cared more about roots music and politics, Kent more about arty innovators. Both shared *NME*'s predilection for U.S. urban rock and British lads' rock. Both were radically independent. Kent especially did much to improve the careers of half-forgotten heroes like Iggy Pop. Above all, Kent became the first rock journalist-as-star, a gifted storyteller who embodied the bohemian myths of rock. Living in the shadow of the artists, he depicts with New Journalism grit their self-destructiveness, callousness, meanness, and stupidity, but also their will to survive, as illustrated in the collection *The Dark Stuff* (1994). Murray arguably was the more self-reflexive of the two, a good pedagogue and a carnivalesque reporter. His wit, knack for visual detail, and extraordinary ear for language often enabled him to reproduce the excitement of a musical event, as the anthology *Shots from the Hip* (1991) bears witness.

As the works of Kent and Murray demonstrate, the aesthetic ideals of the mid-1960s were still effective ten years later. Frith has pointed out that U.S. writers throughout the 1970s judged rock according to its relevance for a mythic sixties community (1981, 176). In Britain the counterculture never was nearly as strong, yet there too 1970s rock criticism lamented a lost paradise or evoked the image of a never-fulfilled promise. But a strong counteractive force existed in glam rock's conscious exploration of artifice. The British critics had considerably fewer problems with glam than many of their U.S. colleagues; in a sense, British pop always had to be "artificial" because it was secondary, a derivative of American rock 'n' roll. The main distinctions in rock writing in the early 1970s appear in how critics related to the imagined rock community, either by hanging on to it or by celebrating its decomposition and replacement with the decadent aesthetic of Bowie, Lou Reed, or the New York Dolls. In fact, both paths connected to the "long, fine flash" of the mid-sixties that Hunter S. Thompson was talking about in *Fear and Loathing in Las Vegas* (1971), and both pointed forward to its second coming: the punk wave.

From Punk to New Pop, The Second Turning Point

Apart from the Beatles, the punk rock era, 1976–78, is probably the most mythologized moment in English pop history. In our view, punk rock represents a crossroads where a modernist aesthetic, intent on making it new, ends up in a postmodern celebration of rock's basic barbarism. Put differently, punk rock was an attempt "to keep in play [both] bohemian ideas of authenticity and Pop Art ideals of artifice" (Frith and Horne 1987, 124). The former, drawing on well-established conventions of re-belliousness, gave rise to a left-wing, realist/populist street politics; the latter, claiming that "the music was about itself now" (Frith 1981, 162), questioned precisely that stance in favor of an avant-gardist/experimental fifth-column politics of deconstructing the pop process. This argument applies to punk criticism as well, only it is possible to see the second strategy slowly becoming more important than the first after 1980. The turning point therefore is a longwinded one, where punk represents a transition to the radically different journalism induced by the advent of New Pop.

In a way, "punk and the music press were made for each other," as *NME* editor Neil Spencer put it (1991, xi). Banned from venues and airplay, punk was dependent on print exposure, while its intricacies provided the music weeklies with a raison d'être: explaining them to a broader audience. In practice, though, punk criticism often stopped at attempts to sort out the poseurs and point to the real thing. Established critics ran the risk of familiarizing and so reducing the complexity of the music, turning the Pistols into the new Stones, the Clash into dole-queue rock, Patti Smith and Elvis Costello into rock poets. On the other hand, the writings of their younger colleagues with no more merit than some writing talent and subcultural credibility mostly remained within a fan perspective, guided by the same authenticity paradigm that had informed their forerunners. As for critical standards, punk did not do much to change things. Yet its advent made a big difference. It vastly increased the market for writing on rock (this was something the press just *had* to cover), and it opened the door to a new breed of critics, who in a few years were to shake the authority of the critical orthodoxy. While *MM* used the resident female, Caroline Coon, *Sounds* recruited Jon Ingham as punk correspondent. *NME* advertised for "two hip young gunslingers" and got hold of Julie Burchill, aged seventeen, and Tony Parsons, twenty-one, in the autumn of 1976 (Savage 1991, 252).

In 1978 Burchill and Parsons published a thoroughly heterodox provocation directed at legitimate taste, a short cult book called *"The Boy Looked at Johnny": The Obituary of Rock and Roll. Johnny* is an "alternative" master narration, its negligible amount of musical analysis compensated for by the usual juicy anecdotes and a lot of scathing, vitriolic abuse, rumored to have brought the authors threats on their lives. The heroes of the tale are the Sex Pistols and especially Johnny Rotten, represented as true rebels and single-handed instigators of the punk movement. In retrospect, one is more taken by the book's fervent feminist thrust. *Johnny* highlights continuity to a point where authenticity becomes a caricature.

Yet, in its style, the book successfully communicates the very artifice inherent in punk that its surface text brands as "posing." Hardboiled and mannered, a carnival of words, it puts an all-pervasive nasty, ironic slant on the wit of forerunners like Charles Shaar Murray, which leaves the reader asking, Is this deep-felt youthful disillusionment or a big con?

If punk journalism did not overthrow the ruling authenticity paradigm, works like *Johnny* certainly put it to the test and paved the way for the new stylish criticism of the early 1980s. When New Pop arrived on the scene, the avant-gardist strategy, based on the legacy of Dada and situationism on one hand and U.S. pop art on the other, had won out. It was originally introduced as a means of subversion by, among others, Sex Pistols manager Malcolm McLaren. Ambiguous from its inception, the project was swallowed up by commerce, as pop musicians and writers with less intellectual aspirations picked up on its stylishness but ditched its theories. The shift became visible on several levels in criticism. In terms of aesthetic standards, the artifice of pop was celebrated, while traditional authenticity was ridiculed. The markers of the high/low split in popular music were redistributed, as the top of the charts became legitimate subject matter for the weeklies and for awhile seemed more important than "underground" or "alternative" rock. New writing styles incorporated avant-garde strategies like cut-up, collage, and stream of consciousness. Interviews tended to focus as much on the star journalist as on the music star. Finally, the *Sniffin' Glue*s of punk were exchanged for glossy new magazines, designed to blur the line between editorials, text, pictures, and ads.

There was still room for serious political and aesthetic reflection, as witnessed by the writings of, particularly, Jon Savage in *Sounds, MM,* and the *Face.* But the spirit of the times was embodied by the eccentric Paul Morley, who perfected both the carnivalesque and the narcissistic impulses inherent in Burchill and Parsons's *Johnny.* He, too, was recruited in the year of punk, and for some time his *NME* pieces hewed to the old authenticity paradigm. But after 1980 his interviewees became the new pop stars, and the write-ups were journalist performances mixed with textual experiments, translating Burchill/Parsons into interview format. Behind Morley the star amuser/abuser, there is someone on the lookout for moments of authentic being, for transcendence at the heart of the media. But this impulse is countered by his fondness for self-mirroring and celebrity. Provocative and funny, but seldom more, Morley transformed interviews—some of them collected in *Ask: The Chatter of Pop* (1986)—into happenings; for example, he bickered with Mick Jagger who had sold out the most, the Stones or *NME.* A sample of his textual experiments: "For the moment: only a moment. What was that? It. For the moment. Be bored with that, brats, and be bored with life. The fleeting moment; the kaleidoscopic light of changing environment and circumstance and perception and . . . what was that? Depeche Mode are absolutely on the brink of 'a'—rather than the—next moment. So absolute, so arbitrary" (1986, 69). Having won fame as a journalist, Morley went on to try his luck as a publicity manager for Art of Noise and Frankie Goes to Hollywood, still with the intention of stirring things up and raising hell at the center of the most commercial pop. The project failed. Each group, in Morley's own words, became "just another group in the charts" (*NME*, 18 February 1984, 25).

The three weeklies covered the advent of punk extensively but found it harder to adjust to New Pop. New types of magazines filled the vacuum. The biweekly *Smash Hits,* founded in 1978, and the monthly style bible the *Face* in 1980, were both glossies started by ex-*NME* editor Nick Logan. Both represented the new "pop sensibility" much better than did the old black/white inkies that gave you dirty fingers. *Smash Hits* did so by reinvoking the teen mag idea of "pop as magic" and avoiding rock criticism in a strict sense, but selling to grown ups. The *Face* embraced a postmodern consumer ideology, conspicuously apparent in its design, where the line between editorial copy and advertisement was unclear and visuals flourished at the expense of text.[9] Summing up the first half of the 1980s, Jon Savage (also a punk recruit) christened the period "the Age of Style" and delivered the critique that style as a personal social experiment had turned into a vacuous celebrity culture (*Face*, October 1985, 121; December 1985, 90).

Finally, the adaptation of avant-garde aesthetics brought with it art theory and philosophy, mainly in the guise of French structuralism and poststructuralism, with Roland Barthes as its most prominent intermediary. In academic criticism, it first appeared with *Let It Rock* writers like Dave Laing and the very influential Simon Frith. *NME* journalists, especially Ian Penman and Morley, began to use a semiotic lingo around 1980, paving the way for what was to become an important aspect of the next turning point.

Diversification and Polarization, The Third Turning Point

By 1985, the style bibles and quality dailies were firmly established channels for rock criticism. Two new trends that have ever since tended to define the field's extreme heteronomous and autonomous poles came to dominate the later part of the decade. The first trend was a still more detailed and commercially motivated *segmentation* of readers with regard to age and genre preferences. The second was a *polarizing* of consumer-oriented criticism aimed at record buyers, and elitist criticism aimed at well-educated connoisseurs of underground, alternative, or avant-garde musics.

Both trends had appeared by 1986. According to its first art director, Andy Cowles, *Q* was launched as an "anti-fashion statement" (*Q*, October 1996, 61) by the giant EMAP publishing group. The concept was taken from men's magazines, and the literary approach reflected professional, objective journalism. At the other end of the spectrum, *MM* hired a group of new writers straight out of Oxford and gave them free reign to write think pieces inspired by French poststructuralists like Barthes and Kristeva, in a florid, literary style. Among these, Simon Reynolds would prove particularly influential. As a reaction to eighties pop gloss, *Q* sought out the old stars; the most prominent, Paul McCartney, was in the magazine's words "umbilically linked with *Q* since Month One" (*Q*, October 1996, 28). Reynolds and friends, on the other hand, advocated a return to the contemporary underground, representing "authenticity" experiences as Lacanian jouissance or loss of self in the sublime moment.

The best example of a conscious segmentation is EMAP's glossy music monthlies, which include *Smash Hits* for teenagers, *Select* (1990–) for young male rock fans, *Q* for more all-round pop/rock fans, *Mojo* (1993–) for old rock fans, *Mixmag* (1986–) for dance enthusiasts, and *Kerrang!* (1981–) for heavy-metal fans. The magazines focus on music-related copy, unlike other important outlets for rock critics during the 1980s: the dailies, the style bibles, and the men's and women's magazines, where rock rubbed shoulders with all things art, smart, and modern. The EMAP magazines all explore the heterogenous pole, with *Q* and *Mojo* wielding the greatest authority. Together with the dailies, they have taken over the dominance of the field; the dailies carry the news, while the monthlies print longer interviews with stars and review extensively.

There was little room for think pieces in the new magazines, while the literary and academic ambitions of a few writers employed elsewhere were growing. Yet another scene opened up in the later part of the decade, as intellectual magazines like *New Statesman* began to publish pieces by rock journalists who had learned the ways of academics.[10]

Q's anti-fashion statement soon found a large readership. The abundant editorial copy was set in a stark black/white grid that contrasted with the ads. (The *Face*'s style of blurring the boundaries between ads and editorial copy has since been adopted, and today it is sometimes hard to find the magazine copy among the advertisements.) The ideal of reportage was realized in interviews in which stars were allowed to speak their minds and the journalists were invisible. *Q* in the 1980s was anti-*Face* and anti-Morley. Its readers were grown men for whom rock was a hobby (e.g., record collecting, factual knowledge suited to pub quizzes) and reading a magazine was entertainment. Rather than placing rock in the middle of the metropolitan lifestyle, *Q* pictured it as a leisure activity, part of a life that also includes work, football, television, and the local pub. The first three covers featured seasoned stars like Paul McCartney, Rod Stewart, and Elton John, choices that reflect the *Q* edition of the rock canon. As essays or historical articles are virtually nonexistent in the magazine, as almost every sentence is in one way or another related to a new product, and as nothing (not even the reviews) is controversial, *Q* has become the ultimate consumer guide for rock and related products —and a model for countless others. Rock is still consumption, as witnessed by the numerous short record reviews, but it is no longer conspicuously so.

Whereas *Q* is targeted at a specific readership on the basis of market research, a specialist magazine like the *Wire* concentrates on a number of genres in the hope of reaching out to readers oriented toward "alternative" music. Its circulation is a tenth of *Q*'s, its readership as masculine but more heterogenous with respect to age and income. The *Wire* started as a jazz magazine in 1982 but in the early 1990s took up experimental music with roots in art music, jazz, rock, or non-Western genres —or to use the editor's own term in a 1999 subscription flyer, "nonmainstream" music. Whereas *Q* dominates the field and thus does not need to demonstrate that position overtly, the *Wire* is expressly against mainstream music journalism and magazines. With this stance and by the choice of music it covers, the *Wire* falls at the autonomous pole of the field. At the same time, the magazine is careful to keep its distance from academia; as editor Tony Herrington told Morten Michelsen in an interview in London, 22 January 1999, it prefers "intelligence to intellectualism."

Q and the *Wire* take up two institutional positions in the field of rock criticism that at present define its heterogenous and autonomous poles. There is not much in between, as the weeklies' role has become secondary. This also implies that the critics at *Q* are relatively anonymous, if professional, journalists, while those at the *Wire* still can make their own taste judgments in a classical sense. Best known among the *Wire*'s freelance writers are Simon Reynolds and David Toop.

The discouragement of personal styles and views at EMAP magazines has made it harder for new agents to influence the field. As Reynolds told Morten Michelsen in an interview in New York on 21 June 1999, he and others had easy access when there was a vacuum at *MM*, but few high-profile writers have appeared since. Although the turn toward "theorization" was instigated by *NME* writers, Reynolds's university background, his interest in French poststructuralist theory, and his flair for essay writing made him one of the first critics to live up to academic standards.[11] His national debut in *MM* did not start with a Burchill-like flamethrower, but with a sensible critique of the "sinister cult of Social Realist Pop" and its defenders in the music press (8 November 1986, 20–21; 15 November 1986, 31). This turn was not nearly as apocalyptic as the previous one, but Reynolds and a few colleagues succeeded in defining an academic position within the field in the later 1980s using the noisiest "underground" rock around (e.g., My Bloody Valentine, Public Enemy, Young Gods) as a steppingstone.

The field of rock criticism seems to have stabilized itself with these positions. New magazines and writers pop up, but they lack the power to overthrow the balance of the field. A good example is composer, musician, and writer David Toop, who has emerged as a major contributor. He has written sporadically since the early 1970s, but only in his 1995 book *Ocean of Sound* has his project become clear. Taking off from anthropology, he weaves the most unlikely musical genres into what he calls "open music" (1995, 22), often in illuminating ways. However, his position borders on the modern art circuit and is therefore rather marginal.

The 1990s have seen new genre complexes like dance and hip-hop manifest themselves commercially, but they have spawned few magazines or writers of consequence in Britain. Rap is covered by small independent magazines, dance by the nationals *Mixmag* (EMAP) and *Muzik* (IPC). The dance magazines do not carry any criticism as we have defined it, as they are a mix of the EMAP style of neutral journalism, entertainment, and *Time Out*. The increase in black critics created by the breakthrough of hip-hop seems to be a U.S. phenomenon, and no later women critics have reached the infamous heights of Julie Burchill.

Marginalization

Writing in 1988, Simon Frith, noting that "rock anthems are used to sell banks and cars," claims the rock era has "turned out to be a by-way in the development of twentieth-century popular music, rather than, as we thought at the time, any kind of mass-cultural revolution" (1988a, 1). It is correct, of course, that the historical situation that gave rise to rock as a privileged cultural formation is largely passé. Yet some very important effects of this "by-way" are not. For instance, rock and rock criticism helped pave the way for the breakthrough of postmodernism and cultural studies, and they made clear that popular music may attain the status of at least semi-legitimate culture.

This legitimation process, we have argued, equals the formation of a field in Bourdieu's sense, including a "clergy" of leading critics and magazines. For the early critics, the problem was how to voice the difference they perceived, faced with a cultural form that obviously exceeded "mere" entertainment. The solution was to resort to the notion of authenticity. However, the insight (suppressed during the reign of counterculture) that rock artists, like any other performers, build on artifice and make-believe was successively to surface in the self-conscious rock music and criticism of the 1970s, giving rise to a pop art aestheticization of commerce that has pervaded the rock field since punk, making it nearly impossible to talk of "authenticity" except as one code among others. In the postmodern supermarket, mainstream rock journalism seems to have returned to the consumer guidance of the early 1960s, while alternative writing increasingly tends toward the opposite pole of academic criticism.

Yet, there are important differences between the trajectories of U.S. and U.K. rock criticism. In retrospect, what strikes an outsider most in the U.S. scene is the continuity: Individual differences aside, the discursive strategies launched by the founders seem to function as well in today's market orientation as they did in the "anti" atmosphere of the 1960s. In Britain, on the other hand, the turning points are rather conspicuous; the critics are more susceptible to fads in model paradigms as well as in music. Simon Frith's observation—that whereas British rock writing is informed by the music's connection to youth subcultures, the writings of U.S. critics depart from the history of American culture—seems to help explain this distinction (1981, 10). It also helps us understand why U.K. critics have privileged a subjective form of criticism, positing themselves as enlightened fans with a knack for stylish, carnivalesque prose and strong judgments (it is no wonder that Lester Bangs has been their most appreciated U.S. colleague), while in the United States critics are expected to grow up with the music, be impartial, and report on things. Generally, the tradition of proper journalism has been stronger in U.S. rock criticism, perhaps because rock writing in the U.S. has been able to relate to a stronger tradition of middle-brow cultural writing. In comparison, rock writing in Britain is poorly paid and has little legitimacy, as Simon Reynolds pointed out in his 1999 interview with Michelsen.

As the record companies are finding new roads to consumers, and as these are differentiated into micropublics and penetrating writing is retreating into the universities, comprehensive rock criticism runs the risk of becoming marginalized. For all its deficiencies, this is a pity. Criticism in the sense of a professional discussion of matters of public interest represents a historical conquest. The future scenario that German writer Alexander Kluge has called the "universal provincialism" of a plurality of micropublics unable to understand each other has as little attraction in the rock field as in any other cultural field.

Notes

1. We would like to thank Simon Frith for initial suggestions concerning turning points. In this essay, whose background lies in a Nordic research project (see Lindberg et al., 2000), "criticism" designates journalistic, more than academic, printed texts with argumentative and interpretive ambitions. News thus is not criticism, nor is practical information or passing commentary; reviews, in-depth interviews, overviews, debate articles, and essays (or think pieces, as rock critics like to call them) certainly are. We have privileged the specialist press and books but left out rock histories, choices that may tend to privilege a specific male and white version of the still unwritten history of rock criticism.

2. According to Regev 1994, the legitimizing strategies of rock criticism's founders were based on four claims designed to make rock appear "authentic": that the music was "subversive" or at least anti-hegemonic; that it was produced by autonomous authorial subjects; that it allowed for the formation of canons of artists and their works; and that it was in possession of its own means of artistic expression (electric sound, studio work, a specific voice-lyric relationship, and stylistic eclecticism).

3. By "habitus," Bourdieu means embodied knowledge, one's taste, style, and way with words. The habitus determines how people think, perceive, interpret, evaluate, and act and is itself determined by their background, their present situation, and their future prospects.

4. The field concept is not unproblematic, nor is Bourdieu's conception of taste. It has also been suggested, particularly by postmodern theorists, that his theories rely on dated empiric material (see Frow 1992). Laermans takes up a balanced position that we share, that postmodern culture still has a power center founded on the educational system, though "alongside the general legitimate culture passed on by the educational system, there are now several 'subcultural' forms of legitimacy," which gives rise to a "polyhierarchical" but still "'centred situation'" (1992, 259).

5. *NME* was a relaunch under its new owner, Maurice Kinn, of the original *Musical Express*, which had been struggling along for six years. By 1952 *NME* had introduced the U.S. practice initiated by *Billboard*'s "Hot Hundred" of a weekly "Top Twenty" chart.

6. The mid-sixties saw in the United Kingdom a boom not only of so-called beat and R&B groups, but also of papers covering the music. *Disc*, a national pop weekly that started in 1958, mainly covered teen idols. *Merseybeat* (launched in Liverpool in 1961), expanded during the early 1960s and in 1965 changed its name to *Music Echo*. *Disc* incorporated *Music Echo* in 1966 and *Record Mirror*, which had published under various titles since 1954, in 1972.

7. See, for example, Ray Coleman, "Where Does Beat Begin and R&B End. Can You Tell the Difference?" (*MM*, 29 February 1964, 7), in which five British bands are asked to account for their views.

8. Kael, of the *New Yorker*, was one of U.S. popular culture's most influential writers in the 1960s; she advocated a subjective, populist approach to film, contrary to that of auteur criticism. Rock critics such as Marcus and Christgau often tip their hats to her.

9. See Toynbee 1993 for a fine analysis of *Smash Hits* and the upheavals around 1980, and Hebdige 1988 and Hoy 1992 for analyses of the *Face*.

10. Angela McRobbie notices that more rock critics "have followed a free-lance route through the music press, the style glossies and the Sunday newspapers to the *New Statesman, ZG* and *Marxism Today*," thus blurring the line between journalists and academics (1989, xv).

11. A number of academic anthologies from the later 1980s reflect the partial dissolution of the border between the two fields. See Frith and Goodwin 1990, which includes articles by Reynolds, Marcus, the Vermorels, Sue Garrat, and Holly Kruse; Frith 1988b; and McRobbie 1989, which includes texts from both academics and critics, including Penman, Frith, Savage, Reynolds, Old-field, Stubbs, and Marcus.

References

Aronowitz, Stanley. (1993). *Roll over Beethoven: The return of cultural strife.* Hanover, N.H.: Wesleyan University Press.

Bangs, Lester. (1988). *Psychotic reactions and carburetor dung.* New York: Vintage Books.

Bourdieu, Pierre. (1984). *Distinction: A social critique of the judgement of taste.* 1979. London: Routledge and Kegan Paul.

Bourdieu, Pierre. (1996). *The rules of art: Genesis and structure of the literary field.* Cambridge: Polity.

Bourdieu, Pierre. (1998). *On television and journalism.* London: Pluto.

Broady, Donald. (1990). *Sociologi och epistemologi: Om Pierre Bourdieu's författarskap och den historiska epistemologin* (Sociology and epistemology: On Pierre Bourdieu's works and the historical epistemology). Stockholm: LHS.

Burchill, Julie, and Tony Parsons. (1978). *The boy looked at Johnny: The obituary of rock and roll.* London: Pluto.

Chambers, Iain. (1985). *Urban rhythms: Pop music and popular culture.* London: Macmillan.

Cohn, Nik. (1996). *Awopbopaloobop alopbamboom: Pop from the beginning.* 2d ed. London: Picador.

Christgau, Robert. (1973). *Any old way you choose it: Rock and other pop music.* Baltimore: Penguin.

———. (1998). *Grown up all wrong.* Cambridge, Mass.: Cambridge University Press.

Davies, Hunter. (1968). *The Beatles: The authorized biography.* London: Heinemann.

Draper, Robert. (1991). *Rolling Stone magazine: The uncensored history.* New York: HarperPerennial.

Frith, Simon. (1981). *Sound effects: Youth, leisure, and the politics of rock 'n' roll.* London: Constable.

———. (1988a). *Music for pleasure: Essays in the sociology of pop.* Cambridge: Polity/Blackwell.

————, ed. (1988b). *Facing the music.* New York: Pantheon Books.

Frith, Simon, and Andrew Goodwin. (1990). *On record: Rock, pop, and the written word.* London: Routledge.

Frith, Simon, and Howard Horne. (1987). *Art into pop.* London: Methuen.

Frow, John. (1995). *Cultural studies and cultural value.* Oxford: Clarendon.

Hebdige, Dick. (1987). The impossible object: Towards a sociology of the sublime. *New Formations* 1, 1:47–76.

Hebdige, Dick. (1988). *Hiding in the light: On images and things.* London: Routledge.

Heylin, Clinton, ed. (1992). *The Penguin book of rock and roll writing.* London: Viking.

Hoy, Mikita. (1992). Bakhtin and popular culture. *New Literary History* 23: 765–782.

Huyssen, Andreas. (1986). *After the great divide: Modernism, mass culture, postmodernism.* London: Macmillan.

Jones, Dylan, ed. (1996). *Meaty, beaty, big, and bouncy! Classic rock writing from Elvis to Oasis.* London: Hodder and Stoughton.

Kent, Nick. (1994). *The dark stuff: Selected writings on rock music, 1972–1993.* London: Penguin.

Laermans, Rudi. (1992). The relative rightness of Pierre Bourdieu: Some sociological comments on the legitimacy of postmodern art, literature, and culture. *Cultural Studies* 6, 2:248–260.

Landau, Jon. (1972). *It's too late to stop now: A rock and roll journal.* San Francisco: Straight Arrow Books.

Lindberg, Ulf, Gestur Gudmundsson, Morten Michelsen, and Hans Weisethaunet. (2000). *Amusers, bruisers, and cool-headed cruisers: The fields of Anglo-Saxon and Nordic rock criticism.* Aarhus: Nordisk institut.

Marcus, Greil. (1975). *Mystery train: Images of America in rock 'n' roll music.* New York: Penguin.

————. (1990): *Lipstick traces: A secret history of the twentieth century.* London: Picador.

McHale, Brian. (1992). *Constructing postmodernism.* London: Routledge.

McRobbie, Angela. (1989). Introduction to *Zoot suits and second-hand dresses: An anthology of fashion and music,* ed. McRobbie. London: Macmillan.

Morley, Paul. (1986). *Ask: The chatter of pop.* London: Faber and Faber.

Murray, Charles Shaar. (1991). *Shots from the hip.* London: Penguin.

Neville, Richard. (1971). *Play power.* London: Paladin.

Nuttall, Jeff. (1968). *Bomb culture.* London: MacGibbon and Kee.

Regev, Motti. (1994). Producing artistic value: The case of rock music. *Sociological Quarterly* 35, 1:84–102.

Savage, Jon. (1991). *England's dreaming: Sex Pistols and punk rock.* London: Faber and Faber.

Spencer, Neil. (1991). Introduction to *Shots from the hip,* by Charles Shaar Murray. London: Penguin.

Thompson, Hunter S. (1971). *Fear and loathing in Las Vegas: A savage journey to the heart of the American dream.* New York: Random House.

Toop, David. (1995). *Ocean of sound.* London: Serpent's Tail.

Toynbee, Jason. (1993). Policing bohemia, pinning up the grunge: The music press and generic change in British pop and rock. *Popular Music* 12, 3: 289–300.

Willis, Ellen. (1992). *Beginning to see the light: Sex, hope, and rock-and-roll.* Hanover, N.H.: Wesleyan University Press.

3

Word Power

A Brief, Highly Opinionated History of Hip-Hop Journalism

Jeff Chang

The neatly manicured lawns and ivy-covered brick buildings of Cambridge, Massachusetts, seem one of the least likely settings for a revolution of sorts. But such are the surprises tossed up routinely by hip-hop history.

In the fall of 1988, David Mayes and Jon Shecter put together a one-page hip-hop music tip sheet to advertise their college radio show, which they grandly named the *Source*. The modest offering was not the first of its kind. In Berkeley, California, radio DJ Dave "Bronx Prince Davey D" Cook put out a biweekly Top Twenty chart that included news and reviews. Tommy Boy Records owner Tom Silverman funded a magazine called *Dance Music Report* to promote house and hip-hop releases. And British zines like *Soul Underground* offered artist features and listed breakbeat charts alongside hip-hop playlists.

But the crew behind the *Source* seemed to grasp the size of the burgeoning audience outside the local magnets of club, radio, and mom 'n' pop record stores. And it moved quickly to fill the gap with aggressive business acumen and an editorial voice of affected bravado. Advertisers, radio DJs, and readers flocked to the magazine. In 1990, the *Source* moved its operations to New York City and quickly secured a lock on print advertising for the rapidly expanding and professionalizing genre. The producers seemed to have a sense of their own authority. The January/February 1990 issue boldly canonized the music's seminal decade, filled 30 percent of its pages with advertising, and declared itself "the voice of the rap music industry." Jon Shecter, now editor-in-chief of the magazine, crowed, "The magazine you are holding in your hands is, easily, the best thing ever published concerning hip-hop."

And it was. There was better criticism in the *Village Voice,* better industry coverage in *Billboard,* better writing and copy-editing in *Spin,* but the *Source* spoke to its readers in its own voice, reflected their concerns and controversies, fed their needs. Most importantly, it captured hip-hop's *attitude*—that brimming street confidence and scowling generational defiance, the abandonment of all the disengaging rules of journalism, the barely secret joy of having something no army of parents, baby-boomer cultural critics, or grizzled rock journalists could ever understand. Hip-hop journalism now had a center.

Strictly Underground, Keep the Crossover

In the beginning, the *Source*'s dual efforts to build a readership and establish itself as a player in the nascent hip-hop industry dovetailed. To reach the national market, the *Source* reached out to local DJs and promoters and gave them "regional scene" columns in exchange for street promotion. These columns gave the magazine a backbone of legitimacy, while demonstrating to skeptical execs the vibrancy of the music.

As a networking device, the *Source* was unparalleled. Industry execs used the regional columns and the radio, retail, and video charts as a roadmap to the new music and as a vehicle to promote its high-risk signings. Urban mixshow and college radio DJs connected with record promoters and each other to strategize how to break new music. Local scene makers tried to extend their reps and increase the viability of the music in their area. But as the *Source* developed its ad base and its readership, it shifted in the direction of full-length features, reviews, and even issue-advocacy journalism. By 1992, the local columns and charts had become a casualty of the increased emphasis on ads and articles.

While many angry scenesters did not think so at the time, the move catalyzed a sea change in hip-hop journalism. The coverage, once shallow and openly fannish, greatly improved. Writers like James Bernard, dream hampton, Upski Wimsatt, Danyel Smith, and Ronin Ro began plying an edgy sort of music writing—one that, unlike mainstream rock writing, foregrounded issues of race, gender, gangs, violence, religion, and the generation gap. Drawing inspiration from the lyrical concerns of the artists, they tracked the rise and influence of the Nation of Islam, looked unflinchingly at black-on-black crime, addressed police brutality and racism, passionately took sides over gangs and so-called gangsta rap.

Their 1990 look at gangsta rap, censorship, and social responsibility was groundbreaking, at odds with the sensationalist national media and closer to its subject than rockist music journalist defenders of the First Amendment. David Mills wrote in the *Source*, "You wonder whether things have gotten out of control, and whether, like radiation exposure, it'll be years before we can really know the consequences of our nasty little entertainments" (1990, 40). But the magazine did not end the debate there. Industry leaders and rappers like the Geto Boys and NWA were given space to answer—a journalistic transposition of just the kind of open-ended exchange inherent in hip-hop music. It was an approach that shunned the star fetishization of most music magazines. Leading up to and after the 1992 riots, the *Source* sometimes was as insightful and prophetic as the rappers it covered.

The *Source*'s emergence as a national magazine with national concerns also fueled the rise of a network of underground zines, mostly from the West Coast. When the *Source* slammed the door on regional reporting, the energy of local taste makers, college radio DJs, graphic designers, and young hip-hop-inspired writers had nowhere to go. Zines, and the multiplicity of voices they brought along, seemed suddenly to bloom everywhere there was a college radio station, a decent record store and nightclub, and a Mac. San Francisco, Los Angeles, New York, and Seattle proved to be the real hotbeds.

Some zines, like the *Bomb, Flavor, Straight from the Lip, Divine Styler,* or *One Nut Network*, were basically bedroom projects handed out to industry insiders and sold in specialty record and clothing stores. Others, like *Rap Sheet, URB*, the *Kronick*, and *Ego Trip*, began as free mainly newsprint offerings given out at clubs, shows, and local record stores. Other bootstrapping magazines like *4080, Stress*, and *On the Go* tried to build outward from regional newsstand sales. In time many of the zines faded, but *URB* and others would build a nationally distributed base of more than 30,000 copies. Corporate-funded magazines like *Rap Pages* (Larry Flynt Publications) or *XXL* (Harris Publications) also stepped in to compete, staffed with veterans of the zine world, able to make profits off print runs hovering around 100,000.

Even as they adopted the kind of brash editorial voice the *Source* had pioneered, these magazines often set themselves up in opposition to the *Source*, which for many now had the backroom odor of the East Coast establishment. To the upstarts, the *Source* was increasingly a symbol of New York–centric navel gazing—using hip-hop's New York origins as an excuse not to hear the sounds of vibrant regional scenes, increasingly intimate with major-label big money to the neglect of the rapidly growing underground. The new magazines were united by an underground sensibility, holding an elitist disdain for all things "crossover" while championing a "keep it real" aesthetic.

The best of them, like Sheena Lester's *Rap Pages* and Raymond Roker's *URB*, fostered a cutting-edge graphic design that split the difference between digital futurism and postgangsta realism, and developed a farm system of opinionated writers whose ambivalence over hip-hop's growing commercial success would underline sometimes bitter fights over the standards of critiquing hip-hop culture. The *Source*'s vaunted album-rating system—five mics was a "classic"—suddenly became a major issue among readers and underground writers. When, in 1994, Nas's first album, *Illmatic*, was awarded the rare classic rating, it was seen variously as proof of the magazine's New York centrism, its irrelevance to far-flung regional scenes, and its easy editorial capitulation to industry pressures.

The last problem came into bold relief in the summer of 1994, when the *Source*'s core group of staffers suddenly left over a dispute with publisher David Mayes. When the editors declined to do an article on a group that Mayes managed, Mayes added the article after the magazine had closed, then rushed the altered book to the printers. Their editorial credibility compromised, a large contingent of staffers who had built the *Source* into a national magazine felt they had no choice but to resign in protest.

The event sent shock waves through the world of hip-hop journalism. Even as they plotted how to woo some of the *Source*'s advertising money away, competitors felt that the staff had done the only principled thing it could do. But the *Source*'s meltdown also seemed to puncture any illusions that hip-hop journalists could separate themselves from the corruption of market pressures. Some imaginary line had been crossed; there was no turning back. Hip-hop was now clearly big business.

The Hip-Hop Generation's Myth Machine

By the mid-nineties, the hip-hop industry was peaking, exploding in market share to more than 10 percent of the domestic music market. Advertising was flowing and magazines were being created to tap it. Even industry magazines such as the *Gavin Report* and *HITS* retooled themselves to reflect hip-hop's gradual takeover of urban radio.

Then, in 1993, Quincy Jones unveiled *Vibe Magazine*, a multimillion-dollar joint venture with Time, Inc., that aimed to become the *Rolling Stone* of the hip-hop generation. It launched with a guaranteed base circulation of 100,000. By 1997, *Vibe*'s circulation had climbed to 700,000. It overtook *SPIN* in both circulation and ad revenue, and purchased its competitor outright for $43 million. The moment was symbolic, the four-year infant swallowing the twelve-year vet, hip-hop crushing rock. *Vibe* even began to outsell *Rolling Stone* on newsstands.

And the mid-nineties boom affected the entire market. The *Source*'s circulation, under the new leadership of Selwyn Seyfu Hinds, exploded to over half a million, with one of the highest sell-through rates of any magazine on the stands. (It even scooped up a National Magazine Award nomination.) In 1998, joining a market already shared by dozens, the *Vibe*-sponsored offshoot *Blaze* entered the market with a circulation of 200,000 (although it would soon crash and burn). The gangsta-leaning *Murder Dog* and the true-gangsta-crime *F.E.D.S.* became the print equivalent of regional hardcore rap, all Q & A transcripts and uncut roughneck lifestyles, reportedly circulating in the hundreds of thousands. *Trace, Vice, Strength,* and the *Fader* served upscale audiences seeking irony, authenticity, and cool clothes. By 2000, dozens of web sites sprouted, ranging from the BET-owned 360hiphop.com to the underground-targeted Platform.net. Hip-hop journalism's future seemed assured. The "hip-hop generation" now spanned preteens to fortysomethings.

Vibe's vault to the top, of course, paralleled the massive shift in pop tastes. It began as a high-brow experiment, mixing edgy hip-hop reportage and glossy investigative journalism with minimalist icon-making photography and disorienting "Madison Avenue takes an Uptown excursion" fashion spreads. The writing was often superb—for example, Joan Morgan challenging Ice Cube on his nationalism, Kevin Powell confronting Death Row Records at its peak, Danyel Smith both documenting and mourning Tupac's tragic career—while the New York–tabloid look made the blood run cold. Critics said the magazine was turning hip-hop into a museum piece—thoughtful but funkless, gorgeous but bourgeois.

But now, with *Vibe* and the hip-hop magazines, the hip-hop generation and the music industry had exactly what they needed: a full-blown mythmaking machine. Editors like *Vibe*'s Danyel Smith, in particular, had definite thoughts about which direction hip-hop journalism ought to take. She wanted to give the music sinew, the culture blood, the texts an aspirational quality. As she would later write in *The Vibe History of Hip-Hop:* "Like hip hop, this book is about the intense kind of aspiration that comes from having little. It's about the ambivalence of having a lot but knowing others don't. About the pain of boxing with brass-knuckled demons while the demons themselves scream that they're shadows. About holding and rhyming into a microphone. Mixing and scratching. Ill shit. Dust coke weed. Guns pain blood. Desire desperation truth true love and too much of the way back but not enough of the way forward. This book is that story. And it's as much about the ones who write it as it is about the ones who live it"(ix).

Hip-hop journalism at its best was deeply passionate—writing that celebrated the performance of blackness, that made myths of the performers themselves. But, often, the pieces were merely ornamental advertisements that fetishized rappers' monetary success and often excused their flaws. Hip-hop artists were presented as postmodern Horatio Algers, rising from the killing streets to enjoy the finer things in life, representing the aspirations of the ghettos from which they emerged, sometimes trapped by those very aspirations, dragged back by the emotions and loyalties of hard-rock life. Even in the underground zines, this kind of writing was pervasive, and disconcertingly coterminous with exactly the kind of shallow celebrity journalism that hip-hop writers once shunned.

Smith's own writing on Tupac Shakur was the model—brilliant, attention-demanding, tortured expert witnessing, full of ambivalence and dissonance. And in the wake of the brutal street slayings of Shakur in 1995 and Biggie Smalls in 1996, hip-hop journalism underwent a soul-searching, agonizing moment of self-criticism, as cover stories for *Rap Pages*, *Vibe*, and the *Source* all attested. They blamed themselves and each other for fostering divisions between the East Coast and West Coast, for exploiting personal and professional rivalries, for glorifying the trife life. Then they retreated. During the late nineties, some of hip-hop's biggest stories, including criminal investigations into Biggie Smalls's killing and exposés of industry backroom deals on gangsta rap, broke outside the realm of hip-hop journalism.

Why Hip-Hop Journalism Sucks in the Twenty-First Century

Hip-hop journalism, at its worst, looks like an endless parade of flossed and glossed ghetto stars, *People* magazine for the new majority. Like the flash and sizzle of a rap video, "keeping it real" in hip-hop writing seems to have become synonymous with confusing surface with depth. But this begs an important question: Have hip-hop journalists been guilty of aspiring to celebrity journalism, or did the increasing star-power of hip-hop artists transform hip-hop journalism?

Hip hop journalists are regularly forced to confront holy-rolling baby-boomers like Joe Lieberman and C. Dolores Tucker whose reactionary politics obliterate the sore to save the cancer. So these kinds of narratives can serve as defense mechanisms: a way of protecting and justifying the existence of a generation debased by outsiders and elders. In fact, many hip-hop writers are cowed by the power that rappers claim in the act of "representing." As Rakim put it: "In this journey, you're the journal. *I'm the journalist.*" Intimidated by such hypertextuality, writers reduce themselves to confirming a rapper's "reality" or conforming to it in order to defend it. Authenticity marks the hip-hop nation's borders. Thus it has proven easier for hip-hop journalists to document the excesses of a Biggie Smalls, Tupac Shakur, or Suge Knight than the racial-uplift programs of a Chuck D, KRS-One, or Sister Souljah.

But this is only a partial answer. It is also important to understand the structural changes that shape the current moment. Hip-hop is now a mature musical genre, one that generates more than a billion dollars in record sales and hundreds of millions more in related revenues yearly. And as the industry has expanded, the critical distance between the music and the journalism has narrowed.

As the number of labels has shrunk, so have the number of signings. Marketing budgets for new-artist development routinely run into the six digits. So it has become customary practice for record labels to bankroll feature-story junkets for magazines and web sites. On the other hand, the sheer number of media outlets can lead to competition for an artist's time, a resource publicists can trade for influence over the way a story eventually runs. In other words, hip-hop journalism, in many ways, *is* inseparable from celebrity journalism.

Yet Danyel Smith's defense of hip-hop journalism is spirited. " 'Hip hop writers' are often accused of being 'too close' to the music, to the artists and to the scene. Hell yes, we're close to it. We love this shit," she writes. "Where else to be but close to the truth?"

In truth, we cannot escape making myths; we can only try to make better ones. If our narratives have taken on the feel of a packaged and spit-shined rebellion, then perhaps it is time to recover the element of surprise so routine in the rhythms of hip-hop history.

References

Eric B. and Rakim. (1988). Follow the leader. On Eric B and Rakim, *Follow the leader.* Uni Records LP.

Mills, David. (1990). The gangsta rapper: Violent hero or negative role model? *Source,* December, 40.

Shecter, Jon. (1990). "Editor's Note." *Source,* January/February, 4.

Smith, Danyel. (1999). Preface to *The vibe history of hip-hop,* ed. Alan Light. New York: Three Rivers.

4

Critical Senility vs. Overcomprehension

Rock Criticism and the Lesson of the Avant-Garde

Robert B. Ray

I should say at this essay's beginning that its *form* gave me the most trouble—it originated, like many of the pieces in this volume, as a conference paper limited to ten minutes. As an academic, I am, of course, used to giving lectures to classes and at conferences where the proscribed length of forty-five to fifty minutes roughly corresponds to the length of a contemporary CD, although at academic conferences, such talks never seem precisely *compact*. But *ten minutes?* What analogies could guide my writing? Not the LP—too long. Not the sound bite—too short.

Finally, I settled on a model whose length might accommodate this assignment—the EP, that 45-shaped mini-album typically consisting of four songs of about two-and-a-half minutes each. In thinking about this form, I remembered that EP meant not only "extended play" but also "European Plan," that arrangement in which a hotel's rates include charges only for the room and not for the meals, a separation of functions implied by this book, whose composition rests on the assumed division of labor between musicians and critics.

Thus, I will ask you to think of this essay as an EP with four brief selections that you can play. Designing in this way also enables me to work in discrete sections that take account of our attention spans, that allow a reader to drop in and out of what I say without losing some single train of thought. If you don't like a section, you can stop reading until something else comes along in two and a half minutes that may interest you more.

Since I am from Memphis, I decided to use as my model the EP that began the rock-and-roll era, *Elvis Presley*, with its four songs: "Just Because," "Blue Suede Shoes," "Tutti Frutti," and "I've Got a Woman."

Track One: "Just Because"

Here is a story. In the 1950s, there was a filmmaker whose movies were more popular than Elvis. In 1956, for example, he released a film that made more money than either *Jailhouse Rock* or *Loving You,* and in 1959, he did it again with another one that was more popular than *North by Northwest, Anatomy of a Murder, Rio Bravo,* or anything Elvis appeared in. This filmmaker, Douglas Sirk, was a German emigré of Danish extraction who between 1952 and 1959 made a group of big-budget, commercially successful melodramas, usually starring Rock Hudson: *Magnificent Obsession, All That Heaven Allows, Written on the Wind, Imitation of Life.* At their release, these movies received no critical attention; like most Hollywood product, they did their job—they entertained, made money, and were forgotten.

In the late 1960s, however, having retired to Switzerland, Sirk began giving a series of interviews (starting with the *Cahiers du Cinéma* in 1967). Sirk now claimed that his movies (which within ten years had dated remarkably, becoming camp reminders of an abandoned style) had, in fact, been subversive, critical, satirical parodies of U.S. "bourgeois values" and Hollywood melodrama. Intentionally or not, Sirk had perfectly timed his play. It was eagerly received by an Anglo-American film studies community flush with two incompatible enthusiasms: auteurism and leftist ideology. Sirk provided a bridge between the two, as an auteur hero whose struggle against Hollywood's "repressive studio system" had involved sly criticisms of middle-class values. The Sirk boom was on, and since then, analyses of his films have flowered in journals and at conferences. By 1978, one film scholar could matter-of-factly refer to Sirk's "famous ironic subtext."[1]

The Sirk phenomenon repeated the founding gesture of postmodernism and conceptual art, Duchamp's designation of the readymade urinal bought at a plumbing supply store as an art work entitled "Fountain" (see Tomkins 1976, 9–68). Sirk had also worked with found objects, which happened to be his own work, and had changed their status and meaning without modifying them in any way. He had simply *said something about them,* thereby confirming Walter Benjamin's famous dictum that "any person, any object, any relationship can mean absolutely any-thing else" (1975, 177). Like Duchamp, Sirk had demonstrated the enor-mous importance of what French literary critic Gerard Genette calls "the paratext," the information (spoken and written) that surrounds and in-flects any work. After Duchamp, criticism had become as important as its objects of study; after Duchamp, it would never be as easy to say you liked something "just because."

Track 2: "Blue Suede Shoes"

Here is another story about critics and criticism. In 1874, at the height of Impressionism, the Palais du Luxembourg (at the time, France's official museum of modern art) had no paintings that we now consider impor-tant: no Manet, no Monet, no Renoir, no Degas, no Cézanne. Over the course of the nineteenth century, a huge gulf had opened up between the official system and the new art so that in 1874, the important critics had entirely excluded precisely that body of work that future genera-tions would come to regard as the best of its time. How could this situa-tion have arisen? How could so many critics with so much training and experience have been so wrong?[2]

In 1956, reviewing Elvis Presley's *Milton Berle Show* appearance, Jack Gould wrote in the *New York Times* that "Mr. Presley has no discernible singing ability. His specialty is rhythm songs which he renders in an undistinguished whine; his phrasing, if it can be called that, consists of the stereotyped variations that go with a beginner's aria in a bathtub. For the ear, he is an unutterable bore, not nearly so talented as Frank Sina-tra back in the latter's rather hysterical days at the Paramount Theater" (qtd. in Hopkins 1971, 136).

Critics who complained about the Impressionists now sound remark-ably like 1950s critics who complained about rock-and-roll and Elvis and songs like "Blue Suede Shoes." Here is a distinguished one, Albert Wolff, writing about the Second Impressionist Exhibition of 1876:

> The rue Le Peletier is out of luck. After the burning down of the Opéra, here is a new disaster which has struck the district. An exhibition, said to be of painting, has just opened at the gallery of Durand-Ruel. The harm-less passer-by, attracted by the flags which decorate the facade, goes in and is confronted by a cruel spectacle. Five or six lunatics, one of them a woman, an unfortunate group struck by the mania of ambition, have met to exhibit their works. Some people split their sides with laughter when they see these things, but I feel heartbroken. These so-called artists call themselves *intransigeants*, "Impressionists." They take the canvas, paints and brushes, fling something on at random and hope for the best. (qtd. in Haskell 1987, 207)

But other critics were less certain of their objections, and here, with Impressionism, the first avant-garde, which offered work whose newness represented a break with certain established forms—at this exact moment appears the first of criticism's two great dangers: the possibility that the critic might simply be *too old* to understand what has arrived, the problem we might call "critical senility." Reviewing the 1868 Salon show, Théophile Gautier, one of the best critics of his generation, diagnosed himself:

> Faced with this paradox in painting, one may give the Impression—even if one does not admit the charge—of being frightened lest one be dismissed as a philistine, a bourgeois, a Joseph Prudhomme, a cretin with a fancy for miniatures and copies of paintings on porcelain, worse still, as an old fogey who sees some merit in David's *Rape of the Sabines*. One feels one's pulse in something of a panic, one runs one's hand over one's belly or head, wondering if one has grown pot-bellied or bald, incapable of understanding the courage and daring of youth. . . . One reminds oneself of the antipathy, the horror aroused some thirty years ago by the paintings of Delacroix, Decamps, Boulanger, Scheffer, Corot, Rousseau, for so long excluded from the *salon*. . . . Those who are honest with themselves, when they consider these disturbing precedents, wonder whether it is ever possible to understand anything in art other than the works of the generation of which one is a contemporary, in other words, the generation that came of age when one came of age oneself. . . . It is conceivable that the pictures of Courbet, Manet, Monet, and others of their ilk conceal beauties that elude us, with our old romantic manes already shot with silver threads. (qtd. in Haskell 1987, 209; Hemmings 1986, 177; and Seigel 1986, 308).

Track 3: "Tutti Frutti"

Here is another story. In 1881, for a rather ordinary effort by his standards—a painting called *M. Pertuiset, the Lion Hunter*—Édouard Manet won the Salon's second-place medal. A few months later, through the intervention of a friend in the Ministry of Arts, Manet was awarded the Legion of Honor.

One art historian, Francis Haskell, has called this event the most important moment in the history of modern art: "Manet, the greatest enemy the Academy had ever known, Manet who had been mocked as no artist ever before him—Manet was now honored by the Academy, decorated by the State, accepted (however grudgingly) as an artist of major significance" (1987, 217–18).

From this point on, critics will be wary, will always have their eyes turned back on past examples, for this event acknowledges that, in Haskell's words, "there had been a war . . . [and] the critics had . . . lost"

(1987, 219). Here is born what Haskell calls the avant-garde's "most potent myth": that initial critical failure is *the sign of worth;* critics picked up on this idea, becoming afraid to condemn what might turn out to be the next Manet. Hence, the second of criticism's two great dangers, what Max Ernst called "Overcomprehension" (qtd. in Seigel 1986, 308) or "the waning of indignation": Advanced critics feel a duty to make up for injustices committed by their predecessors and become afraid of missing the next messiah.

In many ways, overcomprehension has become the ruling mode of rock criticism, as critics eager not to repeat the mistake of those who denounced Elvis and Little Richard (with his nonsense like "Tutti Frutti") praise everything, because *anything*—2 Live Crew, Bikini Kill, Mudhoney, Fiona Apple—might be the next Elvis or Sex Pistols. Certain bands and artists ("critics' faves") have always been subject to "overcomprehension": Arrested Development, De La Soul, Lou Reed (especially his "concept" albums like *New York*), punk-as-a-movement, techno, the Chemical Brothers, rap in general, P. J. Harvey (the new Tracey Chapman). While critics flock to some artists like Beck because their records easily accommodate fashionable notions like "recontextualization" and "grafting," overcomprehension typically involves the overappreciation of lyrics, particularly those involving some "political" theme. Hence the critical support of John Lennon's solo career. Nevertheless, "Tutti Frutti" remains more "revolutionary" than "Woman Is the Nigger of the World": Music's effects always register less at the level of explicit political content than at the level of *sound.*

More than a hundred years ago, in 1882, with overcomprehension just beginning, one very astute critic, Henry Houssaye, spotted the problem:

> How many people see in the Impressionists the renewal and future of French art? If we do not admire the Impressionists, are we then as blind as the critic Kératry who wrote that [Gericault's] *The Raft of "the Medusa"* was an insult to the Salon? Kératry was wrong, but he was sincere, just as we too are sincere. If criticism should aim to be so timid that it will never ever run the risk of having had its judgments faulted, then it would be necessary to praise everything to the skies on the grounds that everything may one day be consecrated by posterity. And in any case, supposing posterity does one day put Impressionism on the same level as Romanticism, who can be sure that posterity is not mistaken? (qtd. in Haskell 1987, 219)

Track 4: "I Got a Woman"

Gregory Ulmer proposes that we should think of cultural information as flowing through something analogous to nature's water cycle—a *pop cycle* that includes the four basic social institutions of family, entertainment, school, and the disciplines of knowledge. Thus, an idea or a theory can appear in one domain—let us say the disciplines—where it will employ a specific logic (formal), a specific medium (writing), and a specific genre (the treatise)—before eventually circulating into, let us say, entertainment, whose logic is mythological, the medium electronic, and the genre popular forms like songs, movies, and videos. The health of the cycle depends on an unimpeded flow; hence, when an idea such as, let us say, feminism (women in control of their own destinies) arises in the disciplines (where it appears as criticism), it will seek out figures or situations that can embody it in entertainment (Ulmer 1994, 193–97). That idea, in other words, wants to say, I got a woman who will illustrate what the disciplines and schools have been talking about; but in return for that figure's allegorizing of a critical idea, criticism will repay in Sirkian fashion, making that woman mean in a critically privileged way. And what woman did criticism discover, as its ideas circulated through the pop cycle? Madonna, of course.

Other disciplinary ideas have been used to justify certain forms of music—the links seem obvious between the academy's politically correct multiculturalism and the paratext surrounding rap and world music (usually African), and Derrida's specific word "deconstruction" has, in its passage through the pop cycle, become an all-purpose term for explaining Seattle bands, rave, industrial, and any music that initially sounds ugly.

But we need to remember that the pop cycle runs in both directions. Ideas and information and knowledge can appear in another institution besides the disciplines, in entertainment, for example, and then they will go looking to the schools and criticism until they can say, "I Got a Theory."

Notes

1. The best analysis of "The Sirk Phenomenon" is Klinger 1994. The most important English-language source for the notion of "Sirk's ironic subtext" is Halliday 1972, a collection of interviews with Sirk that triggered the "Sirk boom." To sense those interviews' effect on the film studies community, see Mulvey and Halliday 1972, a collection of essays devoted to Sirkian-sponsored "re-interpretations."

2. I am relying in this section on Rosen and Zerner 1984, an enormously important essay. My other, and equally important, source is Haskell 1987. See also the sections on Impressionism in Hemmings 1971 and Seigel 1986.

References

Benjamin, Walter. (1977). *The origin of German tragic drama*. Translated by John Osborne. London: NLB.

Halliday, Jon. (1972). *Sirk on Sirk*. New York: Viking.

Haskell, Francis. (1987). Enemies of modern art. In *Past and present in art and taste: Selected essays*. New Haven: Yale University Press.

Hemmings, Frederick W. J. (1986). *Culture and society in France, 1848–1898*. New York: Scribner's.

Hopkins, Jerry. (1971). *Elvis: A biography*. New York: Simon and Schuster.

Klinger, Barbara. (1994). *Melodrama and meaning: History, culture, and the films of Douglas Sirk*. Bloomington: Indiana University Press.

Mulvey, Laura, and John Halliday. (1972). *Douglas Sirk*. Edinburgh: Edinburgh Film Festival '72.

Rosen, Charles, and Henri Zerner. (1984). The ideology of the licked surface: Official art. In *Romanticism and realism: The mythology of nineteenth-century art*, ed. Rosen and Zerner, 205–232. New York: Viking.

Seigel, Jerrold. (1986). *Bohemian Paris: Culture, politics, and the boundaries of bourgeois life, 1830–1930*. New York: Viking.

Tomkins, Calvin. (1976). *The bride and the bachelors*. New York: Penguin.

Ulmer, Gregory L. (1994). *Heuretics: The logic of invention*. Baltimore: Johns Hopkins University Press.

DISCOURSES

5

Consumers' Guides

*The Political Economy of the
Music Press and the Democracy
of Critical Discourse*

Mark Fenster

n his review of a rock concert in 1992, Ron Wynn, then the
rock critic for the *Memphis Commercial-Appeal,* noted that one
of the groups appearing on the bill, Lynch Mob, "was effective and at least played tougher, harder music" than one of
the other bands at the concert, and that "they are a developing, growing band, and the show had elements of rowdiness,
fun and musical frenzy." An innocuous little review, the piece
employed the easily understood (perhaps even clichéd) metaphor of muscularity ("tougher, harder") for the band's hard-
rock musical style and suggested a narrative of maturation
("developing, growing") for the band's career. It also used key
rock-and-roll nouns ("rowdiness," "fun," and "frenzy"), implying that the band delivered on the (presumptive) desires of
the rock-and-roll audience for a good time. All fine and good,
if a bit trite. One problem: The Lynch Mob had failed to show
up for the gig. After his indiscretion had been exposed, Wynn
explained that he had arrived late for the show and asked
other audience members to describe the band he thought he
had missed. This seemingly innocuous review proved to be
Wynn's undoing and led to his firing from the newspaper
(Sweet 1991, 7).

81

I begin with this example to dwell neither on the occasional unethical act by a rock critic, nor on the unfortunate practical joke some fellow concert-goers might have played on Wynn, nor even to make fun of this poor rock critic, who was forced to walk away from a steady job. Instead, the story is helpful and interesting because of what it illustrates about expertise, authority, and repetition in contemporary rock criticism. First, the story demonstrates that one can cut and paste a generic review of a generic rock performance from certain phrases, images, and analogies —not unlike, one could argue, popular music itself, which relies upon (as Adorno and similar curmudgeonly elitists have maintained) the repetition of melodies, chord progressions, and rhythms to communicate to and maintain its audience. Second, and perhaps more interestingly, the story suggests that it was audience members, rather than Wynn himself, who supplied these phrases, images, and analogies. If the critical discourse surrounding popular music is so well-known and accessible from its development in the pages of magazines like *Rolling Stone, Creem, Spin,* and the like, then that writing is available equally to the Ron Wynns and friends of Ron Wynn in the audience of any club or concert hall. On the one hand, the critic is so essential for reporting on emergent trends and figures and new products in popular music that a daily paper feels it must have one; on the other, the critic's role can be appropriated by his friends (or perhaps enemies) and like-minded souls in the audience, so that his absence is noted only when he is exposed.

I want to suggest that the problems of popular-music criticism and journalism that the Ron Wynn case exposes so well are themselves tied to the institutional, economic, and ideological structures of the practices of contemporary popular music. Music critics and journalists operate within the economic structures of the music industry and within the various cultural discourses (with their attendant structures of power) of U.S. mass culture, and they work from certain notions of what makes good and bad "rock" or "pop" (or whatever they are writing about)— notions that the critic may attempt to play with or subvert (see Frith 1981, 165–77). Moreover, critics' and journalists' roles as consumer's guides and professional opinion leaders are themselves continually subverted by the accessibility of evaluative discourse within different genre communities (e.g., the hip-hop community, the indie rock community) and by the opportunity for noncritics to share musical opinions in everyday situations (e.g., to a friend at a concert) and in mediated communications (fanzines, websites, etc.). Accordingly, I want to present some thoughts about why the "bad" example of Ron Wynn actually provides some reason for celebration, or at least hope, for music criticism's present and future.

Critics and Journalists
within the Media Industries

Sociologists have long considered the position of the critic within the culture industries. In a highly influential article in the early 1970s, Paul M. Hirsch argued that critics function as "autonomous gatekeepers" or "surrogate consumers" who serve as "opinion leaders" for their "constituency" or readers (1972, 649). For Hirsch, each critic expresses an individual, autonomous opinion that is used by and has some effect on those who read her or his work. This notion of the critic has permeated the discourse of rock criticism since its beginnings; a particularly good example appears in the editors' introduction to a *Rolling Stone Record Review* collection published in 1971: "The reviewer listens carefully to the music in question, ponders its aesthetic qualities and offers his humble judgement" (1971, 6).

More recent commentators have abandoned Hirsch's formulation. Jon Stratton, writing a decade later specifically on rock critics, argued that their role as "mediators" or "cultural brokers" gives critics a "perceived independence" in their opinions that legitimates their position. This provides them with a "taken for granted credibility" separate from other marketing strategies of the culture industries—strategies with which rock critics themselves are associated, given their roles in promoting records and the proportion of promotional budgets that is spent on sending them free records and other materials (1982, 269).

Indeed, critics and their opinions achieve a certain cultural and economic status through the critics' employment by one or more institutions and their reviews' transmission through print or the airwaves. As capitalist workers in private enterprises, critics are compensated for their work based upon their ability to be "popular"—that is, either to increase or, at worst, to keep steady the profits of their employer. In order to retain the economic position of paid employees, critics must be seen as speaking both *to* and *for* their audience, while standing as representative voices of consumers who may or may not buy the records in question. (One could argue that Ron Wynn lost his job not because of any immediate economic loss he forced his newspaper to suffer, but because of the shame and threats to legitimacy he brought to his employer—which may, in turn, have caused some economic loss and certainly affected the morale and social status of the paper and its editors.)

Rather than autonomous observers, music critics are simultaneously opinion leaders and employees according to their ability to represent their constituencies faithfully, spread information about new records, and impart the status of their opinions to the media outlet that publishes them. Like other aspects of record industry marketing, critics help to circulate new records but speak as seemingly "independent" judges who have particular status and cultural capital. This position makes the critic-reader dialogue a structured one. The public debate of rock critics and rock journalism appears as legitimate and representative of public opinion and the "truth" of rock music by virtue of its establishing standards of values and ideological assumptions that are transmitted via the mass media. As Simon Frith has noted, rock critics attempt to create a "knowing community . . . select in its superiority to the ordinary, undiscriminating pop consumer" (1996, 67). Critics' discursive positions, then, are both as audience members who are presumably *similar* to their readers, and as speakers from a position of expertise and authority that *differentiates them* from their readers.

The critic's economic position within the media industries is equally important. The periodicals and other media outlets the critic works for depend upon advertising, a relatively large portion of which comes from record labels and from other media companies themselves often financially related to, or maintaining ongoing relationships with, record labels. This seems at worst a conflict of interest or the appearance thereof (hence *Consumer Reports'* rejection of advertising as a source of revenue), and at best a dagger that labels can hold over publications in retaliation for negative reviews. Anecdotal evidence and rock critic folklore speak of pressure placed by labels on magazines to suppress negative reviews and reportage; moreover, the implicit threat of advertising withdrawal might lead editors to assign important reviews to reviewers who are less likely to write pieces upsetting to labels.[1] At the same time, however, negative reviews and profiles do appear regularly, making any argument about direct and constant influence suspect.

On a more microeconomic level, critics do not make much money; one of the main reasons that people become and remain critics is for the free promotional material they get, including records, spots on club guest lists, backstage passes to concerts, and so on. Again, I do not want to suggest that such perks always and necessarily lead critics to write fluff (indeed, if every critic loved and wrote a positive review of every free CD received, music magazines would be as large as the phone book, and there would be a lot fewer of those cheap copies of promotional CDs that savvy consumers find at their local used-record store), but the fear of getting cut off by an important label or club is a real one.[2]

The microeconomic position of critics is also deeply affected by those who publish their work. Established periodicals, which constitute the overwhelming majority of paying employment opportunities for music critics, seem inherently conservative in their hiring and editorial practices. Whereas the pop music industry expects that any particular star can disappear within five years, the "stars" of rock criticism who have been with us for years are more likely to get book contracts, featured columns, and editorial and staff positions at magazines and newspapers, or to be able to grind out a living in the extremely difficult profession of freelance writing.

It makes sense; if I am the editor of a rock or general entertainment magazine or of a book-publishing company and I have the choice of publishing an article, review, or book by either an unknown writer or a well-known published writer who is a regular reviewer for a number of magazines, I know whom I would want to have in my magazine or on my book list, so long as I can afford it. Unfortunately, these writers are almost exclusively white males on the other side of thirty, folks like Dave Marsh, Robert Christgau, and Ed Ward, and they are the ones that get the few full-time positions, the good freelance jobs, and the book contracts. Given the very limited number of people who can make a living as music journalists and critics—if not a zero-sum game, it is certainly no booming source of new jobs—there is something of a logjam in the professional ranks. And those who have made it are generally older and less diverse (in age, gender, race, and ethnicity) than the popular-music audience, not to mention the talent pool itself.

The commercial nature of the music and publishing industries structures the possible content of music journalism and criticism. Speaking from a discursive and economic position within the institutions of mass culture, popular-music critics and journalists judge recordings, live performances, music news and current events, and artists' lives according to certain evaluative criteria for consumers. The questions a consumer publication like *Rolling Stone* and *Spin* (as opposed to a trade publication like *Billboard*) ask and try to answer are: Should you buy this record? Should you attend that concert? Is this guy an asshole, and should I therefore like and buy his music more or less? Music criticism is at the center, ultimately, of popular music's role in a consumer society.

More to the point, the discourse of rock periodicals and record companies promotes the sense that one's participation in rock and roll—indeed one's participation in American culture as a whole, given the centrality of popular music in our lives—begins and ends at the point at which we decide whether or not to purchase a record or a ticket to a show. Engagement is equated with consumption. This is not to say that back in the good old days (the fifties, the sixties, the heydays of punk), things were more revolutionary or collective. Clearly, from its start, rock music has operated within the expansion of a market economy and the increase in teenagers' disposable income and leisure time—to varying degrees, that is to say, it has always worked within the conditions of mass production and consumption. It is unsurprising, then, that popular-music critics and journalists are implicated in this system.

In addition to the review or reportage of particular products and acts, popular-music criticism's other important role is to legitimate and canonize, to perform an external evaluation of the music industry's products based upon certain core assumptions about what makes good, important music, and what makes disposable crap (as well as what makes bad important music and good disposable crap). One of rock criticism's accomplishments has been the establishment of a canon of great rock works—it is hard to imagine the faithful reader of *Spin* and the music pages of the *Village Voice* (and similar local alternative weeklies) who has not heard any Velvet Underground or Talking Heads, and at least heard of, say, Pavement or P-Funk or Afrika Bambataa, or the *Rolling Stone* reader who has not heard of REM or U2. Indeed, *Mojo* seems precisely to be about explaining and constructing the rock canon. Comparison to the canon and the genres represented within it serves as a familiar trope of criticism, enabling the conclusion that any particular record succeeds or fails because it is like or unlike other, similar records.

Rock Criticism and the Emergence of Rap

The reaction of rock publications to the emergence of rap in the early 1980s is illustrative of these processes.[3] Rap initially was, and has continued to be, incorporated in rock publications as an emergent form of *rock* music made by blacks. Throughout the mid-1980s, rap was generally explained and judged with the assumed criteria of aesthetically and socially "important" forms of rock music: Rap spoke from and for a specific community, it was innovative, it was "authentic," and it conformed to a continually shifting set of definitions of that which constitutes "rock" music.

The discussions of rap in the *Village Voice* and *Rolling Stone* demonstrate this well. In a March 1981 edition of his *Voice* "Consumer Guide" (a section that briefly reviews and grades approximately fifteen new records), Robert Christgau praised the fact that "indie-label underground R&B"—a movement in which he includes rap—"seems to have been exploding since the collapse of disco as mass culture" (1981, 50). He then gave two- to four-sentence reviews of a number of different albums and twelve-inch singles, many of them rap, assigning grades to each. For example, he gave the Afrika Bambaata/Zulu Nation/Cosmic Force single "Zulu Nation Throw Down" an A minus and described it as "virtually irresistible"; he characterized Grandmaster Flash and the Furious Five as "the hookiest rap band on record," although he criticized their record "The Birthday Party" for not being up to their usual standard; he praised Kurtis Blow's lyrics as "cleverer than the competition"; and he assigned the Funky Four Plus One's record "That's the Joint" an A for showing the band at the peak of their form rhythmically.[4]

Rap was thus incorporated quite easily into a column and a discourse that grades records as potential consumer purchases. In fact, in the introduction of this column, Christgau complained about the prices of twelve-inch singles and stated that the only rap singles to which he was giving positive reviews were those that, if lost or stolen, he would replace —in other words, the records presented in his column were those that he deemed necessary to his collection, good and important enough for him to replay on his home stereo. Rap records could be "graded" and collected alongside the recordings of rock artists and those of other forms of popular music, and thus could be incorporated within the discourses of rock criticism and the system of commodification and consumption of rock music.[5]

Rolling Stone music critic Kurt Loder's September 1982 review of Grandmaster Flash and the Furious Five's "The Message," one of rap's first breakthroughs into the mainstream rock press, evaluated rap alongside and against aesthetic and social standards of mainstream rock practice. Loder identified "The Message" as a social commentary and compared it to accepted standards of rock and pop commentaries: "[It is] the most detailed and devastating report from underclass America since Bob Dylan decried the lonesome death of Hattie Carroll—or, perhaps more to the point, since Marvin Gaye took a long look around and wondered what was going on" (1982, 52).[6] For Loder, "Flash and company" prove that they are great artists through their ability to "report" and make audiences "identify" with social problems; Loder thus immediately applied to rap the well-circulated criteria of the rock criticism of *Rolling Stone* and its privileging of socially important performers like Bob Dylan.

Authenticity, innovation, and successful conformity to rock standards continued to be the central themes in favorable reviews of rap records in *Rolling Stone* throughout the mid-1980s. Having "something to say" and using "drum tracks [that] treat the beat like a basketball being slam-dunked"; offering "more than a tough attitude: he's a good songwriter"; recording "the first truly consistent rap album"; "making rap safe for heavy-metal fans"; and sounding like a "sort of hip-hop Black Sabbath" were all compliments within these standards of judgment, helping to make rap intelligible to the predominantly white audience of a rock publication (Considine 1985, 95; Ball 1986, 68; Coleman 1986, 78; Pareles 1985, 24). In this context, crossover was not merely accepted, not merely praised, but necessary. In order to enter the pages of *Rolling Stone,* in other words, rap had to be comprehensible and explicable within the standards and discourses of rock. Run-DMC's success in receiving attention from the magazine was explicitly tied to its success in adapting rock sounds and reaching white rock audiences (in 1985 and 1986, five out of six of the reviews, interviews, and profiles of rap music and musicians were about Run-DMC). For example, a review of the group's album *King of Rock* identifies "the most resonant moments" as those that "come from the way the trio employs guitar"; similarly, *Rolling Stone* staff reporter David Wild's introduction to his interview with the band praised them for their "smart, accessible blend of rap and rock" and noted that they are one of the most important factors in rap's "coming of age"—a maturation process apparently predicated on its becoming more like a rock band (1986, 20).

For *Rolling Stone,* then, rap was visible to the extent that it proved an "artistically" successful (defined within established [white] rock standards of judgment) and commercially "successful" (defined by the ability to reach and cross over to the magazine's white readership) form of music. Like Robert Christgau, the rock critics and writers of *Rolling Stone,* once they identified rap as an object for discussion, immediately placed the music within the evaluative criteria by which rock is judged. This response to rap illustrates the "commonsense" values of popular-music criticism and journalism that erase race by applying the same standards of judgment to (black-dominated) rap as to (white-dominated) rock, and that simultaneously apply arguably racist notions of both "authenticity" (in the implicit expectation that rap must and, at its best, does, "speak for" the black community) and "maturity" (in assuming that rap artists must become more like "mature" rock artists in order to be worthy of consideration).

This example is especially striking in its demonstration that race—along with gender and sexuality—remains relatively unproblematized in the processes not only of reviewing and discussing a music like rap but in all of popular-music criticism and journalism. The overwhelming number and influence of baby-boomer white males in the rock journalism business makes a comparison like that of Grandmaster Flash to Bob Dylan and Marvin Gaye seem like commonsense to a demographic with a certain background and education and the economic and cultural capital to know the rock and pop music canon. This dominance also permeates the standards of judgment and values of the discourses of rock, including rock criticism. Jon Stratton argues that criticism mystifies the commercial nature of rock through its discussion of rock as art (1982, 269); I would go further and say that rock criticism also often conceals the social hierarchies that underlie many of the accepted assumptions of rock music and its audience: that it is the domain of heterosexual white males of a certain age. This remains among rock culture's and rock criticism's most important and unaddressed problems, extensively articulated only in recent years by an emergent generation of women and gay and bisexual critics.

The Democratic Probabilities of Music Criticism

But does mainstream music criticism and journalism really matter much? Consider that soon after the period described in the previous section, hip- hop began to develop publications devoted solely to its own music and the culture surrounding it, such as the *Source* and, to a much lesser extent, *Vibe*. Moreover, the language and processes of criticism were already alive among rap performers and audiences—indeed, on the turntables and in the samples themselves—while Kurt Loder and Robert Christgau were passing judgment from "outside" the community for the benefit of nonmembers. If criticism is so well-articulated and implicated within the commodification of culture that anyone can perform its functions, then maybe we are all, to a certain degree, critics.

Indeed, music criticism and canon construction are everywhere. VH-1's obsession with narrativizing the lives and careers of virtually everyone who has ever picked up a guitar is merely one example of the circulation of arguments about what matters in popular music's recent history. The proliferation of tribute records, to everyone from Led Zeppelin to Roky Erickson, exemplifies the ways in which artists themselves explicitly employ critical concepts in reworking (or merely reiterating) another's work. The wide range of professional magazines and fanzines written by and for followers of genres and subgenres demonstrates the application of broad critical terms and concepts to ever-narrower tastes. And the vast resources of the World Wide Web allow everyone who can crank a little HTML and can afford to operate a web page to speak her piece about an artist or an entire genre, while the seemingly infinite number of electronic mailing lists devoted to genres, subgenres, and individual artists enables a conversation between fans.

Critical discourse also enters into our everyday conversations with others, and into our own evaluation of music we hear on radio and television, as well as on our own stereos. It is hard to imagine hearing a record or seeing a band for the first time without an initial response filtered through a history of similar experiences, connecting new sounds with those one has heard, and evaluating these sounds according to certain standards and values of judgment. Clearly, such evaluations are conditioned by what one has read and how one has been implicated within the critical discourse of popular music, even if taste remains an intensely personal aspect of one's identity. The accessibility of criticism, then, is inherently democratic—just as democratic, in fact, as popular-music making itself.

The Revenge of the Audience

I have this undoubtedly incorrect vision of Ron Wynn—who by now, you certainly recognize, occupies near-mythical status in my mind as the rock critic as tragic hero—sauntering into the Memphis concert an hour late, at which point some resentful audience member decides he is going to jerk this asshole around by lying to him about that lame opening act. So the guy in the crowd talks some shit about the hard rockin' Lynch Mob, and the poor critic dutifully jots it all down in his notebook. The tragic, absent critic thus symbolizes both the (absent) authoritative critic regularly churning out tired descriptions of commercial popular music to fill the space between ads in a commercial publication, and the ongoing struggle over the participation and activity of those involved in the practices associated with popular music—the revenge of the audience as critic, both of the music and the professional critic himself.

This is not to say that all critics are absent, or that criticism is little more than content-free drivel. I can think of countless musical experiences I would not have enjoyed but for the suggestions and vivid prose of the critics I read while growing up, and that I continue to read. My point, rather, is to note the position of popular-music criticism in the political economy of the entertainment industry, and to assert that increasingly, some of the most interesting criticism comes about when musicians, fans, and listeners—not mutually exclusive groups by any means, nor groups that would exclude a professional critic—formulate and communicate their own critical tastes and desires despite the hierarchical structures that so often place critics and others with greater economic or cultural capital above them.

Of course, this formulation and communication require a language that criticism, aesthetics, and the capitalist mode of production provide. Any revenge of the audience will not be revolutionary, and popular-music criticism will remain a viable and even necessary appendage to the marketing process of popular music, as a filter and commentator useful for audience and industry alike. Nonetheless, at stake in this revenge is the degree to which professional criticism matters in shaping listening experiences and contexts, in making sense of the bands who do and do not show up.

Notes

Acknowledgment: Thanks to Frank Kogan, professional critic *and* zine publisher, for our discussions during my revision of this article.

1. On the relationship between record-label promotion departments and the pop-music press, see Negus 1992 (115–25).

2. Of course, we should recognize that it is the artists themselves, not the labels, who pay for such "free" records to critics (and cheap used records for savvy consumers) by contract (see Passman 1997, 96).

3. For a more extensive account, see Fenster 1995 (223–44). See also Rose 1994 (124–45) for a discussion of mainstream news organizations' response to rap's allegedly inherent violence.

4. Similar reviews can be found in "Consumer's Guides" of the period, including that for 29 July–4 August 1981 (60).

5. Along with *Spin*, the *Voice* has historically been one of the most important general rock music sections or magazines in the coverage of rap. See, for example, the cover story and special section on rap entitled "HipHop Nation" (*Village Voice*, 19 January 1988, 21–33).

6. A longer profile of rap that appeared in *Rolling Stone* less than a year after Loder's review also uses a rock analogy to explain this new music to the magazine's white readership: "Since its breakout in 1979, rap has been as much of a nuisance to urban contemporary radio as New Wave was to album-oriented radio: at once too arty and too rough, and a backwater of inspiration ripe for ripping off" (Carr 1983, 20–25).

References

Ball, Debby. (1986). Record review: LL Cool J's radio. *Rolling Stone,* 10 April, 68–70.

Carr, Tim. (1983). Talk that talk, walk that walk. *Rolling Stone,* 26 May, 20–25.

Christgau, Robert. (1981). Christgau's consumer guide. *Village Voice,* 25 March, 50.

Coleman, Mark. (1986). Record Review: Run-D.M.C.'s raising hell. *Rolling Stone,* 28 August, 78.

Considine, J. D. (1985). Record review: Run-D.M.C.'s king of rock. *Rolling Stone,* 28 March, 95.

Fenster, Mark. (1995). Interpreting and incorporating rap: The articulation of alternative popular musical practices within dominant practices and institutions. *Howard Journal of Communications* 5, 3: 223–44.

Frith, Simon. (1981). *Sound effects.* New York: Pantheon.

———. (1996). *Performing rites.* Cambridge: Harvard University Press.

HipHop Nation. (1988). *Village Voice,* 19 January, 21–33.

Hirsch, Paul M. (1972). Processing fads and fashions: An organization-set analysis of cultural industry systems. *American Journal of Sociology* 77, 4:639–259.

Loder, Kurt. (1982). A message for the times. *Rolling Stone,* 16 September, 52.

Negus, Keith. (1992). *Producing pop*. London: Edward Arnold.

Pareles, Jon. (1985). Run-D.M.C.: Making rap safe for heavy-metal fans. *Rolling Stone*, 18 July, 24.

Passman, Donald S. (1997). *All you need to know about the music business*. New York: Simon and Schuster.

Rolling Stone record review, The. (1971). New York: Pocket Books.

Rose, Tricia. (1994). *Black noise*. Hanover, N.H.: Wesleyan University Press.

Stratton, Jon. (1982). Between two worlds: Art and commercialism in the record industry. *Sociological Review* 30, 2:267–283.

Sweet, Roland. (1991). News quirks. *Indianapolis New Times*. October, 7.

Wild, David. (1986). Run-DMC answers a bum rap. *Rolling Stone*, 11 September, 20.

Between Rock and a Hard Place

Gender and Rock Criticism

Kembrew McLeod

A s a professor and a music critic, I lead a double life and maintain a sort of dual consciousness. Music criticism is an island to which I can swim in order to escape the rigidity of my university life, and I have been reluctant to connect these two worlds. In the past few years I have nonetheless started to cast a critical, reflexive gaze at rock criticism and have begun to use my scholarly training to think more systematically about certain questions that go to the heart of this chapter.

One issue that started me down the path of writing this essay is the fact that the field of rock criticism in North America is still dominated by men. Because of their key role in distributing influential ideas to a wide audience, what and whom rock critics write about is significant. Thinking about this in more depth reminded me of a lesson I learned on the elementary school playground and formulated more articulately in grad school: Discourse plays an important role in structuring and reproducing social relations. Or, to put it in terms that my ten-year-old self understood, *what* is talked about and *how* it is talked about influences who feels comfortable enough to come out and play—how certain cliques form.

The Music Industry, Rock Critic Discourse, and Gender Inequality

Writing rock criticism is an ideological act; the evaluative frameworks that guide the judgments of rock critics connect to belief systems shared by the community of which the critics are a part. Critics often unconsciously rely on descriptive devices that stand in for larger, more overarching concepts associated with traits traditionally ascribed to men. This makes sense, considering that the profession of rock criticism has been dominated by men since its origins. One can get a quick sense of how men dominate the rock journalism establishment by glancing at who is listed as a senior writer or senior, associate, assistant, or contributing editor on the mastheads of major rock magazines like *Rolling Stone, Spin,* and *Raygun.* In 1999, the number of female editors or senior writers at *Rolling Stone* hovered around a whopping 15 percent, at *Spin* and *Raygun,* roughly 20 percent.

Another way to get a relatively accurate picture of who is regularly working as a rock critic is to examine who has contributed to the *Village Voice* Pazz & Jop poll. Between 1978 and 1980 the female participation rate in the poll moved between 6 and 8 percent (this at the end of a decade marked by advances linked to the feminist movement). Of the nearly five hundred writers who contributed to the 1997 and 1998 polls, only about 15 percent were women—a twenty-year growth of only 8 percent. You could probably find a greater percentage of women professionals at one of Jesse Helms's garden parties—a shocking fact, considering the changes in the gender makeup of many other contemporary workplaces. The critics' poll founded in 1997 by ex-*Rolling Stone* editors Dave Marsh and Michael Goldberg—the Rock & Rap Confidential/Addicted to Noise Writers Poll—shows a similar disparity, women critics logging in at roughly 15 percent.

The exclusion of women from the profession of rock criticism is likely not the result of overt discrimination on the part of editors or those who run these critics' polls; for instance, the founders of the R&R/ATN poll intended it to be more diverse and representative. Rather than these polls misrepresenting the number of active female rock critics, the gender ratio they reflect probably represents the reality of working rock critics throughout the country. Who works as a rock critic in large part depends on one's immersion in the social sphere that rock critics inhabit, which in many ways resembles the old-boy networks that for years dominated most businesses.

These statistics attest to one of the most significant trends I have witnessed: the relatively small number of women who enter the music industry generally, and rock criticism specifically. As Will Straw points out in a discussion of record collecting, one of the functions of hipness is to maintain boundaries by requiring for admission a body of specialized knowledge and by understanding when that knowledge is *not* to be shared. "If the worlds of club disc jockeys or rock criticism seem characterized by shared knowledges which exclude the would-be entrant," Straw writes, "this functions not only to preserve the homosocial character of such worlds, but to block females from the social and economic advancement which they may offer" (1997, 10).

Rock critics articulate the attitudes of—and influence—the members of the interconnected music communities I have discussed. Perhaps the most significant aspect of rock criticism is its role in maintaining the circulation of particular discourses, and the content of those discourses helps determine who feels comfortable enough to participate and socialize with those in music communities. Engaging in rock criticism often requires one to employ particular cultural references and be aware of certain aesthetic hierarchies; the lack of that knowledge can put an aspiring rock critic at a decided disadvantage or dissuade one from even considering that career option. The specifics of what is said influence the way taste communities and other networks are formed, which in turn connect with the larger social and economic institutions of the music industry. This discourse is thus one way in which rock criticism helps sustain gender inequality in the music industry, even beyond the relatively small world of rock criticism.

What Rock Critics Talk About and How They Say It

The *Village Voice* Pazz & Jop poll Top Ten offers a kind of historical atlas of rock critic tastes, that is, what and who the critics talk about. Writings about the winning artists in record reviews in *Rolling Stone* (1971–99), *Crawdaddy!* (1971–78), *Creem* (1971–89), and *Spin* (1985–99) gave me a database of 587 reviews; Pazz & Jop–winning albums are favorably reviewed by a number of people across the country, indicating a powerful evaluative framework at work. To these I added reviews about the same artists in *The New Rolling Stone Record Guide* (1983) and *The Rolling Stone Album Guide* (1992), both sources of good examples of mainstream rock criticism and both good overall samples of the attitudes of most mainstream North American rock critics. (The writings about the albums at the time of their release closely correlate with later evaluations of them in the *Rolling Stone* record guides.)

Further, I looked at the artists excluded from the pantheon of critics' darlings and what, if anything, was said about them. From the company of top-selling artists each year who never placed in the Pazz & Jop poll, I created a hit list of some of the most critically despised artists ever. These artists are often not reviewed in rock magazines; when they are discussed, they often serve as scapegoats upon whom writers may heap their harshest criticisms concerning what constitutes "bad" popular music. Because many artists who have placed in the Pazz & Jop Top Ten more than once have also sold a sizable number of albums (e.g., Bruce Springsteen, Neil Young, Prince, Bob Dylan, the Rolling Stones, U2), the mainstream/margin distinction that Frith (1996) proposes to replace the worn-out high/low axis is not as useful when applied to mainstream rock criticism. Granted, rock critics do maintain tastes that include more obscure fare, but a cursory glance at *Rolling Stone, Spin,* and *Creem* during their peak "credibility" years demonstrates that the artists featured on their covers sold massive amounts of records at the time.

The question then becomes, How do critics distinguish "good" multiplatinum artists from "bad" multiplatinum artists? I began with a cluster analysis of favorite terms and concepts in the 587 reviews, especially adjectives used to describe the music or artist, and how those adjectives played off one another—for example, "serious," "raw," and "sincere" rock music as distinguished from "trivial," "fluffy," and "formulaic" pop music —a dichotomy, as we will see, that is implicitly, and sometimes explicitly, gendered. It is the *cumulative effect* of this patterned discourse—not the influence of a particular critic or piece of writing—that is most important to my analysis of rock criticism.

Pazz & Jop Winners and Rock Critic Tastes

Between 1971 and 1998, nearly 200 artists placed in the Pazz & Jop Top Ten (no polls were conducted in 1972 or 1973). Most artists, roughly 150, have been voted in the Top Ten only once. Some of these (such as Arrested Development) made little critical impact after their splashy debuts; many others are well established (such as Aretha Franklin). An artist who places more than once, then, is significant and relatively rare; taken together, they offer a rough picture of the type of artist around which critical consensus coalesces (table 6.1).

Since 1990, more women have been voted into the Top Ten than in the two previous decades combined, and in the 1990s women maintained a sizable—though never an equal—presence. In light of the rather pathetic gain in the Pazz & Jop female critic participation rate over the past twenty years (around 8 percent), this increase cannot be attributed solely to the entry of more female critics into the field, and I do not mean to essentialize the writing practices of male and female critics: One's gender does not predetermine who one will vote for or how one will write about a particular artist. *Who* is consistently singled out by rock

Table 6.1   Pazz & Jop Top-Ten Winners Two or More Times

9	Elvis Costello	3	Nirvana	2	Liz Phair
8	Bruce Springsteen	3	Pavement	2	Paul Simon
8	Neil Young	3	PJ Harvey	2	Pere Ubu
8	REM	3	Public Enemy	2	Pretenders
6	Prince	3	Sonic Youth	2	Randy Newman
6	Talking Heads	3	Stevie Wonder	2	Richard Thompson
6	Bob Dylan	3	The Ramones	2	Rod Stewart
4	Hüsker Dü	3	The Replacements	2	Run-DMC
4	Los Lobos	3	X	2	Roxy Music
4	Lou Reed	3	Beastie Boys	2	Sleater-Kinney
4	Steely Dan	2	Beck	2	The Who
4	The Clash	2	Björk	2	Tom Waits
4	Rolling Stones	2	De La Soul	2	Tricky
4	U2	2	Jackson Browne	2	Van Morrison
3	Graham Parker	2	John Mellencamp	2	Yo La Tengo
3	Joni Mitchell				

critics is significant, and a look at the list of winners lets us make initial assumptions about what types of musical characteristic are valorized. Nevertheless, it is even more telling to examine *how* they are discussed.

To analyze the adjectives used to describe the music, I have organized them as semantic dimensions.[1] I have named these dimensions after words and phrases used by critics, and while some that are used to judge "good" and "bad" music exist along an oppositional continuum, some are not. I view them as existing in a complementary, contradictory, and sometimes independent "play" of signs.

Aggressive Intensity

Critics often valorize music that has "aggressive intensity"—music that is forceful and powerful. For instance, in a *Rolling Stone* review of John Fogerty's *Centerfield*, the song "Zanz Kant Danz" is described by Kurt Loder as imbued with "a sense of personal vengeance that seems near-Biblical in its relentless intensity" (1985, 48). Rob Tannenbaum writes that Hüsker Dü's "*Flip Your Wig* is a product of compulsion—passion seems an inadequate word—and it communicates its savage purpose loud and clear" (1985, 56). About another Hüsker Dü album, David Fricke writes that "there is no mistaking the desperate conviction behind *Zen Arcade*'s almighty roar" (1985, 46). Dave Marsh's review of Neil Young's *Tonight's the Night* states: "If the songs here aren't pretty, they are tough and powerful, with a metallic guitar sound more akin to the abrasiveness of the Rolling Stones than the placid harmonies of CSNY. . . . If anything, these are the old ideas with a new sense of aggressiveness" (1975a, 68).

In a glowing review, Fricke points out that (after a series of relatively mild albums), Costello's *Blood and Chocolate* was "Elvis's most musically aggressive album since *Armed Forces*" (1986, 177). In many instances, rock critics identify anger as the source of this musical and emotional intensity, as Marsh does here: "As angry as it is desperate, [*The Who by Numbers*] moves from song to song on pure bitterness, disillusionment and hopelessness" (1975b, 66). He calls Garland Jeffreys's "Wild in the Streets" "a masterpiece—the kind of pissed-off music the Stones made from 'Satisfaction' to '19th Nervous Breakdown'" (1977b, 93). Rock 'n' roll is often correlated with masculinity, and the favorable adjectives and metaphors in these reviews invoke characteristics traditionally associated with men.

Violence

Although violence and anger are interconnected, critics' pervasive use of metaphors of violence to describe performances positively puts violence in its own (very prominent) dimension. For instance, Paul Nelson writes that "Neil Young makes rock & roll sound both marvelously murderous and terrifyingly triumphant as the drums crack like whips, the guitars crash like cannons and the vocal soars above the blood-red din" (1979, 74). John Landau makes the rock 'n' roll/violence connection explicit when he writes that the Rolling Stones' *It's Only Rock 'n' Roll* is "a rock 'n' roll album because it's so goddamn violent" (1974, 79). When one thinks about the Who's destructive concert-ending closers or Limp Bizkit's notorious Woodstock '99 performance, it is understandable why rock critics use metaphors of violence and masculinity, but there is nothing essential in the sounds made by guitars, bass, and drums that requires such fixed signifiers.

Later in the same Rolling Stones review, Landau writes: "The album has its playful moments but its most characteristic instant is Charlie Watts' first drumbeat on 'It's Only Rock 'n Roll.' It resonates like the sound of a shotgun. That violence—transmitted through the singing, words and music—makes *It's Only Rock 'n Roll* one of the most intriguing and mysterious, as well as the darkest, of all" (1974, 80). Greil Marcus calls Neil Young's *Comes a Time* a great record, but not a "knockout punch like last year's American Stars 'n' Bars" (1978, 59). Of Lou Reed's 1989 solo album, another reviewer writes that "the words of *New York* snap like switchblades" (Passantino 1989, 105). Sometimes critics blur the line between violence and sexuality, as when Landau positively refers to the Rolling Stones's "aggressive sexuality" or when, describing their song "If You Can't Rock Me," he claims that "the chorus turns it back into the anticipated and angry fuck song" (1971b, 42; 1974, 79). This connection between violence, sexuality, and rock 'n' roll is further articulated in a review by David Fricke: "*Goo,* the major-label hello by the ex-indie guitar-rape gods in Sonic Youth, is damn near *musical* by their standards, a brilliant extended essay in refined primitivism that deftly reconciles rock's structural conventions with the band's twin passions for violent tonal elasticity and garage-punk holocaust" (1990, 64).

Rock critics seem to scatter military and gun metaphors like bullets. Kit Rachlis writes, "There's bravado in the way Costello's machine-gun mouth sprays out each image" (1978, 54), and Fricke claims that the Replacements' "guitar-drums gunfire threatens to turn your brain to tapioca" (1987, 52). Lester Bangs refers to the New York Dolls' songs "Trash" and "Personality Crisis" as "neo-submachine classics" (1974, 60); on former Dolls lead singer David Johansen's solo album, "banks of layered guitars hit like bazookas" (Nelson 1978a, 80). Similarly, the song "Careering," on PIL's *Second Edition,* is described by Greil Marcus as "punctuated with gunshot percussion, ending in a barrage" (1980, 55).

Softness

One of the primary ways rock critics dismiss music is to use descriptors like "soft," "weak," "light," "wimpy." In a review of Hüsker Dü's *New Day Rising,* John Leland comments: "Without sacrificing any of the raw power or impassioned flailing that have made them one of the most electrifying bands on the planet, the Huskers have developed into brilliant pop songwriters. After all, there is no rule that says brutal rock songs can't have killer hooks, nor that killer hooks have to be coddled in light arrangements" (1985, 33). In a largely favorable review, Ken Emerson criticizes Joni Mitchell's *Court and Spark* because the "spare integrity of the music at its best is compromised here by silly frills. One of the finest melodies she has ever written, 'The Same Situation,' . . . is irritatingly sweetened by an insipid string arrangement" (1974, 65). In another largely favorable review, John Landau claims that Van Morrison's *Tupelo Honey* "is dominated by an air of intensity that tells us Van feels his current needs with no less passion than he felt past ones, even as the texture of the album sometimes passes into a bubbly lightness" (1971c, 56).

Discussing the genre of the female singer-songwriter, Steve Pond writes: "So now it's time to go further, to make this much-maligned form tougher and more soulful and grittier and more real. . . . And that's where Tracy Chapman and Toni Childs come in" (1988, 69). He implies that this "wimpy" and "wispy" form can only be taken more seriously if it becomes "tougher," "grittier" and "more real." In a review of the Replacements' *Let it Be,* the reviewer similarly uses such contrasts: "In an age when most rock records are studied and wimpy, this rugged album feels truly fresh" (Miller, 1985, 45). A *Spin* critic asks in a review of Arrested Development's debut, "Can rap be authentic when it swings with such an easy lilt?" (Foege 1992, 169).

Many of the adjectives used in these examples are gendered. Another example is this *Creem* review of Suzi Quatro's *If You Knew Suzi . . .* , whose "lackluster production of guitar-castrated foundations, conjures the ulti- mate archetype of feces-rock: 'Stumblin' In' stumbles in and out of the foulest, most wretchedly boring and constipated MOR-mindrot maggots the likes of Helen Reddy and Olivia Newton-John wouldn't sniff at" (Turner 1979, 62). Strong words, indeed. The image of "guitar-castrated foundations" is an evocative one, and it says a lot about the sort of gendered images that many critics associate with guitar-generated rock 'n' roll.

Rawness

Another characteristic critics look favorably upon is a certain raw quality with regard to the overall production sound, the individual instrumental performances, or the emotional vibe conveyed by the lyrics or vocals. For instance, Patti Smith's *Horses* "is an extreme record, a raw collection of epiphanies" (Goldwasser 1976, 72). According to Bangs, it "lunges with raw urgency," and the "general primitivism makes you realize you're a mammal again and glad for it, licking your chops." He goes on, "Which is not to say that there's not musical sophistication working here; it's just that it's *gut* sophistication" (1976, 58). Writing about the Band's *Northern Lights, Southern Cross,* Robert Palmer states that "the overall sound re- mains rustic, due largely to the roughness of Hudson's horns and the country-style close harmony of the vocalists" (Palmer 1976, 45). Of Neil Young's *Tonight's the Night,* Dave Marsh writes, "The music has a feeling of offhand, first-take crudity matched recently only by [Dylan's] *Blood on the Tracks,* almost as though Young wanted us to miss its ultimate majesty in order to emphasize its ragged edge of desolation" (1975a, 67).

Paul Nelson celebrates the Ramones' "deliberately crude and basic" sound, along with David Johansen's "musical primitivism," and he finds Neil Young's *Rust Never Sleeps* so engaging because of its "open embrace of the raw potency of punk" (Nelson 1976, 46; 1978a, 79; 1979, 73). Nel- son and Marsh are not alone in their admiration of Neil Young's raw edge; Kurt Loder claims that "*Ragged Glory* is, in fact, a monument to the spirit of the garage—to the pursuit of passion over precision, to raw power and unvarnished soul" (1990, 101). This "spirit of the garage" is invoked in a discussion of Keith Richards, "the Glimmer Twin with a garage-rock heart, a Rolling Stone for whom rawness isn't just a virtue, it's nirvana" (Fricke 1988, 86). "*Bring the Family* doesn't crack its shaft nearly as hard as [John] Hiatt's previous *Warming Up to the Ice Age,* but thanks to rawness and improved epiglottal rasp," Chuck Eddy writes, poking fun at the conventions of rock criticism, "it's maybe the more credible album" (1987, 20).

Slickness

A critically disdained form of sophistication is labeled slick professionalism or overproduction, considered antithetical to a credible, critically sanctioned "sound." Rod Stewart's *Night on the Town,* which the *Crawdaddy!* reviewer did not like, "retains a bit of the old roughness but, for the most part, presents a homogenized view of rock 'n roll which brims with vapid horn arrangements and omnipresent strings" (Naha 1976, 72). Journey's music is "slick," Kim Carnes sings with an "impersonal Hollywood gloss," and the Carpenters' "clean-cut, inoffensive pop" is dismissed, in part, because of its "chaste arrangements and crystalline production" (Coleman 1992c, 383; Holden 1983b, 81; Coleman 1992b, 112). Maintaining "rawness" or an "edge" can save from critical scorn some music that could be categorized as overproduced. Discussing Steely Dan, Ken Tucker writes, "It has always been the hard nasal edge of both the lead guitar and Fagen's vocals that rescued the band from slickness" (1976b, 66). On the Pixies' *Doolittle,* "the emphasis on more textured production has in no way taken away from the band's intensity" (Mundy 1989, 170). In the writings of rock critics, slick overproduction dilutes the "rawness" and "intensity" of rock 'n' roll and all that it implies (and it implies a lot about the way identities are constructed within certain musical communities).

Blandness

Being bland, boring, or middle-of-the-road flies in the face of what many critics value about rock 'n' roll, which is a sense of rebellion or, at least, excitement. Byron Coley castigates a-ha because he claims they "have birthed a whole new era in which vast numbers of humans actually seem to prefer the bland and puny to the huge and filthy" (1987, 30). A *Creem* reviewer insults Electric Light Orchestra with an interesting simile: "Some of this stuff is so tired it sounds like a menopausal Paul McCartney" ("Electric" 1974, 71). In another castration metaphor, reviewer Robot Hull dismisses John Denver's songs as "boring music played down to the lowest level of the semi-college, semi-double knit, flared-pants, bankteller set, all sung with this adenoidal castrated drone" (1974, 63). The Carpenters are considered both "serenely inexpressive" and "bubbly and bland," and Neil Diamond is castigated for his "MOR [middle-of-the-road] schmaltz" and for his "blandness" (Holden 1983a, 82; Coleman 1992b, 195).

Critics have discounted Barry Manilow as a "middle-of-the-road icon," reviled Journey's music for its "blandness," disparaged the "tunefully sanitized" music of Rick Springfield, and labeled Jefferson Starship's music "faceless, expert and bland" (Coleman 1992a, 447, 1992b, 383; Considine 1992, 663; Evans 1992a, 364). The music of Neil Diamond, the Car-penters, Barry Manilow, Journey, and Rick Springfield, it should be noted, has a significant audience among women. Critics' near-uniform reaction to such artists may be based as much on aesthetic reasons as on the need to carve out a distinct identity for themselves in opposition to these artists' audiences. There is no reason that certain stylized charac-teristics associated with critics' darlings are inherently more musically radical or progressive than various MOR acts. While some critical fa-vorites explore new sonic territories, most occupy distinct musical tradi-tions and employ their own formulas, so much so that a majority of geo-graphically dispersed critics can independently agree on the superiority of particular recordings.

Simplicity

Just as aggressive intensity is related to violence, the dimension of "sim-plicity" is connected with "rawness," though they are not quite the same thing. "Simplicity" refers to lack of excessive aural adornment, direct-ness, and avoidance of "fluffy," "overproduced" sounds, both typically disparaged. For instance, on *Nebraska*, Steve Pond writes, "Springsteen has stripped his art down to the core" (1982, 65); on Wonder's *Songs in the Key of Life*, "the best songs in this collection are love songs, which are classic in their directness and simplicity" (Aletti 1976, 77). Car metaphors as emblematic of simplicity are common in rock criticism; Greil Marcus's 1975 *Rolling Stone* review of Springsteen's *Born to Run* is a notable exam-ple. In a review of the Ramones' debut album, Nelson writes that "the songs are stripped down like old Fords, then souped up for speed" (1976, 47). Stripping one's music to the core and keeping it simple are ele-ments found in early "classic" rock 'n' roll and are something to aspire to. Paul Nelson writes of the Rolling Stones' *Some Girls* that "it's wonder-ful to hear the group blazing away again with little more than the basics to protect them" (1978b, 52).

Personal Expression

Honesty, sincerity, and "speaking from the heart" are highly regarded by rock critics, who use such descriptors to differentiate favored artists from those that employ "formulas" or "clichés" in their music. For example, John Landau argues that even though Carole King's "songs written with Goffin were written with the requirements of AM radio always firmly in mind, they still managed to express themselves in a rich and personal way" (1971a, 40). In his review of Carole King's *Tapestry*, Landau distin-guishes King's earlier songs from other "Brill Building" music—a genre synonymous with "formula" pop. Comparing King's *Tapestry* to Neil

Young's *After the Gold Rush* ("a sustained *tour de force* of self-expression"), Landau writes, "No one has recently expressed its full range of feelings as well as Carole King and she has done it nowhere as finely as on *Tapestry*" (41).

In describing U2's *Joshua Tree,* Steve Pond claims that the Irish group's music is "refreshingly honest" (1987, 72); Joni Mitchell is praised for her "unhampered self-expression" (Swartley 1977, 99). Fricke singles out Lou Reed's *Legendary Hearts* album for "its uncompromising frankness and harsh emotional thrust" and the "gray nakedness of the performances and frayed lyrical nerves" and points out, "That arrogant severity and unflinching honesty, however, are the very qualities that make Reed's fourteenth LP one of the singer-guitarist's most powerful solo statements" (1983, 68).

Seriousness

Many of the reviews refer to the lyrical and musical intelligence of Elvis Costello, REM, Peter Gabriel, Talking Heads, Bob Dylan, and the other usual suspects. In this context, they contrast seriousness to the "vapidity" of critically disfavored pop acts. The headline that accompanied the *Rolling Stone* review of Michael Jackson's *Thriller* reads, "Jackson Gets Serious," and in this review *Thriller* is considered a giant leap away from his more frivolous earlier material. The reviewer claims that Jackson is one of a number of black artists who "have incorporated increasingly mature and adventurous themes—culture, sex, politics—into grittier, gutsier music" (Connelly 1983, 46). According to this reviewer, only "serious" lyrical themes can translate to gritty, gutsy music. A reviewer of Bob Marley's *Natty Dread* claims that every one of his albums is weighted with "lyrical seriousness"; "*Natty Dread* deals with rebellion and personal liberation, using tough and sensual reggae to slam home Marley's bold and dead-serious opinions on exactly what is right and what is wrong" (Davis 1975, 52).

John Mendelsohn argues that "*Who's Next* contains songs that are 'intelligently-conceived,'" (1971, 42), and another reviewer writes, "to listen to [Joni Mitchell's] *Court and Spark* is to encounter an analytical intelligence that is equally rare" (Emerson 1974, 65). Elvis Costello, according to Janet Maslin, "writes short, blunt compositions that don't pretend to be artful, though they are, and don't demand to be taken seriously, even though they're more stunning and substantial than anything rock has produced in a good long time" (1979, 60). Notions of seriousness and intelligence are deeply tied to what is considered "substantive music"—notions that are bound up with other evaluative dimensions discussed here.

Vapidity

"Stupid," "trivial," and "vapid" are adjectives often tossed at critically un-popular pop music (and, sometimes, at its audience). Vapidity is con-trasted against the seriousness of critically favored rock music, and this be-comes quite apparent when an artist disliked by critics covers a song by an artist they take seriously. For instance, a reviewer argues that Suzi Quatro's version of Tom Petty's "Breakdown" "does just that, breaks down bland and gratingly INSIPID" (Turner 1979, 62). Paul Evans claims Poison is "scaling the heights of dim-wit portentousness" (1992b, 550), and the later, criti-cally disfavored, version of Cheap Trick is disparaged because the reviewer claims that "their songs are as dumb and generic as they come" (Dean 1990, 129). Mark Coleman dismisses the Carpenters for their "shallow and undemanding" material (1992b, 113). The mid-to-late 1970s material of the Bee Gees represented the "emotional vapidity" of the 1970s disco era (Holden and Marsh 1983, 35). Dave Marsh calls Journey's music "*Stepford Wives* rock, dead on its feet without any awareness of the utter triviality (not to mention banality) of such a scheme" (1983a, 266).

Traditionalism

Critics show favor to artists by positioning them as grounded in the pres-ent but consciously cultivating a connection with rock 'n' roll's past—in sound or spirit. A reviewer of *Howlin' Wind* argues that, "like all classic rock 'n roll, Graham Parker forces all these revered roots through his own sensibilities" (Glazer 1976, 82). Comparing Los Lobos to the Band (another critical favorite), a reviewer writes that "each band has the abil-ity to take from its roots while looking at the future to express both its personal feelings and its political ideas, to be both traditional and cur-rent" (Malanowski 1987, 32). A review lauds X's Billy Zoom for his "suc-cinct, revelatory guitar lines reclaimed from Carl Perkins, Chuck Berry and every junk guitarist worthy of the name" (Cohen 1981, 44). In a re-view of *Imagine*, Lennon's *Plastic Ono Band* "represented a return to rock's most visceral, and still implicit origins" (Gerson 1971, 48). And Kate and Anna McGarrigle are admired in part because they are "tradi-tionalists in the first order" (Holden 1976, 77). (Not only Kate McGar-rigle is blessed with the "critical adoration gene," but also her son Rufus Wainwright—both have been voted into the Pazz & Jop Top Ten.)

Authenticity

Many rock critics find authenticity suspect as a concept, but it neverthe-less seeps into their writing—even of those identified as anti-authenti-cists. For instance, Lester Bangs writes of Patti Smith's *Horses*: "Each song builds with an inexorable seethe, a penchant for lust and risk that shakes you and never lets you forget you're listening to real rock 'n' roll again at last" (1976, 58). Even if the term "authenticity" does not show up, invocations of "real" or "genuine" music often do, as in a description of Blue Oyster Cult's *Agents of Fortune* as "genuine rock & roll" (Tucker 1976a, 63). A reviewer claims that "Marley's self-appointed mission is to make us take [Reggae] and him seriously, to listen to these wails while we still have the time. His is the *real* soul music, close to the roots of us all and crying to be heard" (Davis 1975, 54). Of course, the word "authentic" itself is no stranger to rock criticism; Paul Nelson writes, "The Ramones are authentic American primitives whose work has to be heard to be understood" (1976, 46). Similarly, a *Spin* critic comments, "One hopes Arrested Development is savvy enough to know that history is paved with pure intentions and energetic enough to stick with its substantial, authentic groove" (Foege 1992, 170).

Commercialism

Rock critics are well aware that rock music is a mass-distributed commodity. Nevertheless, they still raise the specters of "commercialism" and "the masses" to dismiss an artist or album, or an audience who consumes a certain type of music. A *Creem* reviewer claims Midnight Oil's *Diesel and Dust* is "loaded with elements sure to irritate the contemporary domestic audience, which has, of course, been trained to accept NOTHING but brain-killing entertainment and AVOID challenges like the plague" (Young 1988, 26). "As it often seems, however," writes another *Creem* reviewer, "mega-success is frantically followed by the corporate rock blandout process, which scientists have proven seeks the lowest common denominator while thoroughly obeying the laws of diminishing returns" (Knapp 1987, 18). "Divisive, extreme and visionary, the Jefferson Airplane was a band of absolute artists—Jefferson Starship, at its best, became nothing but a band of hitmakers," Paul Evans writes. Instead, "Jefferson Starship chose survival by means of sheer commercialism" (1992a, 364). In a Public Image Limited review, Greil Marcus claims, "A group like the Doobie Brothers has nothing to do with rock & roll—rock & roll as an affront to entropy and a subversion of stasis—but, for millions, the Doobie Brothers are the thing itself" (1980, 55). The Doobie Brothers are targeted to contrast and illuminate certain aspects of Public Image Limited's musical and cultural identity, whose dissonant *Second Edition* album, which represents a challenge to the tastes of those "millions," had no chance of being popular.

Originality

Some critics reserve their most venomous remarks for artists deemed unoriginal. On the flip side, discussing Patti Smith in a review of *Horses*, a

Crawdaddy! reviewer writes, "Like Dylan and the rest of her influences, she is an original" (Goldwasser 1976, 72). Experimentation, inventiveness, and musical rule breaking are traits associated with critically favored artists. Jon Pareles claims that Steely Dan have "outflanked every musical rule they've ever met" (1976, 57), and Bud Scoppa argues that the group, "in a short time, . . . has turned into one of the best American bands, and surely one of the most original" (1974, 73). Greil Marcus praises Elvis Costello and Randy Newman as "two rock & roll singers distinguished by their almost total disregard for the music and marketing strategies of their contemporaries" (1977, 69). Stephen Holden admires Rickie Lee Jones, who "takes imaginative [lyrical] leaps that make most of today's songwriters seem pathetically timid" (1981, 55), and John Landau lauds Van Morrison's "Tupelo Honey" as piece "of such purity and inventiveness that it stands as a sort of landmark in the middle of the album" (1971c, 56). A number of the dimensions discussed to this point exist in opposition to some of the dimensions to follow that are used to disparage the music of certain artists. They are not intended to mirror each other; instead, they exist as part of a larger evaluative framework. They are sometimes played off against one another; at other times, they reinforce and magnify each other.

Formulaic Unoriginality

Formulas are at odds with the notion that the work of artists should reflect honest, sincere, and personal expression, even though familiar song structures guide most critically hailed music. Referring to an earlier, more acceptable version of the band, Dave Marsh argues that "Cheap Trick has already won the battle against the formulaic and pedestrian that punk rock is trying to fight" (1977a, 65). A decade later, critics had cooled toward the band, and in a *Rolling Stone* review, rather than praised for avoiding formulas, they were damned for filling their music with clichés. Discussing their 1990 release, a *Rolling Stone* reviewer states that "Cheap Trick has continued to "ignore the whole realm of originality by singing semi-metal tunes that sound like *Top Gun* soundtrack rejects" (Dean 1990, 129).

Of the late-1980s hair-metal band Warrant, John Mendelsohn writes that "there's precious little to be said for *Cherry Pie,* which comprises a lot of balls-out rockers based on riffs that were already grievously shopworn when Kiss was learning them off the third Alice Cooper album" (1990, 104). Dave Marsh dismisses Judas Priest's music as "for lovers of recycled Led Zeppelin riffs only" (1983b, 267). Stephen Holden disparages Barry Manilow for singing "formula ballads" (1983b, 313), and Dave Marsh claims that Foreigner's later releases rehash "a formula approach that suggests the group belongs in the ranks of the simply banal" (1983c,

183). The originality of critically hailed artists is often contrasted to a vague, generalized mainstream straw figure: "Rickie Lee Jones' *Pirates* arrives like a cloudburst in the desert of Eighties formula pop music and recycled heavy-metal rock, . . . explosively passionate and exhilaratingly eccentric" (Holden 1981, 53). Similarly, Kurt Loder argues that "Prince's rock & roll is as authentic and compelling as his soul, and his extremism is endearing in an era of play-it-safe record production and formulaic hitmongering" (1984, 102).

Sweet Sentimentalism

In popular culture generally, "sentimentalism" is a criticism often leveled at products aimed at, or produced by, women—and this is a relatively common trope used by rock critics. In one of the few favorable reviews of disco albums, the critic finds that Donna Summer's *Bad Girls*'s "only serious lapse is side three, which consists of four sappy ballads, all of them cowritten by Summer. Working with lyrics that are embarrassingly mawkish, the singer overemotes in a painfully flat, syrupy sob, while the Eurodisco-pop synthesis that works so beautifully elsewhere collapses in these lengthy, unstructured weepers" (Holden 1979, 72). Ken Tucker writes that Pere Ubu's *Dub Housing* "coheres as a lyrical work devoid of the sentimentalism that so many lyrical works drown in." In another review he claims that "[Elvis] Costello has always taken pride in giving sentimental clichés a malicious twitting" (1979, 96; 1981, 59). A *Creem* reviewer calls Huey Lewis's "Stuck on You" "a lilting serenade of such unremitting mush and sap that'll make even his most partisan fans grope for the barf bag" (Knapp 1987, 18). And a *Spin* critic notes in a review of the Neville Brothers' *Yellow Moon* that Aaron Neville's "voice—previously noted for syrupy singles like 'Tell it Like it Is'—becomes as powerful as a thunderclap" (Gordon 1989, 84). In this case, "syrupy" is contrasted to "powerful," a gendered dichotomy common to rock criticism.

This Is the End . . .

Rock music magazines like *Rolling Stone* emerged not only from trade papers and teen magazines, but also from the underground press. Significantly, 1960s underground culture emphasized authenticity and authentic expression; Frith states that "rock turned out to be the basic form of underground culture, but in becoming so it was imbued with an ideology that was at marked variance with previous notions of pop: rock was valued for its political stance, its aggression, its sexuality, its relationship to the underground" (1983, 168). This 1960s authenticist ideology has informed rock criticism for many years, and the discursive dimensions detailed in this chapter have been shaped by it. Not all the dimensions can be identified in the writings of all rock critics, and that is not essential to the claims I make. I believe that more important than the short-term effects of a single review is the exploration of how the patterned discourse shapes the consciousness of those in music communities over time.

The dimensions employed to favorably describe an artist or album (aggressive intensity, violence, rawness, simplicity, personal expression, seriousness, tradition, authenticity and originality), as well as those used to dismiss an artist (softness, sweet sentimentalism, blandness, slickness, formulaic unoriginality, and commercialism), tell a story. That is, the *way* critics employ these ideas within the discursive space of reviews tells a story. For instance, the concept of simplicity is not inherently gendered, but the way in which it is used in rock critic discourse is. Critics damn the Carpenters' "saccharine simplicity" and praise RUN-DMC's "brutal simplicity" (Coleman 1992b, 113; Considine 1992a, 611). Returning to the metaphorical discursive playground I mentioned earlier, how particular artists are talked about (as well as which artists are discussed) shapes, early on, who feels comfortable enough to participate in particular musical communities. These interconnected communities act as gatekeepers that restrict entrance into rock criticism and the music industry.

But, based on my analysis of rock critic writings and my own observations as a producer and a consumer of rock criticism, there seem to be cracks in what could be called the dominant ideology of rock criticism. While the dimensions outlined here are still present in rock critic discourse, throughout the 1990s I have found increasingly less reliance on many of them. Here is an extended excerpt from a review by Rob Sheffield of Nirvana's *MTV Unplugged in New York:*

> In the wake of Nirvana, American rockers cling to their own back-to-Africa movement, an escapist fantasy away from fake music into real music. You know the drill: Rock 'n' roll would be so much better if we could just make tapes and give them away at shows, or maybe just hitch from town to town and sing for the kids! This fantasy has done more to bleed the humor and spontaneity out of music than samplers ever did. After all, the blandishments of corporate rock never stopped Boston's "More than a Feeling" from sounding like divine intervention, or prevented ZZ Top's "Rough Boy" and Def Leppard's "Photograph" from communicating recognizably human emotions. If Poison wrote better songs than Beat Happening—and it did—then there's something crippling about the purist scam. (1995, 71)

The popular notion held by many critics that people's lives have been saved by rock 'n' roll (as opposed to "meaningless" pop music) anchors, for instance, Dave Marsh's excellent *Born to Run: The Bruce Springsteen Story,* as well as a host of other rock tomes. This construction of rock 'n' roll is closely tied up with the 1960s counterculture ethos that celebrated attributes associated with masculinity and dismissed as counterrevolutionary or unprogressive cultural expression typically the domain of women. With men defining the discourse of the civil rights and antiwar movements—and of the counterculture, more generally—not surprisingly, men dominated these areas of activism. And because these discourses of the counterculture heavily influenced the rock community, the terms for entry into this area of cultural production were defined early on as, to quote James Brown, a "man's man's man's world." In the critics' sincere commitment to connect their vision of a better world to a particular version of popular music (their version), they unwittingly created the discursive conditions helped reproduce gender inequality.

A brief example of this patterned discourse drawn from a piece of rock writing from outside those I analyzed occurs in Marsh's *Born To Run,* which is very much committed to the idea that "rock and roll has saved lives" (1996, xvi). Of Springsteen's concert-opening stint for the group Chicago early in his career, Marsh writes: "Chicago is a purely commercial proposition; its exploitation of banal rock and jazz riffs in a pop setting qualifies as a kind of cynicism. If nothing else, Chicago is bland, and its appeal is not to people who share Bruce's intense commitment to rock and roll. This slick, adult, middle-class show was the antithesis of Bruce's performance" (67). Rob Sheffield's extended quote just cited (and the writings of the newer critics that it echoes) is in a dialogue with this conception of popular music. In contrast to Marsh's dismissal of the "bland" pop-rock group Chicago (and other pop straw figures that can stand in for Chicago), Sheffield argues that "the blandishments of corporate rock" do not prohibit certain songs from achieving the nirvana that critically sanctioned rock songs conjure. Further, the crass commercialism of particular popular songs doesn't stop them from "communicating recognizably human emotions."

Some of these newer critics have begun questioning and undermining assumptions that have grounded rock criticism by inverting the criteria traditionally used to evaluate rock and pop music, as well as by subverting accepted aesthetic hierarchies (for example, Sheffield's sincere claim that the 1980s hair-metal band Poison wrote better songs than indie-rock favorites Beat Happening). When the music is deserving, this means embracing music that is soft, sweet, bland, slick, formulaic, or commercial but nevertheless moving and life affirming. This shift represents, essentially, an abandonment of the idea that this very culturally and historically situated model of musical identity can alone bring us closer to a better, more liberated world. It is an acknowledgment that everyday people regularly find temporary answers to life's big and small problems in what have been described as trivial and ephemeral pop melodies.

To embrace such a position is to surrender the promise that rock 'n' roll can save the world or individual lives. Instead, it more realistically positions the relationship between popular music and listeners as one that still possesses a liberating potential but holds no guarantees. Rather than understanding popular music as part of a high-stakes war where we must be careful not to wander into enemy territory (like Chicago or Boston), such a position allows us to emphasize popular music's role in helping people survive the small psychological battles, brief interpersonal skirmishes, and other indignities that everyday life holds. In abandoning this older model of rock 'n' roll, it opens up fans, critics, and the rest of us to a less rigid, more inclusive, conception of popular music in which everyone potentially has agency and is invited to join the party.

Note

1. Seitel defined a semantic dimension as "a two-valued set that is used to conceive of and evaluate aspects of language use" (1974, 51), described and analyzed through indigenous literal statements. I came up with an indigenous coding scheme to analyze any discursive context in each review where adjectives conveyed positive and negative evaluations in relation to artists or their music. Without going into the distinctive features analysis I employed (see Seitel 1974; Katriel and Philipsen 1981; Carbaugh 1989), I then outlined the key concepts used to describe music that is considered "good" and "bad," which are tied to particular identity formations with which critics consciously or unconsciously associate themselves in discourse.

References

Aletti, V. (1976). Stevie Wonder: Songs in the key of life. *Rolling Stone,* 16 December, 77–78.

Bangs, L. (1974). New York Dolls: Too much, too soon. *Creem,* July, 60.

Bangs, L. (1976). Patti Smith: Horses. *Creem,* February, 58–59.

Carbaugh, D. (1989). *Talking American: Cultural discourses on Donahue.* Norwood, N.J.: Ablex.

Carbaugh, D. (1996). *Situating selves: The communication of social identities in American scenes.* Albany: State University of New York Press.

Coleman, M. (1992a). Barry Manilow. In *The Rolling Stone album guide,* ed. A. DeCurtis, J. Henke, and H. George-Warren, 446–447. New York: Random House.

———. (1992b). The Carpenters. In *The Rolling Stone album guide,* ed. A. DeCurtis, J. Henke, and H. George-Warren, 112. New York: Random House.

———. (1992c). Journey. In *The Rolling Stone album guide,* ed. A. DeCurtis, J. Henke, and H. George-Warren, 383. New York: Random House.

———. (1992d). Neil Diamond. In *The Rolling Stone album guide,* ed. A. DeCurtis, J. Henke, and H. George-Warren, 194–195. New York: Random House.

Coley, B. (1987). a-ha: Scoundrel dream. *Spin*, February, 30–31.

Connelly, C. (1983). Michael Jackson: Thriller. *Rolling Stone*, 20 January, 46–47.

Considine, J. D. (1992). Rick Springfield. In *The Rolling Stone album guide*, ed. A. DeCurtis, J. Henke, and H. George-Warren, 662–663. New York: Random House.

Davis, S. (1975). Bob Marley: Natty dread. *Rolling Stone*, 24 April, 52–54.

Dean, C. (1990). Cheap Trick: Busted. *Rolling Stone*, 23 August, 129.

Eddy, C. (1987). John Hiatt: Bring the family. *Creem*, October, 20.

Electric Light Orchestra: On the third day. (1974). *Creem*, April, 71.

Emerson, K. (1974). Joni Mitchell: Court and spark. *Creem*, April, 65.

Evans, P. (1992a). Jefferson Starship. In *The Rolling Stone album guide*, ed. A. DeCurtis, J. Henke, and H. George-Warren, 364–365. New York: Random House.

Evans, P. (1992b). Poison. In *The Rolling Stone album guide*, ed. A. DeCurtis, J. Henke, and H. George-Warren, 550. New York: Random House.

Foege, A. (1992). Arrested Development: 3 years, 5 months & 2 days in the life of . . . *Spin*, June, 169–70.

Fricke, D. (1983). Lou Reed: Legendary hearts. *Rolling Stone*, 28 April, 68.

Fricke, D. (1985). Hüsker Dü: Zen arcade. *Rolling Stone*, 14 February, 45–46.

Fricke, D. (1986). Elvis Costello: Blood and chocolate. *Rolling Stone*, 18 December, 177.

———. (1987). The Replacements: Pleased to meet me. *Rolling Stone*, 2 July, 51–52.

———. (1988). Keith Richards: Talk is cheap. *Rolling Stone*, 1 December, 86.

———. (1990). Sonic Youth: Goo. *Rolling Stone*, 9 August, 64.

Frith, S. (1983). *Sound effects: Youth, leisure, and the politics of rock 'n' roll*. New York: Pantheon Books.

———. (1996). *Performing rites: On the value of popular music*. New York: Cambridge University Press.

Gerson, B. (1971. John Lennon: Imagine. *Rolling Stone*, 28 October, 48.

Glazer, M. (1976). Graham Parker: Howlin' wind. *Crawdaddy!* September, 82.

Goldwasser, N. (1976). Patti Smith: Horses. *Crawdaddy!* January, 72.

Gordon, R. (1989). The Neville Brothers: Yellow moon. *Spin*, May, 84.

Holden, S. (1976). Kate and Anna McCarrigle: Kate and Anna McCarrigle. *Rolling Stone*, 26 February, 77–78.

Holden, S. (1979). Donna Summer: Bad Girls. *Rolling Stone*, 12 July, 71–72.

Holden, S. (1981). Ricky Lee Jones: Pirates. *Rolling Stone*, 3 September, 53–55.

———. (1983a). The Carpenters. In *The new Rolling Stone record guide*, ed. D. Marsh and J. Swenson, 81–82. New York: Random House.

———. (1983b). Kim Carnes. In *The new Rolling Stone record guide*, ed. D. Marsh and J. Swenson, 81. New York: Random House.

Holden, S., and D. Marsh. (1983). Bee-Gees. In *The new Rolling Stone record guide*, ed. D. Marsh and J. Swenson, 35. New York: Random House.

Hull, R. (1974). John Denver: Back home again. *Creem*, October, 63–64.

Katriel, T., and G. Philipsen. (1981). "What we need is communication": "Communication" as a cultural category in some American speech. *Communication Monographs* 48: 301–17.

Knapp, K. (1987). Huey Lewis & the News: Fore! *Creem*, January, 18.

Landau, J. (1971a). Carole King: Tapestry. *Rolling Stone*, 29 April, 40–41.

———. (1971b). Rolling Stones: Sticky fingers. *Rolling Stone*, 10 June, 42.

———. (1971c). Van Morrison: Tupelo honey. *Rolling Stone*, 25 November, 56–57.

———. (1974). Rolling Stones: It's only rock and roll. *Rolling Stone*, 19 December, 79–80.

Leland, J. (1985). Hüsker Dü: New Day Rising. *Spin*, May, 33.

Loder, K. (1984). Prince: Purple rain. *Rolling Stone*, 19 July, 102.

———. (1985). John Fogerty: Centerfield. *Rolling Stone*, 31 January, 47–48.

———. (1990). Neil Young: Ragged glory. *Rolling Stone*, 20 September, 99, 101.

Malanowski, J. (1987). Los Lobos: By the light of the moon. *Spin*, May, 32.

Marcus, G. (1975). Bruce Springsteen: Born to run. *Rolling Stone*, 9 October, 74, 77.

———. (1977). Elvis Costello: My aim is true. *Rolling Stone*, 1 December, 69–70, 73.

———. (1978). Neil Young: Comes a time. *Rolling Stone*, 30 November, 56, 59–60.

———. (1980). Public Image Limited: Second Edition. *Rolling Stone*, 29 May, 53–56.

Marsh, D. (1975a). Neil Young: Tonight's the night. *Rolling Stone*, 28 August, 67–68.

———. (1975b). The Who: Who by numbers. *Rolling Stone*, 20 November, 63–64.

———. (1977a). Cheap Trick: In color. *Rolling Stone*, 22 September, 61–63.

———. (1977b). Garland Jeffreys: Ghost writer. *Rolling Stone*, 21 April, 91, 93.

———. (1983a). Foreigner. In *The new Rolling Stone record guide*, ed. D. Marsh and J. Swenson, 182–183. New York: Random House.

———. (1983b). Journey. In *The new Rolling Stone record guide*, ed. D. Marsh and J. Swenson, 266–267. New York: Random House.

———. (1983c). Judas Priest. In *The new Rolling Stone record guide*, ed. D. Marsh and J. Swenson, 267. New York: Random House.

———. (1996). *Born to run: The Bruce Springsteen story*, Volume one. Rev. ed. New York: Thunder's Mouth Press.

Maslin, J. (1979). Elvis Costello: Armed forces. *Rolling Stone*, 22 March, 59–60.

Mendelsohn, J. (1971). The Who: Who's next. *Rolling Stone*, 2 September, 42.

———. (1990). Warrant: Cherry pie. *Rolling Stone*, 18 October, 104.

Millier, D. (1985). Replacements: Let it be. *Rolling Stone*, 14 February, 45.

Mundy, C. (1989). Pixies: Doolittle. *Rolling Stone*, 13 July, 170.

Naha, E. (1976). Rod Stewart: A night on the town. *Crawdaddy!* September, 72.

Nelson, P. (1976). Ramones: Ramones. *Rolling Stone*, 29 July, 46–47.

———. (1978a) David Johansen: David Johansen. *Rolling Stone*, 18 May, 79–80.

———. (1978b). Rolling Stones: Some girls. *Rolling Stone*, 10 August, 51–53.

———. (1979). Neil Young: Rust never sleeps. *Rolling Stone*, 18 October, 72–74.

Palmer, R. (1976). The Band: Northern lights, southern cross. *Rolling Stone*, 29 January, 44–45.

Pareles, J. (1976). Stevie Wonder: Songs in the key of life. *Crawdaddy!* December, 65.

Passantino, R. (1989). Lou Reed: New York. *Spin*, April, 105–6.

Pond, S. (1979). Donna Summer: Bad Girls. *Rolling Stone*, 12 July, 71–72.

———. (1982). Bruce Springsteen: Nebraska. *Rolling Stone*, 28 October, 65–67.

———. (1987). U2: Joshua tree. *Rolling Stone*, 9 April, 71–72.

———. (1988). Tracy Chapman: Tracy Chapman. *Rolling Stone*, 2 June, 69, 71.

Rachlis, K. (1978). Elvis Costello: This year's model. *Rolling Stone*, 29 June, 53–54.

Scoppa, B. (1974). Steely Dan: Pretzel logic. *Rolling Stone*, 23 May, 73.

Seitel, P. (1974). Haya metaphors for speech. *Language in Society* 3: 51–67.

Sheffield, R. (1995). Nirvana: MTV Unplugged in New York. *Spin*, January, 71.

Straw, W. (1997) Sizing up record collections: Gender and connoisseurship in rock music culture. In *Sexing the groove: Popular music and gender*, ed. S. Whiteley, 3–16. New York: Routledge.

Swartley, A. (1977). Joni Mitchell: Hejira. *Rolling Stone*, 10 February, 99–100.

Tannenbaum, R. (1985). Hüsker Dü: Flip your wig. *Rolling Stone*, 7 November, 56.

Tucker, K. (1976a). Blue Oyster Cult: Agents of Fortune. *Rolling Stone*, 14 July, 63–65.

———. (1976b). Steely Dan: Royal Scam. *Rolling Stone*, 1 July, 66–67.

———. (1979). Pere Ubu: Dub housing. *Rolling Stone*, 14 June, 96.

———. (1981). Elvis Costello: Trust. *Rolling Stone*, 2 April, 58–59.

Turner, G. (1979). Suzi Quatro: If you knew Suzi. . . . *Creem*, July, 62.

Young, J. (1988). Midnight Oil: Diesel and dust. *Creem*, July, 26–27.

1

Exclusive! The British Press and Popular Music

The Story So Far . . .

Martin Cloonan

The relationship between the British national press and popular music has always been an uneasy one (see Cloonan 1996, 259–70; Rimmer 1985b; Shuker 1994, 72–92). On the one hand, the press has reported popular music and thus helped to promote it; on the other, pop has often offended the press's sensibilities, and this has led to occasional press calls to curb pop's alleged excesses. More often that not such calls have been prompted by pop's attendant features rather than by the music itself.[1]

A Tale of Five Decades
The 1950s

By the time rock 'n' roll arrived in Britain, the British press had a rich tradition of critiques of, and opposition to, various aspects of popular culture, including music (see, e.g., Pearson 1983, 63; Godbolt 1984, 2; Hustwitt 1983, 13; Vermorel and Vermorel 1989, 10). When rock arrived, the critiques intensified and could reach the heights of hyperbole. In the wake of rock 'n' roll riots during screenings of *The Blackboard Jungle,* the *Daily Mail* of 5 September 1956 commented: "It is deplorable. It is tribal. And it is from America. It follows ragtime, blues, jazz, hot cha-cha and the boogie-woogie, which surely originated in the jungle. We sometimes wonder whether this is the negro's revenge."

In many ways, this quote captures some of the hostility with which the British press greeted America's latest cultural export. Rock was attacked for being foreign, alien; Pearson (1983) has shown that such reactions frequently accompany the advent of new social phenomena in Britain. While the mainstream press defended Britain's heritage, the music press endeavoured to defend British jobs. In line with its tradition of attacking new musical forms and defending established musicians, it colluded in attacks on rock 'n' roll. The *Melody Maker* urged the BBC to be wary of the "cheap and nasty lyrics" of rock and called it "one of the most terrifying things ever to have happened to popular music" (Martin and Segrave 1988, 53). It began, says Chambers, "a campaign to silence rock 'n' roll" (1985, 19–20).

Elsewhere, newspapers became concerned with the apparent demonic powers of popular music. Thus the *Sunday Pictorial* asked whether the singer Johnny Rae was a mass hypnotist (Vermorel and Vermorel 1989, 26–27). Indeed, the effect upon audiences was a prime concern, and much of the press's coverage of rock 'n' roll concentrated on the behavior of fans and the "riots" the music allegedly caused, rather than on the music itself. For example, Whitcomb (1972, 226–27) notes that the press exaggerated a "riot" by teddy boys on Tower Bridge in 1956, and Wicke (1990, 58) reports that a number of cinema owners reacted to this press hysteria by banning the early rock 'n' roll film *Rock around the Clock*. Inaccuracy in reporting is something of a subjective matter, but allegations of such inaccurate reporting have plagued popular music over the years and militated the reception of various forms of pop in Britain.

Inaccuracy was often accompanied by hysteria. A key incident came in May 1958 when Jerry Lee Lewis toured Britain accompanied by his thirteen-year-old wife, his second cousin, Myra. This relationship inspired a need by the British press to show that Britain was not the same as the southern United States (White 1995, 56–66). The *People, Daily Sketch,* and *London Evening Star* all called for Lewis's deportation; only four concerts went ahead before the tour was cancelled. MPs asked questions about Lewis in the House of Commons, and the Rank Organization, which had booked the tour, explained that it had cancelled the remainder because of "unfavourable audience reaction and other reasons" (60). Lewis later wrote an open letter in *Billboard* as part of a five-page advertisement to resuscitate his career.

Instances of the antics of performers, rather than of the music itself, attracting fierce press criticism continued, with the music press again fanning the flames. In the 3 February 1959 issue of *New Musical Express,* the columnist Alley Cat attacked the home-grown act of Cliff Richard on Independent Television's *Oh Boy!* in December 1958 as "some of the most crude exhibitionism ever seen on British TV . . . hardly the kind of performance any parent could wish their child to witness." The *Daily Sketch* picked up this criticism and eventually forced the show's producer, Jack Good, to get Richard to tone down his act.

Bradley (1992, 90) claims that there were *no* favorable reports of rock 'n' roll in the press before 1962. However, the potential of the press to play another role, that of promoter of pop (especially if it was British), was also apparent in the 1950s. Thus Melly (1989, 49–50) notes that the press encouraged and spread the phenomenon of screaming at Tommy Steele gigs and so helped domestic rock to prosper. After an initial hostility, the press seemed to be moving toward a more ambivalent attitude, promoter as well as critic, and this continued in the next decade.

The 1960s

By the 1960s, the press was able to praise as well as condemn an increasing number of home-grown rock stars. Most of the praise went to the Beatles, whose success was widely covered and engendered the first press attempts to treat pop seriously *as* music. The *Times* was something of a barometer here, and William Mann's anonymous 1963 article is symptomatic of attempts to discuss the Beatles in purely musical terms. However, Beatlemania again made audience reaction a focus of attention, and pop was again attacked on nonmusical fronts. For example, the *Daily Telegraph* attacked it as something Hitler might have found useful (Everett 1986, 48).

The Beatles were generally portrayed as home boys who made good (Cloonan 2000), and press scorn was reserved for the Rolling Stones, who found the press eager to play along with their bad-boy image. Early British tours by the Stones witnessed a number of audience disturbances, and segments of the press put the blame firmly upon the band's shoulders. In August 1964, after fights between mods and rockers at a Stones gig at the Tower Ballroom in New Brighton, the *Daily Mirror* referred to the band as "a menace to law and order" and spoke of "the mob violence they generate" (Wyman 1991, 301). Wyman (1991) reports a great deal of hostility from the paper toward the band, and Laurie (1965, 107) notes that the press often distorted accounts of the band's gigs. Again the inaccurate or hysterical reporting of events was apparent and caused resentment amongst both musicians and fans.

In early 1967, *Melody Maker,* by now a champion of new music, complained on 7 January that "newspapers and magazines are continually hammering pop music and its exponents." A few weeks later stars such as Vince Hill and Alan Price objected in particular to the press's treatment of the use of drugs by musicians (*Melody Maker,* 11 and 18 March 1967). Segments of the press seemed to be assuming the role of moral guardian.

In January 1967 the *News of the World* launched a four-week series on drugs and popular music—Hall et al. (1978, 239) would later describe 1967 as "the year of the English (moral) 'panic' about drug use." The series made a number of claims about pop's causing fans to take drugs, targeted Donovan as a particular mover in this area, and on 29 January suggested the banning of his "Sunshine Superman" single. The series prompted one reader to write in suggesting that pop stars should be tested for drugs—like horses and greyhounds—before they went on stage (*News of the World,* 26 February 1967). The paper also criticized the BBC's television program *Juke Box Jury* for playing the Mothers of Invention's "Can't Happen Here" single, which was allegedly made under the influence of LSD. It also attacked the Game's *anti*-drugs record, "The Addicted Man," which was withdrawn by Decca soon afterward in light of media hostility (Cloonan 1996, 45, 260).

Toward the end of the series, the paper reported a police raid on the Sussex home of an unnamed major pop star. This turned out to be Keith Richards's Redlands house in Sussex. There is a great deal of evidence that the *News of the World* itself tipped off the police that there would be drugs in the house (Wyman 1991, 520). After Mick Jagger and Richards were jailed for one night before being released on appeal, two hundred fans protested outside the newspaper's office (529). Again, the attack was not on the music, but its attendant features.

While segments of the British press are still keen to pursue a moralist agenda, it is almost inconceivable that in the late 1990s a British newspaper would take a similar action against a band. But in 1967 the *News of the World* had some specific aspects of pop in its sights. The UFO Club in London's Tottenham Court Road, an important site for London's underground movement (Nuttall 1970, 119), was forced to move after the paper ran a story that an "orgy" had taken place there, and the owner subsequently refused to renew its licence (*Melody Maker,* 28 October 1967). After a brief spell at another location, the club closed.

The process was not all censorious, however. Some in the press defended pop and its excesses. William Rees Mogg, editor of the *Times* (at this point still the establishment's daily newspaper), wrote an editorial titled "Who breaks a butterfly on a wheel?" in defense of Jagger and Richards at the time of their imprisonment. This famous piece is often portrayed as something of a watershed in the establishment's support of pop. While there is some justification for this, it is less often recorded that a few weeks later the paper informed its readers that "the world of pop has its own freakish laws" (Jassell 1967).

Nevertheless, after 1967—with the Beatles' landmark *Sergeant Pepper* album and the beginning of the "Is pop art?" debate—some of the more highbrow broadsheet newspapers seemed to feel that pop was worthy of consideration and began to review it seriously. For example, the *Observer* reviews of Jimi Hendrix's *Electric Ladyland* album and "All along the Watchtower" single were quoted in an advertisement by his label, Track (*Melody Maker*, 23 November 1968). Chambers (1985, 84) notes that between 1966 and 1971 professional critics arrived on the scene, legitimating pop as an art form, and newspaper coverage shifted toward pop as music rather than pop as social phenomenon.

The 1970s

By the early 1970s, a backlash against the permissiveness of the mid- to late 1960s had begun. One victim was the British underground movement, which was allied to some forms of popular music (Cloonan 1996, 14). This backlash was exemplified by the temporary imprisonment of the three editors of *OZ* for obscene libel in publishing the infamous "School Kids" edition of the magazine (Palmer 1971). The *Daily Telegraph* displayed its establishment credentials by suggesting in an editorial that the "*OZ* three" might need mental-health treatment (de Jongh 1991). In 1972 the same newspaper attacked McGuinness Flint's protest song against the internment of political prisoners in Northern Ireland, "Let the People Go," as "matchless in idiocy, inanity and feebleness" and praised the BBC for banning it (*Melody Maker*, 11 March 1972).

But the major preoccupation of the press in the early 1970s was one of pop's attendant features: festivals. Hall et al. (1978, 250) report that the press described the 1968 Isle of Wight festival as containing "just-about every permissive demon that had ever haunted the imagination of the morally indignant." As Arnold commented in 1971, "for sheer prurience, the reportage of the rock festivals . . . would be hard to equal," and Wale pointed out in 1972 that in Britain, pop festivals were "never helped by the popular Press who, instead of reviewing the music . . . dwelt on pot smoking, bad LSD trips, odd outbreaks of violence and the VD figures" (15). There were frequent letters to the music press complaining about press distortions of events at festivals (see, for example, *Melody Maker*, 10 June 1972). Eventually the fans' concerns got official recognition, as a 1973 government report on festivals noted that the press "have behaved with great irresponsibility and have to a certain extent created the problems surrounding pop festivals" (Advisory Committee 1973, 8–9).

Damage to the public image of pop by inaccurate and sensationalist reporting continued in the late 1970s, when punk set off the worst cases of press excess in the decade. National press coverage of punk took off on 15 October 1976, when the *Sun* called it "the craziest pop cult of them all." The same month, the *Daily Mail* referred to prominent punks Siouxsie Sioux and Steve Severin as "the wreckers of civilisation' (Savage 1991, 252).

But it was the Sex Pistols' appearance as interviewees on the *Today* television program of 1 December 1976, airing in London in the early evening, that really set the press on to punk. During their interview, the band cursed several times. This was a major violation of normal codes of behavior for such programs. It interrupted "family viewing" (see Laing 1985, 36) by introducing swearing "with Nan and the kids around," as the *Daily Mirror* put it (3 December 1976). The following day, 2 December, the press reacted in a virulent manner and was uniformly hostile: "Four Letter Group in TV storm" and "The Punk Horror Show" (*Daily Mail*), and "4 Letter Words Rock TV" (*Daily Telegraph*).

While again it was not the music that attracted attention, one effect was to thrust punk onto the national scene. What had been largely a London phenomenon now went nationwide. The coverage also changed the careers of the Sex Pistols. As guitarist Steve Jones put it, after the *Today* appearance, "it was different . . . it was the media" (Savage, 1991, 260).

One theme that characterized the press coverage of punk was that of a hapless audience being manipulated by a money-mad business, a frequent allegation of would-be censors (Cloonan 1996, 27–28). The *Daily Mail* argued that "the only notes that matter come in wads" (Usher, 1976)—the same edition carried a feature on its "Femail" page on how to "Tempt Him with Silk" at Christmas—while the *Daily Express* headlined "Punk? Call It Filthy Lucre" and said that the real four-letter word behind punk was "CASH" (Pearce and Clancy 1976). This theme was taken up in the *Times* by Ronald Butt, who wrote: "Exploitation comes in many guises. The masses were once exploited by being made to work too hard for too little pay. Today it is their children's minds which are exploited, to make quick bucks by the millions for the record companies, the promoters, the agents, the cinema chains and some publishing houses" (1976).

After the Pistols' television appearance, EMI was continually asked by the press when they were going to sack the band. In January 1977 the Pistols flew to Holland and the *London Evening Standard* (4 January 1977) carried a story that they had vomited in public at Heathrow airport prior to departure.[2] This was vehemently denied by the band but appears to have been a contributory factor in their dismissal by EMI. Following a letter from Tory MP Robert Adley to EMI chairman Sir John Read asking him to control the band, they were sacked by the label.[3] (Another factor in the sacking was the appearance of the band on the front page of the *Los Angeles Times,* which had put in jeopardy an EMI brain-scanner project [see Savage 1991, 285].) In his definitive work on punk, *England's Dreaming,* Savage (1991, 287) contends that this sacking was a victory for the press. There certainly seems to be some truth in this. EMI itself cited press coverage and distortion of events as one factor in the sacking (Wood 1988). Leslie Hill, its managing director, said, "I was shocked by the misrepresentation" (Vermorel and Vermorel 1978, 204).

In the press's defense, the *Daily Mirror's* Jack Lewis explained that the paper did not cover the band's music, as this would not be of interest to its readers (Vermorel and Vermorel 1978, 201)—an admission that pop is often of interest to the (tabloid) press not as music, but as sensation. But according to Lewis, the coverage also helped to publicize punk, and the *Mirror* at least tried to understand the music by linking it to unemployment in a June 1976 editorial that spoke of a punk future (195). It also carried an interview with Sid Vicious that attempted to understand his motives (153–55). Savage (1991, 195) claims that while the press and the Pistols mirrored and fed off one another, the press began to print true stories about the band only after they had been sacked by EMI (287).

If the press and punk *did* have a symbiotic relationship, it was consummated in the summer of 1977 with the release of the Sex Pistols' "God Save the Queen" single. The lyrics—which talk of "making you a moron"—were widely (mis)reported as referring to the queen herself (Wood 1988). In apparent response, the *Sunday People* ran a three-week series on punk, which concluded that it was "dangerous," "sick," and "sinister" (19 June 1976). The *Sunday Mirror* (12 June 1977) headlined "Punish the Punks," and a series of attacks on members of the Sex Pistols and other punk musicians followed (Laing 1985, 137). The same edition of the paper claimed that punk songs "cause violence," although the following week's edition carried letters blaming the press for promoting punk by giving it widespread coverage.

The *Sunday People* (26 June 1977) ran a story claiming that patriotic teddy boys were itching to take on punks, while the *Daily Mirror* (1 August 1977) ran one saying that it did not want to see a punk-against-teds battle to replicate those between mods and rockers in the early 1960s; so, says Hebdige (1979, 157), the press managed to recycle an old moral panic. Press distortion again came under fire. Robson's contemporary account reported that "the bands bitterly attack newspapers that they claim have fabricated scare stories. Many punkers argue that the current spate of street fights between punks and Teddy boys in London would not have happened if the papers had not sown the seeds of the idea" (1977).

As "punk" became something of a dirty word in the press, some within the scene began to call it "new wave" in order to counter negative images. But the *Sunday People* (19 June 1977) warned that "new wave" was "punk in sheep's clothing" and raised a familiar theme by accusing record companies of "exploiting teenagers' weaknesses for their own profit." The *Sunday Times* saw new wave as "punk deodorised and re-packaged" (Laing 1985, 101). But the press always kept one eye on sales. If sensationalism was one way to make money from punk, another was to sell it as a fashion. Thus the *Sun* began an A-to-Z of punk in November 1977 and, although it also complained that a court decision not to convict the cover of the band's album *Never Mind the Bollocks* was "astonishing" (Savage 1991, 425), in January 1978 it began serializing the Vermorels' book on the band.

The press also took on another of its occasional roles, that of comforter after the initial fright. Hebdige (1979, 98) describes how the press managed to bring punk back into the family: The *News of the World* and the *Sunday People,* for example, ran stories about good punks and punk weddings. At a local level, the *Islington Gazette* carried a heartwarming interview with Johnny Rotten's mum (*NME,* 4 June 1977), and the *Nottingham Evening Post* ran a story about punks attending church (*NME,* 10 December 1977). As early as July 1977 the *Sunday Times* ran a thoughtful article on punk that presented it as just another business—albeit one with a number of peculiarities (Burn 1977).

But some things remained beyond the pale. The *News of the World* refused to print the name of the punk feminist band the Slits (*Guardian,* 6 November 1991), and it also attacked the comic band Alberto y Los Trios's punk parody "Fuck You" (*NME,* 7 October 1978). In 1979 the *Sun* was active in getting Kevin Coyne's "Babble" show cancelled because some of its lyrics dealt with the Moors murderers, Myra Hindley and Ian Brady (Cloonan 1996, 265), but the press's obsession with punk was long over by this time.

The 1980s

Some of the press first got pop back within their sights in early 1981 when fascist infiltration of rock gigs was widely reported (Tyler 1981). Oi music soon got particular attention. A spin-off from punk, Oi was heavily backed by *Sounds* magazine, which promoted the compilation album *Strength Through Oi.* A number of Oi bands were also involved in extreme-right politics. Three of these bands—the Business, Last Resort, and the Four Skins—played a gig in the London borough of Southall, which has a large Asian population, in July 1981. The gig was attended by a large number of supporters of the extreme right, and violence broke out between them and local Asian youths that resulted in the burning down of the venue for the performance—the Hamborough Tavern (Cloonan 1996, 173).

The *Daily Mail* headline the next day (4 July 1981) read "Terror in Southall," and the paper put the blame for the violence on the music and its promoters, rather than on the politics that surrounded it. Something of a backlash against Oi followed (*NME*, 18 July 1981). The *Mail* called for—and got—the withdrawal of the *Strength* album by the Decca-owned subsidiary Deram.

The political background here is important. As the first Thatcher administration struggled to implement its New Right agenda and as unemployment rose, the summer of 1981 witnessed a series of riots in Britain's inner cities. These were accompanied by the usual search for causes, and pop was implicated. Even the generally liberal-inclined *Observer* postulated that "the *casus belli* of a youth war lies in unemployment, bad housing, the breakdown of morality, of family/school discipline, a more rebellious attitude toward authority in this generation, overreaction by the police, the violence of youth culture, of some rock music" (Muncie 1984, 84).

In the *Daily Express,* the right-wing columnist George Gale blamed the permissive 1960s for the riots (Pearson 1983, 4). It is often columnists who inveigh against popular music (see, for example, Levin 1987), and Gale was no exception. In May 1985 he wrote: "Minds indeed become mindless when stuffed with the trash poured out by the pop industry everyday, without restraint, without control, without decency without discipline" (Street 1986, 14).

Meanwhile, the *Daily Mail* was one of the prime movers in the campaign to clamp down on video nasties, which resulted in the 1985 Video Recordings Act (Newburn 1992, 183) Although not directly an attack on pop, the scare over video nasties did impact upon the type of pop video that could be shown on British television (Cloonan 1996, 153). Columns in the *Mail* also condemned pop as "the new pornography" (Blanchard 1983, 35) and informed readers that "the entire pop world is geared to titillating the young" (Potter 1983).

But while there were unreconstructed attacks on pop that resonated with the Victorian values espoused by Thatcherism, other sections of the press were attempting to get back into bed with pop in order to fulfill another tenet of Thatcherism—naked commercial self-interest. This was the era of New Pop artists, who were generally much more amenable to the press than the punks had been. Record company publicists sought to exploit this to the full by getting the backing of the British press in a new attempt to fulfill the pop myth of conquering America (Rimmer 1985a; Kohn 1983). "Integration' was the open agenda (Rimmer 1985b, 154).

One of the main stars of New Pop, Boy George, was later to suffer cruelly at the hands of the *Sun* when his heroin addiction was revealed (Boy George 1995, 399), but initially it seemed that a more easy relationship might prevail. This courting of the tabloids still continues but is fraught with danger for those doing the courting. The press is interested in sales and will help an artist's career only if these two agendas coincide.[4]

An instance of the two *not* coinciding came in the early 1980s when a number of tabloid newspapers expressed concern that the Smiths' "Handsome Devil" dealt with child abuse (*NME*, 6 January 1990). The *Sun* erroneously reported that the BBC had banned the record (*Record Hunter/Vox*, July 1991).

Again, such reports were often one-offs by newspapers with their eye on sales. This appeared to be the case in the *Daily Mirror*'s attack on the Beastie Boys in 1987. The *Mirror* ran a story—which no other paper followed—of the band's verbally abusing disabled children at the Montreux festival in Switzerland. The *Mirror* then backed a campaign by Conservative MP Peter Brunivels to prevent the band's entering Britain for a planned tour and editorialized that "the CBS record company ought to have nothing more to do with them. . . . The least it can do now to save its reputation is to cancel their tour at once and stop putting out the group's records" (15 May 1987).

Although this campaign was unsuccessful, the *Mirror*'s reporting contributed to a growth in public hostility toward the band. This reached a peak when the tour climaxed in violence at Liverpool, where some of the crowd threw objects at the band and sang, "We're the Scouse army and we've beaten the Beastie Boys" (*NME*, 6 June 1987).

A year later the press turned its attention to raves and acid house. Initially, some of the press, especially the *Sun,* welcomed raves. On 14 September 1988 it offered readers acid-house clothes, and it published a "Hit List for Acid Boppers." But after the drug-related death of a young girl, Janet Mayes, at a Surrey disco, all this changed. The *Sun* on 1 November 1988 ran a front-page headline: "Shoot These Evil Acid Bastards" (see also *NME*, 29 October and 12 November 1988; Collin 1997).

While there were calls to ban the music (see Melechi and Redhead 1988; the *Sun,* 26 October, 1 and 3 November 1988), again it was something additional to the music that captured most media attention—in this case, drugs, especially ecstasy. While there was no doubt that drugs were prevalent on the rave circuit (Collin 1997), it is also apparent that some of the press saw drugs, rather than music and excitement, as the *only* attraction. In this they were wrong, and in November 1988 New Scotland Yard called an unprecedented press conference to confirm that the police's major concern with raves was not drugs, but safety (*NME*, 26 November 1988).

But there was evidence to suggest that, after their initial criticism of the press, segments of the police were accommodating press demands to clamp down on raves. *Q* magazine reported in January 1989 that a number of police raids on raves followed the *Sun*'s denunciation of them. This perception was shared elsewhere. Rock journalist Steven Wells asked if the police had become the puppets of the press: "Not so, says a Met(ro-politan Police) spokesman. It is apparently a mere coincidence that three separate and independent forces decided to concentrate vast manpower on smashing up Acid parties all on the same weekend. . . . The Met don't pander to the whims and fancies of the tabloid press. Of course not" (1988, 24).

Around this time the BBC was reported to have banned the word "acid" (*Record Mirror,* 5 November 1988) following tabloid coverage of raves. The band Children of the Night were denied a spot on Independent Television's late-night *Hit Man and Her* program in November 1988 with their "It's a Trip" single, which was thought to be inappropriate during this time of moral panic (*NME,* 3 December 1988). The local press was an important player in a ban on raves at Birmingham's Mecca ballroom (*NME,* 17 September 1988), while the same city also saw a ban on NWA playing their "Fuck Da Police" track live following a *Sun* report on them (*NME,* 9 June 1990).

The coverage of raves helped generate attempts to clamp down on them. Certainly, MPs could not simply ignore them. The first anti-raves law was the Entertainments (Increased Penalties) Act, which came into force in 1990. But this proved ineffective, as was shown by a week-long rave in Castlemorton, Worcestershire, that attracted 25,000 people and further widespread press coverage. Subsequently the 1994 Criminal Justice Act was passed, with clauses that clamped down further on illegal raves. Sensationalist press reporting was again implicated in these moves.

The 1990s

The coverage of raves bridges the 1980s and 1990s and shows that while the press generally covers pop in a much more sympathetic way than it did in the 1950s, it has lost none of its taste for sensationalism. For example, the *Sun* described attempts by Manchester's Chief Constable to close down the city's popular Hacienda club as "fascist" (*NME,* 4 August 1990). Such condemnation would have been unthinkable in the 1950s. It was also reported that the *Sun* had to rebuild its relationship with the industry after being successfully sued by Elton John in 1998 for untrue allegations about his sex life (George, 1993). This formed part of a public debate about the press intrusion in the private lives of celebrities (Cloonan 1998). A toning down of the *Sun*'s coverage of pop celebrities took place. This did not, however, prevent its headlining an article on

Sinéad O'Connor "Sinéad the She Devil" (*NME*, 23 February 1991). The press's censorial role also continued elsewhere, and in 1990 American theatrical band GWAR had several gigs cancelled following sensationalist tabloid coverage of its act (*NME*, 26 May).

The press also expects loyalty in times of national crisis, and one of its regular tactics is to ask MPs for comments on the latest pop outrage in order to legitimize its moral crusades. In 1991, with the Gulf War in progress, the *Daily Star* covered the remarks of Tory MP Sir Ivor Stokes on the Rolling Stones "High Wire" single, which criticized governments who sold arms to Iraq. Stokes called the single "appalling in the time of war" (NME, 23 February 1991). Subsequently, the record did not receive the type of coverage on radio and television that a Stones single might normally expect. (Johnny Beerling, the controller of BBC Radio 1, said that the song would not be played because of the fear of media headlines accusing the BBC of "supporting the enemies of freedom," the *Sunday Times* reported on 17 February 1991.)

Indeed, the *Star* seemed to take up the mantle of moral arbiter that had previously been the domain of the *Daily Mail*. It was a *Star* report that led to the ban of a single by the band Skin Up called "Blockbusters" that parodied a popular television series and led to an injunction from the program's makers, Central TV (*NME*, 24 August 1991). The *Star* also labeled Liverpool band the 25th of May "the sickest band in Britain" (*NME*, 12 October 1991), accused EMF of encouraging its fans to take ecstasy (*NME*, 11 January 1992), greeted the arrival of Snoop Doggy Dog in Britain with "Ban This Evil Bastard" (*Star*, 12 February 1994), and gave prominence to attempts to ban the Outhere Brothers' *1 Polish 2 Biscuit and a Fish Sandwich* album (*Star*, 28 July 1995).

But the *Mail* was not to be outdone. In 1991, it reported the allegedly obscene content of NWA's *Efil4zagin* album. A police raid on the premises of the album's distributors, Polygram, followed. The record was taken to court but found not to be obscene under British law (Cloonan 1995). The *Mail* has since unsuccessfully tried to get the films *Natural Born Killers* and *Crash* banned from British screens (Toohey 1996). The *Sun* also continued the tradition of giving prominence to MPs' views of aspects of pop. It headlined "Fury at Radio One Pop Poofs" after the station's special program on gay artists drew fire from Tory MP Terry Dicks (*Vox*, March 1993, 8). Its sister paper the *Sunday Times* gave widespread coverage to U.S. film critic Michael Medved, who had a censorial agenda that included pop.[5]

Sensationalist coverage of pop continued elsewhere. In 1994 a horrific knifing attack on a school classroom by a Middlesborough man, Stephen Williams, resulted in the death of a young girl, Nikki Conroy. Some newspapers implicated rock in the attack. The *Star* (30 March

1994) said the murderer was "obsessed by Iron Maiden," while the *Sun* (30 March 1994) dwelt on the murderer's links with the "bloodchilling" songs of Sepultra, especially the album *Schizophrenia,* which it described as "scary." Subsequently, pop was *not* implicated in this murder.

By 1995, the press appeared to have rediscovered the enthusiasm for pop that it had sometimes shown in the early 1960s, as the success of— and apparent rivalry between—Blur and Oasis engendered widespread press coverage (*NME,* 26 August 1995, 9).[6] Again, pop was wrapped in the Union Jack and used to sell newspapers, and the press played a role in articulating 1990s Englishness in pop (Cloonan 1997). However, the new romance appeared to be in jeopardy in September 1995 when Pulp issued its "Sorted For Es and Wizz" single. This song refers to the drugs ecstasy and amphetamine sulphate, and there was much speculation in the press that it would be banned by the BBC's Radio 1, but it was not. However, a plan by Pulp to include an inner sleeve with instructions on how to make a wrap similar to the type used for sniffing sulphate hit the *Daily Mirror* (20 September 1995) front page: "Ban This Sick Stunt." The *Mirror* again launched an independent campaign against the record, which included a poll that asked whether the single should be banned. Yes, said 2,112 *Mirror* readers, while 770 opposed it (Orr 1995, 16), and the band's label, Island, withdrew the sleeve (*NME,* 30 September 1995). However, the *Mirror* later printed "Jarvis Is Innocent" t-shirts after Jarvis Cocker invaded Michael Jackson's performance at the annual Brits awards (Armstrong, 1996).

Drugs returned as an issue in January 1997 when Brian Harvey, singer with East 17, was temporarily sacked after he admitted taking several ecstasy pills in one night (Donegan 1997). Harvey later apologized and was eventually reinstated after the media backlash subsided.

The horrific murder of fifteen people by two young men at Columbine High School in Littleton, Colorado, in April 1999 saw the British press looking for the causes. While the murderers' Internet and Nazi affiliations were seen as their prime inspiration, the fact that both were fans of the band Marilyn Manson was also noted. The British press also linked the bands KDFM and Rammstein to the murders (Younge 1999). The *Mirror* spoke of the "Rock King of Evil the Kids Adore" (Sutherland 1999, 23). The *Sun* headlined, "Killers Worshipped Rock Freak Manson" and asked readers not to buy his records as a mark of respect to the dead (24). The *Daily Telegraph* (22 April 1999) spoke of a "violent sub-world fed by sadistic rock and films," and its columnist of "artists who have used the [U.S.] free speech guarantee to bulldoze not just traditional mores, but the whole concept of good and bad taste" (Gurdon 1999). The *Mail* said that Manson "promotes violent death in almost every song he sings" (Jeffreys 1999). The *Guardian* (22 April 1999, 3) reported claims about backward messages in songs made on the band's Internet site, and the *Sunday Herald* said that Manson "may have the most explaining to do" (Gibb 1999, 13). While there was some speculation that Manson would not be allowed to perform as planned at a British festival in July, this gig eventually went ahead without problems.

If the coverage of the Columbine murders showed the press returning to its sensationalist instincts, then some progress seemed to be made in other areas. In June 1999 a story broke that Boyzone singer Stephen Gateley was gay. Although it was clear that Gateley did not think this a matter of public concern, the reaction from the previously homophobic *Sun* was instructive; it supported Gateley as it broke the story (see Greenslade 1999). While the *Sun* certainly had an eye on sales, it had also moved on from the time when its television writer (and former rock journalist) Garry Bushell proclaimed, "The single most important message we should be teaching our children is that sodomy kills" (Leith 1993).

In sum, at the end of the 1990s the ambivalent relationship between pop and the press continued. Pop is still a means to sell newspapers, the more so if its attendant features can provoke moral indignation or salacious interest. To these characteristics of the press's coverage of pop across the years can be added several others, as we will see.

The Same Old Story? Common Features of the Coverage

Overall, pop has engendered more sympathetic coverage by the U.K. press as the years have passed, but within this overall pattern a number of common features emerge. Generally, the tabloids (such as the *Express, Mail, Mirror, Sun,* and *Star*) are the keenest to cover the more sensationalist aspects of pop, while the broadsheets (the *Guardian, Independent, Telegraph,* and *Times*) tend to be more involved in carrying aesthetic criticisms and reviews of pops. Another characteristic of the British press's coverage of pop—the way in which pop has attracted sensationalist coverage through its attendant features rather than for its artistic achievements—has already been noted. Four others merit attention.

Moral Panic

One aspect of the press that has also already been alluded to is its role as an instigator of moral panic. As Hebdige (1979, 84–85) notes, "The media play a crucial role in defining our experience for us," and in particular it is the press that can alert the public to the dangers of any phenomenon—pop or otherwise. In pop, it was the press that fanned the censorial flames with festivals, punk, and raves and, in the latter case at least, helped to engender changes in the law. So one perennial role of the press is that of moral arbiter.

Moral-panic theory is generally associated with the work of Stanley Cohen (1973) on mods and rockers. Here, Cohen describes how the press can compile a list of isolated incidents, present them as a problem, and demand that something be done about that problem. Hall et al. (1978) built on Cohen's irrationalist/pluralist model of panic by presenting the "mugging" scare of the 1970s as a response to a *political* problem. By 1988 Cosgrove was describing moral panics as something of a British institution, and by 1994 McRobbie was arguing that moral panic had become the normal, rather than the deviant, way for the tabloids to address their readers.

While the range of moral panic has been wide—from drugs to mugging via male violence and lager louts—youth culture and the pop music that surrounds it has been something of a perennial favorite. The press has always been concerned about large gatherings of youth, and common themes in moral-panic theory are excess and misuse (Clarke and Critcher 1980, 120), both phenomena often associated with pop.

Certainly moral panic has surrounded aspects of pop. At the time of the Sex Pistols cursing on television, there was concern about declining standards in general, which led to the axing of the children's pop program *Pauline's Quirkes* by one independent television company (Cloonan 1996, 283–84). Laing (1985, 3) applies the term "moral panic" to events after the Pistols television appearance, while Hebdige (1979, 142) dates the start of a moral panic around punk as the blinding of a girl at London's 100 Club in September 1976.

In the 1980s the panic apparently returned with raves. *Q* magazine (January 1989) suggested that raves had engendered the biggest moral panic since glue sniffing. Certainly, aspects of moral panic were evident in the press's coverage of raves—the concentration on drugs and the compiling of isolated incidents were familiar features. So was the panic legislation that often follows moral panic (Sutherland 1982, 157; Pearson 1983, 143–44).

The semiotics of moral panic are also of note. Popular-music phenomena are generally in the press's sights once they go beyond being a "craze" to become a "cult." I have commented upon the use of the latter word elsewhere (Cloonan 1996, 262), and it has been widely applied in press condemnations of pop. It was used in the *News of the World*'s coverage of pop and drugs (12 February 1967) and widely used against punk. The *Mirror* (2 December 1976) used the term, as did the *Telegraph* (4 December 1976), while the *People* and *Sunday Mirror* both used the word on the same day (12 June 1977) when referring to punk. The *Mail* (9 July 1981) used the term to attack Oi, the *Mirror* (14 May 1987) used it against the Beastie Boys, and the *Sun* (1 November 1988 and 3 July 1989) against raves. So the word "cult" serves as a warning and is a key labeling term.

Aesthetics

The press also performs the role of aesthetic arbiter. On the positive side, the rise of the critic helped popular music gain artistic credibility. This began with the *Times* reviews of the Beatles and grew, especially from 1967. By 1999, the "quality" press was regularly carrying reviews of popular-music gigs and albums and so was playing a key role in keeping pop in the public consciousness. But it also has kept pop in its place. In the broadsheets, pop is usually reviewed *as* pop and seldom, if ever, as *music*. Here the demarcation lines between popular and classical music are drawn as firmly as ever.

But it is the tabloids that provide the harshest criticisms. Usher's (1976) *Mail* article on punk exemplifies how aesthetics can be used to reinforce moral arguments. Claiming that pop was about attitudes and beliefs, not music, Usher argued that punk was "simply no good" even by pop's own low standards. The *Sun* on 22 December 1976 informed its readers that the Sex Pistols were "foul sounding," the *News of the World* called punk "puke rock" (Burn 1977), and the *People* on 12 June 1977 argued that punk "required little musical talent." A similar line of attack was evident with acid house, described by the *Sun's* Johnathan King as "sheeit" on 27 October 1988 and "dreadful" on 3 November 1988. The *Daily Telegraph's* coverage of Marilyn Manson made sure to put the word "art" in inverted commas (Gurdon 1999). Aesthetic critiques help to undermine pop and are used by the press as a means to discredit pop phenomena that it opposes.

Pop as Manipulator

The portrayal of pop as dangerous has already been noted (Butt 1976; Pearce and Clancy 1976; Usher 1976; Street 1986, 14). In particular the press has often alleged that pop is endangering children. The *News of the World* on 29 January 1967 expressed concern that "impressionable youngsters" would take drugs if their idols did. The *Mirror* on 2 December 1976 portrayed punk as a threat to the young via a story focusing on Dee Generate, the fourteen-year-old drummer of Eater. Usher (1976) referred to pop as opium and to punk as heroin, which an unscrupulous business was feeding to impressionable, defenseless youngsters. The *People* on 12 June 1977 also accused punk of exploiting its audience. The *Mail* on 9 July 1981 portrayed Oi as exploiting its audience, and Potter (1983) portrayed the pop industry as a manipulator of its young fans. Such claims can also surface in the broadsheet press, as the following quote about a heavy-metal show from the *Independent* for 28 December

1989 shows: "The huge volume of the music, the mechanical hammering of its rhythm, its sheer physical impact and total lack of nuance left an audience to trail out at the end in a state of complete mental stupor, drugged and impervious to feeling."

Condemnation by the Stars

Should pop be seen to be getting out of hand, a tactic of the tabloid press is to get condemnatory quotes from some within in the business. Thus in 1964 the *Daily Mirror* condemned mods and rockers with the headline "They Are Just Louts, Says Dreamer Freddie" (Cohen 1973, 119). The *Evening Standard* got a condemnation of punk from Bill Haley as "going too far" (Vermorel and Vermorel 1978, 48) and during the early days of acid house the *Sun* on 1 November 1988 got quotes condemning the phenomenon from members of Bros and Radio 1 DJs.

Conclusion: Friend and Foe?

It would be wrong to portray the press as always opposed to pop and the subcultures surrounding it. As Hall et al. (1978, 73) note, the press is ambivalent to subcultures. It will patronize them, as it did with teds and mods (73) and with acid house. The press is often alarmed but fascinated by youth cults and plays a key role in shaping public reactions to them (Muncie 1984, 21, 23). Hebdige (1979, 92–93) argues that the press's reactions range through dread, fascination, outrage, and amusement. Certainly these characteristics can be seen in its reaction to pop, as has been the case with punk and raves and continues to be the case with contemporary artists such as Oasis, the Spice Girls, and Robbie Williams.

I have suggested that the press has generally moved from opposition to accommodation, but the harm that can take place during times of opposition needs to be acknowledged. To somewhat understate the case, the press did not make things easy for festivals, punk, and raves. But the press has also promoted pop. This essential ambivalence looks likely to continue. Pop and the press need one another in order to sell. This does not mean that their agendas will always coincide. Thus we can confidently expect further campaigns in the British national press, both against pop and encouraging it.

Notes

1. Here, I concentrate on Britain's national press and largely ignore the regional press and the national music press, which also play important roles in covering popular music.

2. In May 1977 the same newspaper ran an article by John Blake entitled "Rock's Swastika Revolution" that called punks "fascists." It provoked a furious letter in response from Malcolm McLaren (Savage 1991, 334).

3. Adley was not so prudish in another area. In 1986 he was one of the major opponents of a bill that would have outlawed the publication of pictures of topless women in newspapers (Short 1991, xvi–xviii).

4. See Negus 1992 (122–23) and Rimmer 1985b (162–63) for more on the relationship between artists and the press.

5. See Medved 1993 and the Sunday Times of the previous three weeks.

6. For the overexposure of Oasis, see *NME,* 7 September 1996; Beaumont 1997.

References

Advisory Committee on Pop Festivals. (1973). *Report and code of practice.* London: HMSO.

Arnold, F. (1971). Pop go the festivals. *New Statesman,* 2 July.

Armstrong, S. (1996). Pulpable success. *Guardian,* 15 March.

Beaumont, M. (1997). Looking back in anger. *NME,* 13 September, 17.

Blanchard, J. (1983). *Pop goes the gospel.* Welwyn: Evangelical Press.

Boy George (1995). *Take it like a man.* New York: Harper Collins.

Bradley, D. (1992). *Understanding rock 'n' roll.* Buckingham: Open University Press.

Burn, G. (1977). Good clean punk. *Sunday Times Magazine,* 17 July, 28–33.

Butt, R. (1976). The grubby face of mass punk promotion. *Times* (London), 9 December.

Chambers, I. (1985). *Urban Rhythms.* Basingstoke: Macmillan.

Clarke, M., and C. Critcher. (1980). *The devil makes work: Leisure in capitalist Britain.* London: Croom Held.

Cloonan, M. (1995). I fought the law: Popular music and British obscenity law. *Popular Music* 14, 3 (October): 377–91.

———. (1996). *Banned!: Censorship and popular music in Britain, 1967–1992.* Aldershot: Arena.

———. (1997). State of the nation: Englishness, pop, and politics in the mid-1990s. *Popular Music and Society* 21, 2: 47–70.

———. (1998). Privacy and media intrusion in a democratic society: The Calutt reports. *Democratization* 5, 2: 62–84.

———. (2000) You can't do that: The Beatles, artistic freedom and censorship. In *The Beatles, popular music and society: A thousand voices,* ed. I. Inglis, 126–149. London: Macmillan.

Collin, M. (1997). *Altered state.* London: Serpent's Tail.

Cosgrove, S. (1988). Forbidden fruit. *New Statesman,* 3 September.

Cohen, S. (1973). *Folk devils and moral panics.* London: McGibbon and Kee.

de Jongh, N. (1991). In those crazy old days of Oz. *Guardian,* 9 November.

Donegan, B. (1997). Sorry East 17 singer goes west. *Guardian,* 18 January.

Everett, (1986). *You'll never be sixteen again.* London: BBC.

George, I. (1993). Friend of the world . . . as he knows it. *NME,* 2 October 1993: 19.

Gibb, E. (1999). Jury's out on violence link as movies and bands face music. *Sunday Herald,* 25 April.

Godbolt, J. (1984). *A History of Jazz in Britain 1919–1950.* London: Quartet Books.

Greenslade, R. (1999). "Surprising, my sun." *Guardian,* 21 June 1999, media sec., 2–3.

Gurdon, H. (1999). Don't blame the guns . . . it's life imitating art. *Daily Telegraph,* 22 April.

Hall, S., C. Critcher, J. Clarke, and B. Roberts. (1978). *Policing the crisis.* London: Macmillan.

Hebdige, D. (1979). *Subculture: The meaning of style.* London: Methuen.

Hustwitt, M. (1983). Caught in a whirlpool of aching sound; the production of dance in music in Britain in the 1920s. *Popular Music* 3, 1: 7–32.

Jassell, A. (1967). The world of pop has its own freakish laws. *Times* (London), 11 September.

Jeffreys, D. (1999). A nation corrupt to the core. *Daily Mail,* 22 April.

Kohn, M. (1983). Hip little Englanders. *Marxism Today,* November, 37–38.

Laing, D. (1985). *One chord wonders.* Milton Keynes: Open University Press.

Laurie, (1965). *Teenage revolution.* London: Anthony Bland.

Leith, W. (1993). Kenny and Holly find positive ways to face up to a new kind of fame. *Independent,* 11 April.

Levin, B. (1987). Popping up all over. *Times* (London), 21 September.

———. (1994). My rock and roll secret. *Times* (London), 14 May.

McRobbie, A. (1994). Folk devils fight back. *New Left Review* 203: 107–16.

Mann, W. (1963). What songs the Beatles sang. *Times* (London), 27 December.

Martin, L., and K. Segrave. (1988). *Anti-rock: The opposition to rock and roll.* Hamden: Archon Books.

Medved, M. (1993). The corruption of rock. *Sunday Times* (London), 22 February, sec. 8, 23–25.

Melechi, A., and Redhead, S. (1988). The fall of acid reign. *New Statesman,* 23 and 30 December.

Melly, G. (1989). *Revolt into style.* Oxford: Oxford University Press.

Muncie, J. (1984). *The trouble with kids today.* London: Hutchinson.

Negus, K. (1992). *Producing pop.* London: Edward Arnold.

Newburn, T. (1992). *Permission and regulation: Law and morals in postwar Britain.* London: Routledge.

Nuttall, J. (1970). *Bomb culture.* London: Paladin.

Orr, D. (1995). Mea pulpa. *Guardian,* 21 October, weekend sec., 12–16.

Palmer, T. (1971). *The trials of Oz.* Manchester: Blond and Briggs.

Pearce, G., and P. Clancy, (1976). Punk? Call it filthy lucre. *Daily Express,* 3 December.

Pearson, G. (1983). *Hooligan: A history of respectable fears.* London: Macmillan.

Potter, L. L. (1983). It's the era of the teeny temptress. *Daily Mail,* 21 January.

Rimmer, D. (1985a). How pop learned to love the media. *New Society,* 25 October.

———. (1985b). *Like punk never happened.* London: Faber and Faber.

Robson, E. (1977). A night out with the punks. *Listener,* 4 August, 165.

Savage, J. (1991). *England's dreaming.* London: Faber and Faber.

Short, C. (1991). *Dear Clare* . . . London: Hutchinson Radius.

Shuker, R. (1994). *Understanding popular music.* London: Routledge.

Street, J. (1986). *Rebel rock.* Oxford: Blackwell.

Sutherland, J. (1982). *Offensive literature.* London: Junction Books.

———. (1999). Sympathy for the devil. *NME,* 1 May.

Toohey, C. (1996). Boycott Sony. *Daily Mail,* 21 November.

Tyler, A. (1981). Rock gets Nazi smear again. *NME,* 7 March.

Usher, S. (1976). The mercenary manipulation of pop. *Daily Mail,* 3 December.

Vermorel, F., and J. Vermorel. (1978). *The Sex Pistols.* London: Universal.

———. (1989). *Fandemonium.* London: Omnibus.

Wale, J. (1972). *Vox pop.* London: Harrap.

Wells, S. (1988). Get right off one chummy. *NME,* 19 November.

Whitcomb, D. (1972). *After the ball.* Harmondsworth: Penguin.

White, C. (1985). *Killer!* London: Century.

Wicke, P. (1990). *Rock music: Culture aesthetics and sociology.* Cambridge: Cambridge University Press.

Wood, L. (1988). *The Sex Pistols day by day.* London: Omnibus.

Wyman, B. (1991). *Stone alone.* London: Penguin.

Younge, G. (1999). Black Tuesday. *Guardian,* 23 April.

8

Abandoning the Absolute

Transcendence and Gender
in Popular Music Discourse

Holly Kruse

As a woman who writes about rock and pop music, I have been struck by the degree to which women have been mentioned only briefly in discussions of rock and roll, primarily because control over the discourses and institutions of popular music is still exercised almost exclusively by men. Both popular and academic rock and pop discourses have been generated largely from masculine subject positions. Throughout my years as a fan of pop and rock in general, and specifically as a participant in alternative music subcultures, I have found much of what is written about popular music irrelevant to my own experience because it assumes a male reader. I want in this chapter to examine how the experience of rock and pop on the whole has been gendered in popular and critical texts. Specifically, I discuss the assumption in much popular and academic discourse that rock's aesthetic is essentially a transcendental one, and one that is comprehensible only by men.

Popular Rock and Pop Criticism

Most rock and pop fans, including academics, first encounter critical discourses about music in the popular print media: newspapers, magazines, and books. Popular critical accounts help determine how fans (and nonfans) situate themselves in relation to various genres, artists, and songs. The ubiquity of popular criticism means that the ways in which it articulates gender can have a significant impact on how people are socialized into pop and rock music.

In 1973, popular-rock critic Robert Christgau noted that he was "struck by how little writing has appeared on the subject of women and popular music." Christgau also observed that his essay on the topic should have been written by a woman, but that he wrote it because "no woman has written it yet, and I've felt for at least a year that somebody had better" (113). Almost thirty years later, men constitute the majority of writers in the popular media writing on women and music. Traditionally, popular male-generated criticism has tended to view women from a few different angles, all of which seem to assume at some level that women involved in rock and roll are anomalies, "others," and therefore can be talked about in ways that would be unthinkable for speaking of male artists and fans. For instance, it remains permissible for male critics to review female musicians' bodies, attire, and sexual desirability as well as (and sometimes in lieu of) their songs. A *Village Voice* review describes a video by the British female-led band Lush in this way: "You see . . . long thin arms and a torso—a crisp, ample bust inside a dress made of clear fish scales that look like a layer of milk. You strive to see a nipple, knowing full well that none is there, and you turn up the sound—a wash of electrified cream and harmonies—and wait for the legs and the go-go boots to come back. There's only the boy playing drums. Splat" (Howland 1991, 87). Similarly, the male reviewer of a concert by Hole notes that band leader Courtney Love wore "a silky pink wraparound skirt and sequined halter," in which she "pouted and flirted like a hyperactive tart on a losing streak" and "[inhaled] lustily on a cigarette" (Moon 1999, C6).

Even "serious" reviews of "serious" female artists may use objectifying terminology, as in the case of the interviewer who traces the trajectory of Sonic Youth bassist Kim Gordon's career as a metamorphosis "from junkie Sheba to wild-at-heart sex symbol" (Kelly 1990, 34). In a review of Lester Bangs's *Psychotic Reactions*, Brenda Johnson-Grau identifies this style of rock criticism as "testosterone-induced ramblings" (1988, 61).

Female pop and rock fans fare little better than female singers and musicians in popular critiques. Fred and Judy Vermorel have noted that music journalists generally treat fans with derision, and if the sample of fans in their book *Starlust* is any indication, the truly passionate fan (the fanatic) is more than likely female, or that is, at least, the popular critical construction. Such girls, as described in Dave Rimmer's account of *Culture Club and the New Pop,* are fiercely competitive and often pathologically devoted to their idols, to the point of losing their own identities: "[The girls'] self-esteem is always tied up with the fortunes of the group they've chosen to follow" (1985, 103).

However, most male critics are not blatantly sexist in their prose. Despite his rather degrading portrait of teenage female fans as mentally unstable, Rimmer notes that pop fans are not stupid and tend to resist media manipulation (1985, 108). At the same time, the frequency of generalizing, patronizing, objectifying terminology points to an underlying supposition in most popular criticism that rock is fundamentally rooted in male experience and governed by an aesthetic that only a man can understand. Because most rock criticism is anchored in male experience, critics tend to see rock as essentially male. For Greil Marcus, it is about escaping from the reality that will catch up with you sooner or later—a "pregnant girlfriend and a fast marriage" (1976, 154); the form itself arose because some whites "have been attracted to another man's culture" (177). Women are ill suited to rock. In Elvis Presley's movies, Elvis "makes all the women snap their fingers (though curiously, none of them can keep time)" (193). Even members of the all-girl punk band the Slits are characterized by Marcus as giggly amateurs, albeit rebellious in their own way (1989, 32). In Marcus's *Lipstick Traces,* a book described by one reviewer as a tribute "to the energy of young manhood desirous of destroying the symbols that would commodify and stultify those desires" (Erikson 1989/90, 135), the author refers to the X-Ray Spex's punk anthem "Oh Bondage up Yours" several times, but he never discusses its radical gender politics; his critique instead compares and contrasts the X-Spex's performance of the song to dadaist art.

Many other critics seem to agree with Marcus's implicit assumption that women's involvement in rock can be only peripheral, because rock itself is fundamentally male. Robert Christgau, in the very essay in which he laments the lack of writing on women and rock, celebrates the liberating power of rock, at least for men, because "even if the energy of rock is nothing more than sublimated (or not so sublimated) machismo, such machismo can be a step on the way out, a naive reaction against apparent sources of oppression, and in that way it is beautiful" (1973, 117). A step on the way out of what? For whom? Obviously, not a step for women on the way out of patriarchal oppression, if the energy of rock is indeed defined as male in nature.

The problem we encounter is in fact the way popular critics define rock, because hand-in-hand with intimations that rock *is* primarily a mode of male expression and understanding is the assumption that rock is governed by a more or less transcendental aesthetic, which, it therefore follows, only men can comprehend. This sort of rock aesthetic posits great figures like Elvis Presley, who are not bound by the limits of time and history; as Greil Marcus explains: "Historical forces might explain the Civil War, but they don't explain Lincoln, they might tell us why rock 'n' roll emerged when it did, but they don't explain Elvis . . .

what a sense of context does give us . . . is an idea of what that person had to work with; but for myself, it always seems inexplicable in the end anyway" (1976, 147).

Since context is ultimately peripheral, a transcendental rock aesthetic is a timeless standard of "good rock" that can be applied to any song from any decade—for Dave Marsh this means that with "My Generation," "Pete Townshend had come up with the only statement *any* rock band ever needed to make" (1980, 292). Whatever the particular song, according to Greil Marcus, a good record is "one that, entering a person's life can enable that person to live more intensely"; a bad record is one "that is so cramped and careful in spirit that it wants most of all to be liked" (1985a, 86). Judging from the examples used in Marcus's writings, this means that there were more good records made in the United States in the mid-sixties and Britain in the mid-seventies, and more bad ones made in the United States during the mid-eighties. But the view that good music transcends contextual boundaries and allows ordinary (male) people to exist beyond the limits of daily existence is certainly not restricted to Marcus. British critic Fred Vermorel, in his biography of Kate Bush, notes—quite evocatively—that pop hits are "black whirlpools of affectivity, luminous moments which lift ordinary lives to transcendence" (1983, 57).

While one might want to argue that Vermorel, Marcus, Marsh, and Christgau ignore how music is understood differently at different moments in history and by people of different races, genders, classes, and generations (among others), the view of rock as transcendent is somehow attractive. Music's meanings are personal meanings, and for fans, pop and rock often indeed seem to be transcendent entities that refuse to be bound by historical and social contexts. Yet a transcendental rock aesthetic is also highly problematic. Rock/pop music cannot be fully understood outside of its contexts. To me, what is important about rock and pop is how the music becomes integrated into our everyday lives and thus becomes part of our lived experience. To condemn the experience of rock and pop as "existing merely [in] the milieu of everyday diversion" (Marcus 1985b, 9) is to ignore how much pop and rock matter as everyday diversion. If rock makes everyday life more bearable, it may be because it helps us make sense of our lives, not because it is completely divorced from life. For people who perceive themselves as at least partially constituted by a set of social relations that are based on shared musical taste and knowledge, music does not simply enable them to momentarily transcend their lived experience—it is fundamental in the construction of their subjectivities.

There is also a dangerous link between the assumption that rock adheres to a timeless standard and the assumption that women are rock outsiders, that rock can best be understood by men. The aesthetic is assumed to be a male aesthetic: Rock is constructed as an essentially male form of expression and pleasure. From the reviews of the Lush video and the Hole concert to Marcus's musings on Elvis Presley movies and Marsh's declaration that "My Generation" is the ultimate rock statement, popular rock and pop criticism has traditionally presented its subject matter in a way that assumes writer and reader coexist in a phallocentric world in which women are peripheral. Women musicians' bodies are available to be reviewed as sources of pleasure, women are relegated to the margins of Elvis movies and Who songs, and thus the threat they pose is lessened. In the narrative of "rock," the notable women who are usually included—from Chrissie Hynde to Heart to Joan Jett to the "riot grrrl" bands—are positioned as anomalies and dwarfed by Elvis Presley, the Beatles, the Rolling Stones, the Who, the Ramones, the Sex Pistols, Bruce Springsteen, Public Enemy, R.E.M., Prince, and Nirvana, artists who comprise traditional rock criticism's canon of the transcendentally great. Moreover, as Lori Twersky, cofounder of the women's rock fanzine *Bitch* once observed, one of the highly problematic "Rock Writer's Irritating Generalizations" is that male-defined "good" bands are ones about which women as a group tend to feel ambivalent (1995, 178).

Academic Rock and Pop Criticism

On the whole, men in academia have historically tended to be more careful to consider issues of gender and context when discussing popular music, though certainly this is not always true. In the 1987 collection *Popular Music and Communication,* none of the articles were written by women, and only two mentioned gender-related issues at all. Similarly, a 1990 study that claims to address the research question "Who are America's pop music critics?" notes only parenthetically, and at the very end of the article, that pop-music critics are predominantly male (Wyatt and Hull, 1990).

But what I want to do here is look at four male critics—George Lipsitz, Simon Frith, Larry Grossberg, and Simon Reynolds—each of whom uses a particular theoretical framework to understand popular music's social and cultural implications. I begin with Lipsitz, because his perspective is in many ways most akin to those discussed in the preceding section. For Lipsitz, rock and roll embodies a dialectic process of active remembering. Musical forms emerge to express specific ideological positions, and therefore one needs to look at the music itself to find dialogic traces of the past (1990, 109–16). Though Lipsitz cites poststructuralist critics like Bakhtin, his thesis is oddly prestructuralist: Meanings are inscribed in texts themselves, and he describes a rock essence, one formed when "rock and roll historically merged with resistance to capitalism in the past and a spirit of independence in the present to stimulate utopian hopes for the future" (1982, 220). Lipsitz's own vision of rock is quite utopian. He believes the anti-apartheid single "Sun City" "displayed the same ability to draw upon the rock-and-roll past to reinforce its capacity for mixing races and cultures in progressive unity in the present" (1990, 131).

And where do women fit into the tale Lipsitz's history of rock and roll tells of the emergence of a form in terms of race and class? There are no important women. The heyday of girl groups like the Ronettes and the Crystals, from 1959 to 1964, is precisely the period condemned by Lipsitz as one during which popular music "became whiter, blander, and less working class" (1990, 127), in other words, less "authentic." The only women of any importance in Lipsitz's "dialogic" history of rock are those who were members of the hippie counterculture, a movement Lipsitz claims granted women new freedoms, apparently because of its style innovations (128). This perspective seems strangely ignorant of the ways in which hippie culture oppressed women by largely confining them to traditionally female roles like food preparation and child care.

Self-Reflexive Approaches

A critic who cannot be accused of ignoring the role of gender and sexuality in popular music is Simon Frith. With Angela McRobbie, he wrote one of the seminal works on the topic, "Rock and Sexuality," in 1978. Frith is quite aware that, historically, women have played an important role in rock and pop music, and he is also conscious of the problem created by his positioning as a male in relation to this subject matter. For instance, Frith admits that "as a man, I've always taken it for granted that rock performances address male desires, reflect male fantasies in their connections of music and dance and sexuality. The first time I saw a woman's band perform I was made *physically* uneasy by the sense of exclusion" (1988, 155).

At the same time, Frith realizes that much popular music is based upon the kinds of male fantasies that gendered divisions create. The feeling of being outside female culture creates a desire to know precisely what it is that goes on between girls. Frith notes that girl-group songs of the sixties cater precisely to this desire: "[In these songs] we get to listen in as the girls talk—in the toilets, in their bedrooms, in the whispering booths of coffee bars. I have no idea if girls did/do talk in those terms, but it was/is a satisfying male fantasy (and one written and produced, of course, by men)" (1988, 152).

No matter how self-reflexive one is about how popular music is organized along gender lines, there are moments when it is tempting to lapse into generalizations about what pop and rock may mean to males versus females. Simon Frith is no exception. At one point in *Music for Pleasure,* he declares: "I'm sure that pop romance, of all sorts, means more to men than women. In youth cultures it is the boys who draw the sharp distinctions between 'casual' sex and 'true' love, who possess their partners with a special fervour. Girls' fantasies are about babies, home-making; they have no illusions about husbands" (1988, 160). Certainly individual lived experience is not reducible to sweeping generalizations that presuppose a particular social, economic, historical, cultural, and psychological position. As a rule, however, Frith avoids reducing pop and rock experience to simplistic formulations that follow traditionally constituted gender lines. Instead, his overriding argument is that the pop experience is one of being drawn into affective alliances—that pop songs are open to personal appropriation in a way that other cultural forms are not. Although people generally see a good song as one that transcends social forces, in fact, popular music's power comes not from its freedom from social forces but from its patterning of them (1987, 136–44). Most pop and rock criticism, as I have shown, depends upon a myth of transcendence; Frith on the whole contends that music cannot be lifted from the historical conjuncture in which it is produced and consumed. And the organization of gender and sexuality is a key feature of any cultural formation.

Another scholar who thinks that meanings can be found only within social contexts is Larry Grossberg. Grossberg suggests that rock music is made sense of first within a particular social and historical site, and second within a range of apparatuses. Apparatuses bring together musical texts and practices, fan and performer images, aesthetic conventions, social and economic relations, ideological commitments, and so on. For Grossberg, there is no necessary correspondence between a text and its meaning, or between a text and its effects: The array of overlapping apparatuses constitutes the music and its effects. It is rock's affective economy that therefore allows an individual listener to transcend the conditions of daily life (1984, 100–103). The music itself is *not* transcendent. It has no essence, no meaning, outside of the apparatus.

The apparatus model is conducive to use in discursive analyses of the gendering of popular music and its constellation of texts. Grossberg himself, however, tends to overromanticize rock and pop's conditionally emancipatory potential. According to Grossberg, "Youth in rock and roll is a celebration of its own impossible existence" (1984, 108); in the post-war years "the privileged place of youth enabled it to resist its own subordination by foregrounding the sense of its own difference, a difference which had been constructed for it" (1992, 178). Conclusions such as these are problematic because they posit a category, "youth" (specifically, children of the baby boom), and generalize from that categorization across lines of gender experience. For example, "the street" is celebrated as the place where youths can enact ever-changing identities and transgress cultural, sexual, and gendered constraints (1984, 108). This mythic "street" bears little relation to real urban streets, where girls and women often feel physically threatened, not empowered.

This is not to say that Grossberg never explicitly addresses gender issues. The apparatus model provides for the possibility of female pleasure, because, "if the 'pleasure' of rock and roll is already coded as male, there is the possibility of a doubled pleasure in its reappropriation as female" (1984, 102). Indeed the potential for reappropriation does exist, but the whole process appears to be abstract—exactly how would a woman go about appropriating, say, Ice Cube's "You Can't Fade Me," and therefore heighten the level of pleasure? On the whole, gender issues are raised but remain unexplored.

If critics tend to address any moment in rock history as particularly liberating for women, it is the emergence of British punk music in the mid-1970s. Punk is often, and correctly, viewed as a genre that created a space for nontraditional female musicians, singers, and fans. Julie Burchill and Tony Parsons have quite rightly argued that "punk rock in 1976 was the first rock and roll phase ever not to insist that women should be picturesque topics and targets of songs" (1978, 74). Yet Dave Laing points out that punk did not altogether restructure the organization of gender and sexuality in rock music. Though punk songs tended to avoid traditional romantic and sexual content, this cannot be equated with a recognition of the sexist bias within these themes. Male punk bands simply chose not to address the topic. While the possibility existed for female punk performers to create a tension between their objectified positions and their song content or mode of performance, these women frequently fit traditional female roles (as the object of the voyeuristic gaze, for instance), and attempts to parody conventional femininity were often misinterpreted. The primary punk image remained that of the aggressive adolescent male, an index of punk's conservative sexual politics (see Laing 1985). Yet punk remains a critical reference point for participants in musical cultures, including girls and women who consider themselves outside, or in opposition to, the pop/rock mainstream.

Often, male writers who are products of the post-punk era seem more keenly aware of the importance of acknowledging the legitimacy of girls' experiences of rock and pop music than their predecessors. Steve Redhead, in his book *The End-of-the-Century Party: Youth and Pop Towards 2000*, observes that in the eighties, "the male notion of 'the people' in folk, and the patriarchal values it enshrines was undercut . . . by the pop context and forms used by 'post-punk' folksingers like Michelle Shocked who have helped move feminist commitments out of the commercial ghetto of 'women's music'" (1990, 57). In rock, the unconventional voices of Kristin Hersh and Björk gained acceptance in at least the alternative music scene in the late eighties.

Of this newer crop of male critics, Simon Reynolds is among the most prominent, and he seems to straddle the popular/academic divide. His numerous critical pieces have appeared in *Spin,* the *Village Voice,* and many other publications, and during the 1990s he wrote books on techno music and on gender and popular music. Reynolds uses deconstruction and postmodern theories to chart the emergence of new musics and cultural formations in the eighties and nineties. To Reynolds, bands as diverse as Throwing Muses, A. R. Kane, Public Enemy, and Metallica have been the salvation of rock music. Because he declares that though he wants to draw on the best work of his antecedents, he is also making a conscious break with the critical approaches to popular music represented by Simon Frith, Greil Marcus, Lester Bangs, and Fred Vermorel, Reynolds gives himself free rein to "broaden rock crit's narrow notion of 'politics' so as to include the occult and obtuse politics of gender, desire, the body" (1990, 11–12). And throughout his collection of essays, *Blissed Out,* Reynolds remains keenly aware both of how rock and pop discourses have traditionally situated women and their experiences of music, and of how he is positioned in relation to female participants in rock culture. His desire seems to be that women be heard as voices of universal experience in the same way that men are presently heard. In praising one of his heroes, Kristin Hersh, Reynolds offers this: "Women in rock are forced to speak as women. Men are allowed to assume a neutrality, to wield truth on behalf of everybody. But maybe Kristin Hersh will be one of the first female artists whose alienation transcends gender . . . someone whose vision of adolescence comes to represent all our experience. And with this would come a second liberation for women, the freedom to . . . recover the right not to be strong, independent, immaculately in control. The right to be as fucked up as men" (1990, 35).

This passage points to a few of Reynolds's strengths and weaknesses. Clearly, here he is, a man, calling for changes in the way female musicians are understood. He also, however, acknowledges later that Kristin Hersh has no interest in being "someone whose vision of adolescence comes to represent all our experience." Hersh herself notes the existence of a societal paradox in which women are limited by sexism but at the same time are bombarded by images telling them they have to achieve, the very paradox into which Reynolds puts Hersh when he imagines her the leader of a new musical liberation movement for women. Her desire is not the desire Reynolds projects onto her, to earn "the right to be as fucked up as man," but rather "just to be regular" (34–35).

In an article about Simon Reynolds, Robert Christgau remarks that "the stunned, dreamlike intoxication [Reynolds] celebrates makes more sense for whiteboys . . . than for those excluded from status and opportunity (blacks, women, gays etc.)" (1990). Reynolds does not have to live within power relations in the same way as do the marginalized groups whose music he champions. Furthermore, his writing style tends to cover over such relations of power in its effusive celebration of sites such as the dance floor, his post-punk version of "the street," where he sees "a magical dissolution of class and difference" (Reynolds 1990, 154–55). Reynolds works outside the school of rock criticism firmly entrenched in the tradition of Anglo-American literary criticism, with its values of proportion, symmetry, restraint, and economy, and its tendency to close off meanings and possibilities through language, rather than open up music's meanings through the gaps and inadequacies of language. This approach to criticism is counter to the traditional, and patriarchal, approach already described and is therefore free of many of the assumptions about the gendered aesthetic of rock music, and the gender positions of its important producers and audiences. Instead, Reynolds plants himself squarely within more recent trajectories of literary theory— namely, deconstructionism and postmodern theory—as the following description of the Blue Orchids' music illustrates: "Here consciousness is not mingled but dissipated, the borders of the self expanded to the point of dissolution. Noise/horror undoes the self by confronting it with the other that dwells within it, the monstrous potential latent in us all, waiting to be catalyzed by an extreme predicament" (61).

In reviewing *Lipstick Traces,* Jon Erikson criticizes Greil Marcus's writing for tending "toward the hyperbolic, myth-making tone of the rock journalist elevating his idols to world historical importance" (1989/90, 135). This criticism is equally applicable to Reynolds's writing. But while Reynolds can be castigated for excessive prose that obscures the realities of lived experience and for exalting forms like hip-hop precisely because "the hip hop ego is the male ego in extremis" (1990, 159), Reynolds's awareness of the context within which he is positioned as a member of a particular generation, his approval of "the deadly seriousness, the piety, the need for something sacred in your life" (15), and his desire that rock in the nineties "confront or at least apprehend the times we live in" (1991, 87) make his vision of contemporary rock and pop worth taking seriously.

Feminist Interventions

Up to this point in the chapter, popular-music criticism has been represented as an exclusively male preserve. Of course, this is not true. In the popular media there is a tradition of female critics that includes notable figures from the late 1960s through the 1990s, like Ellen Willis in the United States and Julie Burchill in Britain, and more recently women like Gina Arnold, Ann Powers, and Evelyn McDonnell. McDonnell notes, however, that women still make up a very small percentage of critics represented in popular anthologies and histories, and that in the music press women still often find themselves treated as tokens, with their pieces "shunted to the fringes" (1995, 6–7). In the academic community there is also a recent tradition of feminist analyses of the relationship of girls and women to popular music. In both the popular and academic arenas, there is the potential for women writers to, as Ann Powers describes it, "throw into doubt the hierarchies of taste and experience that order pop's history, and challenge the order that, paradoxically, relies on their willingness to be seduced without allowing their full participation" (1995, 462). While some of the best work on music written by female academics and popular critics fails to problematize gender, many women writing about popular music work at least in part from a feminist perspective.

One can identify at least two traditionally dominant feminist approaches to the academic study of popular music. The first arose as a response to the variety of subculture theory that came out of Birmingham's Centre for Contemporary Cultural Studies in the mid-1970s and is associated with Angela McRobbie. While subculture theorists made the case that British postwar subcultures were and are a way in which working-class youths could appropriate lifestyle elements, language, clothing, music, and other cultural artifacts to create styles that attempted to "magically solve" the contradictions of growing up working class in a society that celebrates upward mobility, McRobbie argued that this account fails to adequately take into consideration issues of gender. Against the street, a male domain and the privileged site of subcultural analysis, McRobbie posited "the bedroom" as an equally important space—it is the space in which teeny-bopper culture is accommodated, where pop records are the background music of domestic tasks like babysitting and housework, as well as of teenage bonding experiences like practicing with makeup (see McRobbie and Garber 1976; Frith and McRobbie 1978–79). Popular feminist criticism has also acknowledged the importance of the bedroom in girls' experiences with popular music. Ann Powers, for instance, describes how many girls of the 1960s and 1970s first engaged with popular music by sneaking transistor radios under the covers and listening to AM radio at night after the lights were out (1995, 459).

The bedroom culture intervention has been embraced by some male critics, most notably Simon Frith and Iain Chambers, and it is important because it points out not only that girls and women may engage with popular music differently than men, but also that girls *do* engage with popular music. Problems, however, arise when this is seen as the only way in which girls are involved in pop. McRobbie, for instance, claims that the degree to which girls are marginalized in male subcultures makes attractions like thrills, hard, fast rock music, drugs, and alcohol scant compensation for involvement, but it seems to me that many adolescent girls are attracted to rock culture precisely because of these features.

Class and cultural differences affect the ways in which girls engage with popular music forms: The bedroom culture scenario cannot be assumed to apply to even a majority of girls and women who count themselves pop or rock fans. In her book *Gender Politics and MTV,* Lisa Lewis attempts to transfer McRobbie's argument to a U.S. context: "Middle-class and lower-class girls in the United States grow up in a culture in which women's work in the home is a constant, yet devalued, activity, and work outside the home is still underpaid and limited in scope" (1990, 37). Lewis is attempting here to parallel American girlhood and British working-class girlhood so that the bedroom culture scenario is still applicable, but she is not entirely successful. While the points she makes are valid, when one begins to consider the degree to which women in the United States have entered the work force in recent decades, the growing number of women in the professions, and the steady increase in the number of single-parent families, the home environment for adolescent girls in the United States begins to look markedly different from the British working-class home life described by McRobbie. This is not to say that the work of American women both in and outside the home is not undervalued; it is merely to argue that girls in the United States increasingly grow up expecting to have careers outside the home, and boys and girls find themselves having to do their share of domestic chores to fill in the gaps left when both parents (or the only parent) work.

Feminist analyses such as Lewis's that attempt to broadly generalize experiences across cultures and historical moments also fail to take ethnic differences into account, and every feminist struggle has a specific ethnic context (Anthias and Yuval-Davis 1990, 103). Ann Phoenix points out that black children's acquisition of gender identity is qualitatively different from that of white children, and that black children are exposed to a variety of positive gender models. Black women's participation in the labor market means that black children traditionally tend to have grown up accepting that mothers can also be employed; and because black children are more likely than white children to live with other relatives (in addition to one or both parents), they have a wider variety of people with whom to interact and form close relationships (1990, 128).

At the same time, black women who write about popular music find themselves taking on similar sorts of gender issues in music as white women. In a powerful essay, Danyel Smith describes a hypothetical young African American who wishes she could turn the word "bitch" as it is used in so many rap songs into an empowering term, a "badge of honor," but instead to her the word says, "'We don't like you and you're not included'" and "racism is still getting fed huge portions of patriarchy" (2000, 104). Variations of class, ethnicity, and culture indicate that examining the differences, as well as the similarities, between the contexts within which girls are involved with popular music is crucial.

A second vein of feminist popular-music criticism focuses on texts and images. There is a long tradition in both popular and academic criticism of lyric analysis, and critics like Ann Powers have noted the feminist themes in the lyrics of musicians like Courtney Love and Polly Harvey. In the 1980s, academic critics like E. Ann Kaplan and Lisa Lewis analyzed music videos, looking especially at both the ways in which gender is constructed in video texts and at the structure of video narratives—and using feminist film criticism as a major tool in the project. More broadly, some research looks at female performers themselves as texts. For instance, how can we read Madonna? The emphasis on style seems implicitly to confirm Simon Frith and Howard Horne's problematic pronouncement that the new women in pop during the 1980s "were more style experts than musicians" (1987, 156). Beyond images, Susan McClary has also looked at musical performances, such as those of Laurie Anderson, as narratives, and at the musical structures of songs themselves.

All of these approaches recognize the substantial role played by female musical artists in our recent popular culture, but they also foreground textuality and therefore put the critic in a position of having privileged access to the text's meaning, or range of possible meanings. The emphasis tends to be on image and presentation, not on the ways in which female musicians and fans are part of rock- and pop-music culture, how they live this experience. I want now to turn to how we might approach this question.

Understanding Female Experience

Feminist theorists in recent years have given us a wealth of tools to use in understanding female experience. Simone de Beauvoir concluded years ago that men "mistake their descriptive perspective for absolute truth"

(Bovenschen 1985, 26); knowledge and reality have therefore been constructed as if men's experiences are normative, as if being human means being male (Personal 1989, 3). Thirty years ago, Shulamith Firestone pointed to the crux of this problem: "Women have no means of coming to an understanding of what their experience *is*, or even that it is different from male experience. The tool for representing, for objectifying one's experience in order to deal with it, culture, is so saturated with male bias that women almost never have a chance to see themselves culturally through their own eyes" (1970, 157–58). The recognition that human experience is in fact gendered provides the starting point for most feminist critical work. Understanding the gendered dynamics of society necessarily entails listening to the stories of individual women, stories that, as the Personal Narratives Group has found, "illuminate the significance of the intersection of individual life and historical moment, [and] address the importance of frameworks of meaning through which women orient themselves in the world" (23).

Moreover, the life story that matters in feminist critical practice is not just the one of the subject under scrutiny. Angela McRobbie states that "feminism forces us to locate our own autobiographies and our experience inside the question we might want to ask" (1991, 70). The writer or researcher must be aware of the way she is interpellated into the networks of power and knowledge under study (see Walkerdine 1990, 196). For me, this awareness includes acknowledging that I am a post-baby-boom product of the white American middle class; and it also means acknowledging my identification as a female academic, one who often finds herself asserting her academic credentials in dealing with research subjects in the music business in order to differentiate herself from "the average fan."

Writers and researchers cannot step outside society's power relations when engaged in projects. If anything, researching and writing about socioeconomic contexts historically coded, in this case, as male make women quite palpably aware of their still-relative powerlessness within patriarchy, and certainly also serve to normalize for male researchers and writers in these contexts the "essential" maleness of milieus like rock clubs and recording studios. A truly critical perspective on discourses of rock and pop music thus requires that its authors, both male and female, analyze their own relationships to structures of patriarchal power that have helped define notions of what constitutes rock music and "good" rock music.

Part of the subjective awareness for feminist critics of texts generated by women and girls must also be an awareness of how feminist critical practices differ from traditional modes of analysis. Critical practice, as Janet Wolff observes, has consistently undermined women's work and failed to recognize that because it comes from a marginal position, women's work differs significantly from the work of men (see 1984, 43; 1987, 6). Chantal Akerman describes this difference: "When women concretise their modes of seeing, the result is very vehement, very violent. It is just that this violence manifests itself differently than it does with men. Women's violence is not commercial, it is beyond description" (qtd. in Bovenschen 1985, 35). Akerman could be describing two U.S. punk shows that Greil Marcus recounts in *Lipstick Traces:* In one, an apparently pregnant female singer comes on stage, squats, emits a gusher of fake blood, and gives birth to a cow bone; in the other, a naked woman on stage pulls a tampon from her vagina and hurls it into the crowd, to the disgust of the males in the audience. To Marcus, "That was punk after the Sex Pistols broke up, after Johnny Rotten had taken the show as far as a show can go" (1989, 213). Feminist critical practices should seek to question these sorts of limits on what constitutes acceptable and meaningful generic forms of expression.

Critical practices, however, have increasingly become less rigid, as many critics are willing to explore different subject positions, shifting back and forth from hetero- to homosexuality, blackness to whiteness, masculinity to femininity. Suzanne Moore labels this practice "gender tourism" and sees it primarily as a means by which male theorists are able to take trips into the world of femininity. Thus, Roland Barthes could claim that "the future will belong to the subject in whom there is something feminine (Moore 1988, 167). This sort of claim is not new; Christine Battersby in *Gender and Genius* reminds us that Romanticism affirmed the notion that the great artist is a feminine male; he "is like a woman who procreates . . . but is *not* a woman who procreates" (1989, 131). Male "feminist investigations of female subjectivity, while admirable, often fail to recognize that the term 'feminist' itself becomes depoliticized in an appropriation that makes the 'feminine male' a transcendent state of being," Battersby argues. "Being female involves not some collection of innate (or acquired) psychological or biological qualities. It is rather a matter of being consigned—on the basis of the way one's body is perceived—to a non-privileged position in a social nexus of power" (145). So while the oppressor envies the oppressed, what he envies is an exotic fantasy, not the reality of living under oppression (Walkerdine 1990, 208). What is left out, according to Moore, "is the uncomfortably prickly notion of power. Male power" (1988, 185).

"Gender tourism" that ignores power relations ultimately has little to do with the lived experiences of young women and girls involved in rock culture. In fact, even female theorists often lose touch with the material realities of how women and girls experience a patriarchal, sexist society (see McRobbie 1991, 70–72). And because active female participants in rock culture (fans, artists, fanzine editors, promoters) tend to be young women, it is important that feminist studies not patronize them. Many young women refuse to adopt the feminist label because they do not like to give their views political labels. For example, several female rap artists will not call themselves "feminists," despite their strong, prowoman lyrics and images and instead prefer the less politicized term "womanist." Such positions should not alienate older feminists from the voices of a younger generation of women, including the voices of female musicians, fans, and writers.

Women, Girls, and Popular Music Culture

Girls and young women participate in pop and rock music culture on a number of levels and can be as emotionally invested in it as their male counterparts. Yet the experience of rock culture can be significantly more contradictory for girls. Girls tend to differ in many ways from boys in their involvement. In their adolescent years, in general boys talk about music, instruments, and equipment, while girls generally talk more about a song's words, about whether the song is a good one to which to dance, and about the stars themselves (Steward and Garratt 1984, 110–12). For aspiring female musicians, then, it is harder to find a way into understanding pop and rock, because girls traditionally have tended not to talk as much about musical structures and techniques as boys have (110–12). Mavis Bayton's study of female pop musicians reveals that unlike men, few women learn to play songs from listening to records because they lack confidence in their ability to work the songs out; this is largely because girls tend not to be in rock-music-making peer groups. The incentive to learn songs in this way comes primarily from being in a band (1990, 243). Moreover, once girls and women identify themselves as musicians, they are more likely to feel as though they can legitimately talk to male musicians at shows and not be seen as groupies (254).

As fans at these shows, women of course have mixed experiences. In describing a girl who, upon being taken by her boyfriend to see the Clash, fell asleep with her head in a puddle of beer, Gina Rumsey and Hilary Little argue: "This hardly has the ring of rock myth, but it's difficult not to feel that such inattention had less to do with apathy in the face of the much touted conflagration [of punk] than with the simple perception by this woman that what was going on was irrelevant to her: nobody ignores what's important to them, even if they've never heard of the band before" (1988, 241). Rumsey and Little pinpoint a key problem with rock discourses, including academic ones: Rock's vocabulary lacks a record of female experiences, and women and girls lack an emotional investment in male experience. So traditionally, if women did not feel inclined to identify with male spokespersons, they fell by rock's wayside (242).

The subjectivity of female rock fans, however, is not singly determined by gender, and many in fact *do* identify with male spokespersons. In a classic 1975 article, *Creem* editor Jaan Uhelszki described the experience of donning full makeup and going onstage with Kiss as intoxicating and empowering, but importantly as one in which the band came to see her as "one of the boys" and in which the fantasy fulfilled was not of a woman sleeping with a rock star, but of a woman being, for a night, that rock star (1995, 37–43). A young woman writing in the British feminist magazine *Spare Rib* in the 1980s claimed that she came to feminism through the music of the punk gay activist Tom Robinson, whose involvement in Rock Against Racism also brought Rock Against Sexism to her attention. Yet despite her feminist identification, the young woman wrote: "The bands I still like best though are bands with all men in them. I've always liked the Clash—I'm still punk. They of all bands sum up best what I personally feel about being working class—that we're not inferior, and that people with money don't know it all" (Hemmings 1982, 51). Even though rock—and thus by extension some pop—discourses tend to exclude women, and even though girls are not socialized into popular music in the same ways that boys are, male-generated rock and pop can still speak to the experiences of its female fans. After all, gender identity is only one of a number of crosscutting discourses that position music producers and consumers.

Furthermore, it is important to note that female rock fans endure despite the assumption by record companies that the "real" audience, the serious audience, for rock music is male. Historically, girls and women have been important pop and rock music consumers, a fact that music journalism, written mainly by men, is inclined to forget (see Steward and Garratt 1984, 142–50). In discussing the relationship between music reviews and female fans, Brenda Johnson-Grau exposes the silliness of the assertion that men are the real rock audience. A reviewer who declared Edie Brickell a college boy's dream date is taken to task by Johnson-Grau for creating "an image he thought 'everyone' would understand." She adds: "But I don't readily see what value this information has for someone considering buying their records or going to see them in concert (unless concert reviews are now supposed to be a sort of playboy's guide). . . . Is Brickell a dream date or not? Or is the question unacceptable in civilized journalism? Women buy as many records, tapes, and CDs as men, but they are probably smart enough not to read as much 'music' criticism" (1990, 82).

Johnson-Grau underscores the fact that, except for a few critics, assumptions about rock's liberating power, history, and, in many cases, transcendence, are unquestionably tied to patriarchal notions of liberation, history, and transcendence. The personal narratives of women involved in popular-music cultures have the power, however, to subvert some of these assumptions. These women, intentionally or not, reveal how they live the contradictions of being situated within music cultures primarily defined by discourses of masculinity. As a fan and journalist writing about Janis Joplin, Ellen Willis celebrates the singer because "unlike most female performers whose act is intensely erotic, she never made me feel as if I were crashing an orgy that consisted of her and the men in the audience." At the same time, Willis found Joplin's performances troubling because "Janis sang out of her pain as a woman, and men dug it. Yet it was men who caused the pain, and if they stopped causing it they would not have her to dig. In a way, their adulation was the cruelest insult of all" (1980, 277). Willis cannot resolve within herself the contradiction that Janis Joplin lived and represented. Neither could Joplin.

Thirty years after Joplin's death, new generations of female artists have emerged, some in the genres of popular music most constructed as masculine. Rap, for instance, has consistently proven itself to be among the most misogynistic musical forms. Rap also frequently talks about violence, some of it directed against women, as in the much-cited "You Can't Fade Me" by Ice Cube ("Nine months later . . . why did I bang her? Now I'm in the closet looking for the hanger"). Yet women like Missy "Misdemeanor" Elliot have been able to use rap to make their own interventions and talk about their realities. Queen Latifah, one of the most successful female rappers, came to music by appropriating a traditional space of male bonding. When not on the court with the other members of her New Jersey high school basketball team, Latifah (who then went by her given name, Dana Owens) and her friends from the team would "go into the locker room and harmonize. We'd sing 'Betcha by Golly Wow' and Delfonics stuff. Me and my posse all had different names, you know, like superhero names. I think I was Wonder Woman. We had Bat Girl, Zana, Jane—all those crazy names" (Rose 1990, 16). Such friendships are in fact a far more important element in female-dominated bands than in male ones; male bands place a higher priority on "professionalism" (Bayton 1990, 256).

Not only in rap, but also in hard rock, female artists are making their presence known. Several hard-rocking all-female groups popular on the indie circuit, such as Sleater-Kinney, emerged in the 1990s. These bands are no longer novelties, but their followings are still confined largely to the underground scene. The advantage is that underground musicians can stay with smaller record labels and more or less remain in control of their music and their images. As Babes in Toyland drummer Lori Barbero observes, "I like female bands, but not when they have to exploit themselves like they have stagewear and shit" (Marshall 1991, 81). Female-led rock bands often are formed because of female musicians' bad experiences playing in predominantly male bands.

Sonic Youth's bass player, Kim Gordon, theorizes "that women make natural anarchists, because they are outside of the system in so many ways" (Kelly 1990, 34). If Gordon is right, maybe there is hope that female fans, musicians, writers, producers, promoters, and record company owners can successfully rearticulate popular music discourses. On the rock and pop criticism front, Evelyn McDonnell and Ann Powers write in the preface to their 1995 anthology *Rock She Wrote* that the project of collecting the overlooked and neglected contributions of women to rock's critical discourse was "a way of breaking into the canon and restoring the women who belong there to their rightful place" (1995, 1).

In the past decade or so, women and girls who write about popular music have created more spaces in which they can make their voices heard. In the 1980s and 1990s the growth of cheaply produced and distributed fanzines was fueled in large part by rock music zines put out by women and girls, perhaps most notably those zines like *Bikini Kill* that were associated with the riot grll movement of the early 1990s. More recently, women and girls have used the Internet to establish sites that feature information for women musicians and rock-music criticism by and about women, including GoGirlsMusic.com ("cuz chicks rock!") and Rockrgrl.com, which not only promotes the print edition of *Rockrgrl* magazine but provides a message board and links to other World Wide Web resources for women and girls interested in rock music. These sorts of interventions are slowly increasing in number, and they indicate that by the end of the twentieth century, women in rock and pop music culture had found a space in which to more actively engage in the production of themselves, ourselves, as subjects.

References

Anthias, F., and N. Yuval-Davis. (1990). Contextualizing feminism: Gender, ethnic, and class divisions. In *British feminist thought*, ed. T. Lovell, 103–18. Oxford: Basil Blackwell.

Battersby, C. (1989). *Gender and genius: Towards a feminist aesthetics.* Bloomington: Indiana University Press.

Bayton, M. (1990). How women become musicians. In *On record: Rock, pop, and the written word*, ed. S. Frith and A. Goodwin, 238–57. New York: Pantheon.

Bovenschen, S. (1985). Is there a feminine aesthetic? Translated by B. Weckmueller. In *Feminist aesthetics*, ed. G. Ecker, 23–50. London: Women's Press.

Burchill, J., and T. Parsons. (1978). *"The boy looked at Johnny": The obituary of rock and roll.* London: Pluto.

Chambers, I. (1985). *Urban rhythms: Pop music and popular culture.* New York: St. Martin's.

Christgau, R. (1973). *Any old way you choose it: Rock and other pop music, 1967–1973.* Baltimore: Penguin.

———. (1990). Supernova. *Village Voice,* 11 December, 88.

Erikson, J. (1989–90). Review of *Lipstick traces: A secret history of the twentieth century,* by Greil Marcus. *Discourse* 12, 1: 129–36.

Firestone, S. (1970). *The dialectic of sex: The case for feminist revolution.* New York: Bantam Books.

Frith, S. (1987). Towards an aesthetics of popular music. In *Music and society: The politics of composition, performance, and reception,* ed. R. Leppert and S. McClary, 133–49. Cambridge: Cambridge University Press.

———. (1988). *Music for pleasure: Essays in the sociology of pop.* New York: Routledge.

Frith, S., and H. Horne. (1987). *Art into pop.* London: Methuen.

Frith, S., and A. McRobbie. (1978–79). Rock and sexuality. *Screen Education* 29 (winter): 3–19.

Grossberg, L. (1984). "I'd rather feel bad than not feel anything at all": Rock and roll, pleasure, and power. *Enclitic* 8, 1/2: 94–111.

———. (1986). Reply to the critics. *Critical Studies in Mass Communication* 3 (March): 86–95.

———. (1992). *"We gotta get out of this place": Popular conservatism and postmodern culture.* New York: Routledge.

Hemmings, S. (1982). *Girls are powerful: Young women's writings from Spare Rib.* London: Sheba Feminist Press.

Howland, D. (1991). Everything's lush. *Village Voice,* 19 February, 87–88.

Johnson-Grau, B. (1988). Lester Bangs' *Psychotic Reactions,* a book report. *Onetwothreefour* 6 (spring): 56–64.

———. (1990). Dreams that poison sleep . . . *Onetwothreefour* 8 (winter): 80–83.

Kaplan, E. A. (1987). *Rocking around the clock: Music television, postmodernism, and consumer culture.* New York: Methuen.

Kelly, M. (1990). Sonic Youth's flashy Gordon. *Interview,* November, 34.

Laing, D. (1985). *One chord wonders: Power and meaning in punk rock.* Milton Keynes: Open University Press.

Leppert, R., and S. McClary. (1987). *Music and society: The politics of composition, performance, and reception.* Cambridge: Cambridge University Press.

Lewis, L. A. (1990). *Gender politics and MTV: Voicing the difference.* Philadelphia: Temple University Press.

Lipsitz, G. (1982). *Class and culture in cold war America: "A rainbow at midnight."* South Hadley, Mass.: Bergin.

———. (1990). *Time passages: Collective memory and American popular culture.* Minneapolis: University of Minnesota Press.

Lovell, T. (1990). *British feminist thought: A reader.* Oxford: Basil Blackwell.

Lull, J. (1987). *Popular music and communication.* Newbury Park, Calif.: Sage.

Marcus, G. (1976). *Mystery train: Images of America in rock 'n' roll music.* New York: Dutton.

————. (1985a). Corrupting the absolute. *Artforum,* April, 86.

————. (1985b). Speaker to speaker. *Artforum,* November, 9.

————. (1985c). Speaker to speaker. *Artforum,* December, 13.

————. (1989). *Lipstick traces: A secret history of the twentieth century.* Cambridge: Harvard University Press.

Marsh, D. (1980). The Who. In *The Rolling Stone illustrated history of rock and roll,* ed. J. Miller, 285–92. New York: Random House.

Marshall, M. A. (1991). Foxcore. *Spin,* March, 72.

McClary, S. (1991). *Feminine endings.* Minneapolis: University of Minnesota Press.

McDonnell, E. (1995). The feminine critique: The secret history of women and rock journalism. In *Rock she wrote: Women write about rock, pop, and rap,* ed. E. McDonnell and A. Powers, 5–23. New York: Delta.

McDonnell, E., and Powers, A. (1995). Preface. In *Rock she wrote: Women write about rock, pop, and rap,* ed. E. McDonnell and A. Powers, 1–4. New York: Delta.

McRobbie, A. (1980). Settling accounts with subcultures: a feminist critique. *Screen Education* 39 (spring): 37–49.

————. (1991). *Feminism and youth culture: From Jackie to Just Seventeen.* Boston: Unwin Hyman.

McRobbie, A., and J. Garber. (1976). Girls and subcultures. In *Resistance through rituals,* ed. S. Hall and T. Jefferson, 208–22. London: Hutchinson.

Miller, J., ed. (1980). *The Rolling Stone illustrated history of rock and roll.* New York: Random House.

Moon, T. (1999). Hole: Deliciously abrasive rock and roll. *Philadelphia Inquirer,* 17 May.

Moore, S. (1988). Getting a bit of the other: The pimps of postmodernism. In *Male order: Unwrapping masculinity,* ed. R. Chapman and J. Rutherford, 165–92. London: Lawrence and Wishart.

Personal Narratives Group. (1989). *Interpreting women's lives: Feminist theory and personal narratives.* Bloomington: Indiana University Press.

Phoenix, A. (1990). Theories of gender and black families. In *British feminist thought,* ed. T. Lovell, 119–33. Oxford: Basil Blackwell.

Powers, A. (1995). Who's that girl? In *Rock she wrote: Women write about rock, pop, and rap,* ed. E. McDonnell and A. Powers, 459–67. New York: Delta.

Redhead, S. (1990). *The end-of-the-century party: Youth and pop towards 2000.* Manchester: Manchester University Press.

Reynolds, S. (1990). *Blissed out: The raptures of rock.* London: Serpent's Tail.

————. (1991). Future redux. *Village Voice,* 19 February, 87.

Rimmer, D. (1985). *Like punk never happened: Culture Club and the new pop.* London: Faber and Faber.

Rose, T. (1990). One queen, one tribe, one destiny. *Village Voice rock and roll quarterly,* spring, 10+.

Rumsey, G., and H. Little. (1988). Women and pop: A series of lost encounters. In *Zoot suits and second-hand dresses: An anthology of fashion and music,* ed. Angela McRobbie, 239–44. Boston: Unwin Hyman.

Smith, D. (2000). Dreaming America. *Spin,* April, 104.

Steward, S., and S. Garratt. (1984). *Signed, sealed, and delivered: True life stories of women in pop.* Boston: South End Press.

Twersky, L. (1995). Devils or angels? The female teenage audience examined. In *Rock she wrote: Women write about rock, pop, and rap,* ed. E. McDonnell and A. Powers, 459–67. New York: Delta.

Uhelszki, J. (1995). I dreamed I was onstage with Kiss in my Maidenform bra. In *Rock she wrote: Women write about rock, pop, and rap,* ed. E. McDonnell and A. Powers, 31–43. New York: Delta.

Vermorel, F. (1983). *The secret history of Kate Bush (and the strange art of pop).* London: Omnibus.

Vermorel, F., and J. Vemorel. (1985). *Starlust: The secret fantasies of fans.* London: Comet.

Walkerdine, V. (1990). *Schoolgirl fictions.* London: Verso.

Willis, E. (1980). Janis Joplin. In *The Rolling Stone illustrated history of rock and roll,* ed. J. Miller, 275–79. New York: Random House.

Wolff, J. (1984). *The social production of art.* New York: New York University Press.

———. (1987). The ideology of autonomous art. In *Music and society: The politics of composition, performance, and reception,* ed. R. Leppert and S. McClary, 1–12. Cambridge: Cambridge University Press.

Wyatt, R. O., and G. Hull. (1990). The music critic in the American press: A nationwide survey of newspapers and magazines. *Mass Communication Review* 17, 3: 38–43.

9

The Politics and History of Hip-Hop Journalism

Kembrew McLeod

[I'm] in their faces calling out the racists
   at Rolling Stone, SPIN, Details and other places.
KRS is the source.
Fuck these magazines leading hip-hop off course.
You print about black mayors and black senators.
Why you got no black editors?

—KRS-One, "Bulworth"

n the title track of the *Bulworth* motion-picture soundtrack (a posse cut with Method Man, Prodigy, and KAM), hip-hop veteran KRS-One offers a bitter indictment of the state of hip-hop's representation in mainstream music magazines. He has a beef with the mainstream media's treatment of hip-hop, and that attitude is echoed by many other artists, fans, and participants within hip-hop culture. This negative perception is rooted in the fact that magazines and newspapers like the *New York Times, Los Angeles Times, Time,* and *Newsweek* have historically cast hip-hop in a negative light, and when they have attempted a more even-handed approach, these publications inevitably get something significantly wrong. These media outlets tend not to hire editors with much of an understanding of hip-hop and the culture from which it comes; also, as KRS-One charges, there is a lack of black editors controlling what these papers and magazines print, something that impacts how hip-hop is covered.

The misrepresentation of hip-hop is so prevalent that the leading hip-hop magazine, the *Source* (to which KRS cleverly referred in the epigraph), has a long-running column titled "Media Watch: A Survey of the Mainstream Media's Coverage of Hip-Hop." Each month, the column examines articles from various places such as *New York Magazine, Washington Post,* and the *New York Times* to point out inaccuracies and biased views or, in some rare cases, to commend a particular paper for getting it right. But if the reception of the music is poor today, it was worse in previous years, and it is out of this environment—the lack of good, knowledgeable writing about hip-hop—that hip-hop magazines emerged.

In this chapter, I place the profession of hip-hop journalism and criticism in the context of both hip-hop culture and the larger media institutions that ignored or misrepresented the music over the years. By addressing discourses of authenticity and street credibility, media ownership, and the occasionally rocky relationship between artists and critics, I hope to provide a foundation on which further discussions can take place.

A Brief History of Hip-Hop Journalism

Although hip-hop had developed in New York City by the mid-1970s and the first of many hip-hop records was released in 1979, there were no significant magazines devoted to hip-hop in the decade that followed. In this vacuum, some hip-hop criticism emerged in places like the *Village Voice*, where Nelson George (1998) claims that senior music editor Robert Christgau recognized the importance of hip-hop music early on. Nevertheless, hip-hop never dominated the *Voice*'s music section. During the 1980s, stray reviews of albums by RUN-DMC and other major hip-hop artists occasionally appeared in *Rolling Stone* and (after it was launched in 1985) *Spin*. But, overall, there were no magazines that focused their editorial content on hip-hop.

Although a tiny handful of fanzines dedicated themselves to hip-hop music and culture in the late-1980s, the *Source* is the most obvious place to begin a history of hip-hop journalism because of its early and continued prominence. By 1997, this magazine boasted the highest circulation via newsstands of all music periodicals in the United States, almost doubling *Rolling Stone*'s numbers (the *Source* averaged 317,369 copies per issue compared to *Rolling Stone*'s average of 169,625). With its glossy pages and full-color ads, it has come a long way from its origins as a two-page newsletter published by two white men (John Schecter and David Mayes) and a black man (Ed Young) (George 1998).

In its first issue, in August 1988, the *Source* touted itself as "Boston's First & Only Rap Music Newsletter," and the three men circulated their publication using the mailing list from Mayes's hip-hop show on Harvard University's student radio station, WHRB. At the very beginning, the *Source* was primarily an information sheet with very little criticism. The first issue contained release dates, information on upcoming concerts, and a "hot picks" section that listed singles now recognized as classics (Public Enemy's "Night of the Living Bassheads," Eric B & Rakim's "Follow the Leader," and EPMD's "Strictly Business" rounded out the top three). Issue number one also featured a brief news story about a DJ and MC battle held in New York City (the now legendary "Battle for World Supremacy," hosted by the New Music Seminar).

The *Source* moved from Boston to New York City in the early 1990s and began publishing as a monthly magazine with content. Mayes dealt with advertising and promotion, while Schecter headed the editorial division, and soon they had put together a largely African American staff of talented editors, writers, designers, and photographers (George 1998). It continued to dominate the hip-hop magazine market, but, Nelson George (71) writes,

> The Source suffered a major blow in 1994 when the editorial staff, supported by Schecter, battled with Mayes over his fierce loyalty to the mediocre Boston rap crew the Almighty RSO. . . . Moreover, members of the Almighty RSO camp, aware of the low regard in which they were held and frustrated that Mayes couldn't help them more, were accused of threatening several members of the editorial staff. This soap opera came to a conclusion when an article written by Mayes on the Almighty RSO was published in the magazine behind the backs of the editorial staff. After some nasty open letters and much shouting, Schecter and the editorial staff quit en masse while Mayes and Young retained control of the magazine.

Despite this setback, the *Source* continued to flourish, even though its editorial content faltered for a time after the major rift. Another point of controversy for some is the *Source*'s East Coast bias; for instance, roughly one-half of the magazine's covers from 1988 to 1997 featured artists from the New York or tri-state area. In 1991 *Rap Pages* began publishing in Los Angeles under editor-in-chief Dane Webb, who swore his magazine would "give *The Source* a run for its money" (Lester 1996, 6). Subtitled "the Magazine with an Attitude," *Rap Pages*'s first issue had on its cover a scowling Ice Cube, a West Coast artist who cofounded the seminal gangsta rap group NWA.

This magazine challenged, to a certain extent, the *Source*'s New York centrism, though many of *Rap Pages*'s early covers featured East Coast artists (KRS-One, EPMD, Big Daddy Kane, etc.). Nevertheless, there was a greater percentage of cover artists representing the West Coast and the South than what appeared on the covers of the *Source*. *Rap Pages*, at first published bimonthly, moved gradually to publishing every six weeks, and, in October 1995, it became a monthly magazine with a sizable readership.

Urb, a magazine that primarily focused on underground hip-hop and electronic-dance music, began publishing in 1991, and important writers like Jeff Chang and Joseph "Jazzbo" Patel contributed to it. *Urb* championed the L.A. and San Francisco underground during its peak years in the early 1990s, covering artists like the Freestyle Fellowship, Pharcyde, the Alkaholiks, and the Invisibl Skratch Piklz (long before Invisibl Skratch Piklz member Mix Master Mike joined the Beastie Boys to be their DJ). *Urb* is one of the longest running and most respected magazines devoted to hip-hop, and it continues to be at the cutting-edge of underground hip-hop.

Another small but notable West Coast magazine was the *Bomb*, which came out of San Francisco during the first half of the 1990s. Run by Dave Paul, the magazine covered many underground Bay Area and West Coast artists like Blackalicious, Peanut Butter Wolf, and Mystik Journeymen— artists who later appeared on a CD titled *Bomb Hip-Hop Compilation*, released in 1994. Even though the magazine folded by the mid-1990s, Dave Paul began the Bomb Hip-Hop label, which released the widely successful and influential *Return of the DJ* various-artists CD series. *Flavor*, which was based in Seattle, thrived from 1992 through 1996, putting up-and-coming hip-hop artists on its cover before most larger national magazines did so. Significantly, and unusually for the music industry, the zine was run mostly by a staff of women. Other important zines of the early to mid-1990s were the *Kronick* and *One Nut Network*, which were superceded by *Feds* and *Murder Dog*, both of which were published in the late 1990s and continued into the next decade.

In terms of circulation and advertising revenues, *Vibe* positioned itself as *the* major competitor of the *Source* when it began publishing in 1992. (Quincy Jones and Time-Warner unsuccessfully tried to buy the *Source* before they founded *Vibe*.) Although *Vibe* focused on hip-hop, it also emphasized R&B, as well as some contemporary jazz and alternative rock, to create a crossover audience that would appear more friendly to advertisers and the magazine's financial backers. Spinning off of *Vibe* was *Blaze*, a magazine launched in the fall of 1998 by the same publisher that now owns *Vibe* and *Spin*.

For reasons I will explain, *Blaze* launched its first issue amidst a storm of controversy under the leadership of editor-in-chief Jesse Washington. The tacit understanding in the magazine industry was that *Blaze* would allow *Vibe* to deemphasize the less advertising-friendly world of hardcore hip-hop and instead cultivate an image that would generate more advertising revenues.

Reginald Dennis, James Bernard, and other key African American editors who left the *Source* after the Almighty RSO drama founded a competing magazine, *XXL*, in 1997. These editors cultivated an offbeat format and an impressive lineup of writers, earning respect in the hip-hop community (unfortunately, the founding editors soon resigned in another conflict with the publisher over editorial control) (George 1998). *XXL* survived this exodus and continued to feature solid writing, and in 1998 the magazine pulled off the near impossible under the leadership of Sheena Lester.

In an attempt to reprise Art Kane's famous photograph of the 1958 gathering of dozens of jazz greats, *XXL* successfully brought together more than two hundred hip-hop artists on the same block in Harlem captured in the original photo. The photograph, used as *XXL*'s cover (which folded out three times), featured the artists, including members of old-school acts like the Cold Crush Brothers and Grandmaster Flash and the Furious Five, as well as a veritable who's who of hip-hop artists of the past two decades (A Tribe Called Quest, Pete Rock, the Beatnuts, Wyclef, Marley Marl, and the late Fat Joe, to name a few). Not only was this a moment of great cultural significance, it was also a logistical nightmare-turned-miracle, because anyone who has ever tried to schedule and conduct interviews with hip-hop artists knows that many tend to be tardy or fail to show up at all. (My personal experience was that for every successful interview I pulled off, one had to be cancelled because the hip-hop artist was either extremely late or a no show. For instance, after I waited by the phone for more than two hours, MC Eiht's publicist called me to say Eiht couldn't make it because he was "still tied up in court.")

Ego Trip emerged in the mid-1990s, and in its brief four years, this irreverent magazine gained a devoted audience and an exceptional stable of writers, most notably Chairman Mao and Sacha Jenkins. (Jenkins cofounded *Beat Down* in 1992, a hip-hop newspaper that lasted ten issues and whose title was an overt reference to the jazz magazine *Down Beat*.) By the mid-1990s, a lot of venture capital poured into existing major hip-hop magazines as well as emerging magazines like *Stress, Trace,* and *Blaze.* As it turned out, neither *Blaze* nor *Trace* lasted much longer than MC Hammer's short career. *Blaze* folded in the summer of 2000 because, according to the publisher, it "fell short of circulation and advertising goals" (Louissaint 2000). Add to the glut of hip-hop magazines competing for limited market space their difficulty finding well-funded advertisers, and one has a recipe for failure.

Near the end of the 1990s, several key hip-hop writers such as kris ex, Jeff Chang, and the Blackspot began migrating to new online hip-hop sites such as Rebirthmag.com, Hookt.com, 360hiphop.com, and UBO. net. Before those sites came along (some of which were well funded), many people set up their own hip-hop web sites to counterbalance what they saw as the slickness and commercialism of magazines like the *Source* or *Vibe*. Davey D created a well-traveled site, *Davey D's Hip Hop Corner*, and Warren Peace's *Hip Hop Site* also provided an alternative to print magazines. But despite the proliferation of many grassroots hip-hop sites, better-funded sites like 360hiphop.com and the online versions of the *Source* and *Vibe* netted the most traffic. Almost as quickly as they arrived, however, many of these sites folded after the dot bomb collapse.

Hip-Hop's Relationship with the Mainstream Media

Since KRS-One released his first album with Boogie Down Productions in 1986, hip-hop has seen a dramatic rise in popularity. After a decade on the margins of mainstream popular culture, hip-hop music sales began to rise. Within only a few years, hip-hop music was transformed from an aspect of a small subculture identified with young city-dwelling African Americans to a genre that had been absorbed into mainstream American popular culture. Everything from soft-drink commercials to "white" pop music appropriated hip-hop's musical and visual style.

By 1999, exactly twenty years after the first hip-hop record was released, hip-hop music and the culture from which it sprang were firmly entrenched in mainstream American culture. In the course of one month, *Time* magazine devoted a largely favorable cover story to hip-hop, Fugees member Lauryn Hill took home the first "Album of the Year" Grammy awarded to a hip-hop artist, and MTV (which a dozen years earlier had been reluctant to air hip-hop music videos) devoted seven days to the music during its much-hyped "Hip-Hop Week" (Farley 1999). In 1998, hip-hop music sales continued to outpace music industry gains in general (a 31 percent increase over the previous year, compared to the music industry's 9 percent), and hip-hop outsold what had previously been the top-selling format, country music (Farley 1999).

African Americans have been at the center of virtually every major form of twentieth-century American popular music, but, unfortunately, black artists have historically *not* been properly compensated for their efforts. The legacy of exploitative race relations in the United States makes many blacks deeply suspicious of white musicians who are heavily influenced by African American music. It was this concern that prompted a letter to the editor of *Spin* magazine by Harry Allen, who went on to become the "media assassin" for the black-nationalist hip-hop crew Public Enemy. Responding to a cover story on the Beastie Boys in 1987, Allen wrote,

> Your decision to put a white crew on the cover of your magazine as *Spin*'s front-page presentation of hip-hop [Beastie Boys, March 1987] betrays: 1) the inherent phoniness of your "alternative" stance; 2) your lack of facility with nascent black musical forms; and 3) your own racism. American musical history is running over with contradictions. One just hopes that those of us who watched this music (rap, hip-hop) grow off the sidewalk will remember that, despite thousands of recordings, concerts, and park jams by individuals who were and are far more innovative, creative and black than the Beastie Boys, the first rap crew on *Spin*'s cover was not only white but white-faced. (2000, 154)

When one compares the amount of mainstream music magazine coverage that hip-hop artists receive to the number of hip-hop artists found on *Billboard*'s album and singles charts in any given week, it is clear that periodicals like *Spin* and *Rolling Stone* have historically underrepresented hip-hop artists. Even worse, the coverage of hip-hop artists in nonmusic newspapers and magazines tends to focus on negative issues, if they are covered at all. For instance, much of the mainstream news coverage of the murders of Tupac and Biggie didn't go beyond cliched surface observations or more familiar demonizations of a "dysfunctional" African American culture. The editors and writers who wrote about the deaths were likely not well acquainted with hip-hop culture and were probably more likely to have believed before his death that Biggie was a paper towel brand than an important MC.

A *New York Times* editorial published after the death of Tupac states: "The rappers insist they are merely telling it like it is and 'reporting' the news from the ghetto streets. Maybe so. But they were also making a billion-dollar industry into an apparatus for a gang war. The transformation is unprecedented in pop culture; historians will be writing about it for a long time to come" (Staples 1996). Later that month, on 29 September 1996, the *Los Angeles Times* ran a story headlined "FBI Probing Rap Label for Ties to Gangs, Drugs" about how the FBI was reportedly probing death-row records for connections to street gangs and drug trafficking. It is this kind of treatment of hip-hop that has led hip-hop community members to value publications they can call their own.

Authenticity, Street Credibility, and Ownership

Bold letters at the bottom of the *Source*'s masthead state that the magazine is "dedicated to true hip-hop." Authenticity is extremely important in hip-hop, particularly because it was a rebellious youth subculture associated with blacks that went on to become one of the most significant elements of the mainstream music industry. Subcultures threatened with assimilation, particularly musical subcultures, tend to emphasize authenticity within discourse to create in-group/out-group boundaries that help protect the "purity" of the culture. By invoking authenticity, one affirms that even though hip-hop music was the top-selling music format in the late 1990s, hip-hop culture's core remains relatively untouched by mainstream U.S. culture. Hip-hop artists can balance large sales and mainstream success with a carefully constructed authentic self.

Faced with the very real threat of erasure via misrepresentation by outsiders like Vanilla Ice, major label executives, and out-of-touch advertising agencies, hip-hop community members attempt to protect their culture by distinguishing between authentic and inauthentic expression. The sense that hip-hop culture might be transformed into something undesirable led to an increase in authenticity claims throughout the 1990s, the period directly connected with hip-hop's commercial ascendancy (McLeod 1999).

Thus, the *Source*'s de facto motto that associates the magazine with "true" hip-hop is an explicit attempt to maintain its credibility in a community that highly values authenticity and is suspicious of outsiders. For instance, a hip-hop fan wrote to *Davey D's Hip-Hop Corner* that *Stress, Subculture,* and *XXL* were the three "realest hip-hop magazines [because] they represent the entire culture." The same writer claims that the *Source* and *Vibe* are not authentic because they are "too overly commercial" (Soulflower 1998). Authenticity weighs heavily in the discourse of fans and artists; another reader wrote, "I feel that hip-hop media should be doing more to show hip-hop's true image rather than do what they need to sell magazines etc. I mean, the top selling mags out there are the *Source* and *Vibe* . . . which both cater to commercialized, watered-down 'hip-hop'" (Bomb Digi 1998).

Many fans single out those two magazines for having too much advertising—advertising that impacts editorial content. But while the *Source* and *Vibe* both have a hefty number of advertisers, Nelson George distinguishes between the advertisements found in *Vibe* and the *Source* as representing a dichotomy between larger white merchandisers and grassroots ethnic designers: "*Vibe*'s higher ad rate and more mainstream orientation meant its advertisers were mostly larger national brands. . . . *The Source*'s clothing constituency included a few national names but was largely composed of smaller boutique companies (555 Soul, Pure Playez, PNB), many of which were either partially or solely minority owned" (1998, 156).

Although the *Source* may claim that it is "dedicated to true hip-hop," *Rap Sheet* trumpets on its cover that it is the "Only Black Owned National

Hip-Hop Publication." Most major hip-hop magazines are owned by white-dominated corporations, as are the record companies that distribute the biggest-selling hip-hop releases, including Def Jam—the home of Public Enemy, LL Cool J, Slick Rick, EPMD, and other important artists. The evolution of Def Jam reflects many of the business-related trends in hip-hop, and it supports Nelson George's argument in *The Death of Rhythm & Blues* that major labels inevitably absorb the most vital black-owned labels if they prove profitable.

By the late-1980s, Def Jam co-founders Russell Simmons and Rick Rubin had parted ways, and Simmons became the sole owner of the Def Jam until 1996. That year, Simmons sold 50 percent of Def Jam (a company that started as a grassroots label that he cofounded with a $5,000 investment) to the major label PolyGram for $33 million (Simpson 1992; Rawsthorn, 1994; Trapp, 1994). In 1998, the German beverage giant Seagram purchased PolyGram, and in 1999, the company bought Universal Music, reducing the number of major U.S. labels from six to five.

Around this time, Seagram paid Def Jam a reported $100 million for the remaining shares of the hip-hop label, completely dissolving Def Jam into the corporate structure of the Universal Music Group. Motown Records followed a quite similar path, and by 2000 both Motown and Def Jam—two of the twentieth century's most important and culturally significant black-owned record labels—had become reduced to mere arms of the same corporate behemoth. With regard to business practices, the story of Def Jam is in many ways the story of hip-hop.

Even magazines that began as black-owned publications ended up being bought out by white-owned publishing companies. Larry Flynt Publications purchased *Rap Pages* in 1995, but in December 1999 the publisher closed the magazine down due to slim profits and lagging advertising revenues. In an interesting turn of events, *Rap Pages* was bought in early 2000 by Timaj Publications, a black-owned company based in Los Angeles, and original editor-in-chief Dane Webb was brought back to head the magazine (Stephens 2000). Aside from *Rap Sheet* and *Rap Pages,* though, it is a largely white world, just as is the case with record companies.

Relationship Between Hip-Hop Artists and Critics

In Public Enemy's "I Stand Accused," on their 1994 *Muse Sick'n'Hour Mess Age* album from Def Jam, Chuck D ranted, "Cross a line and dis my rhyme/ and they ass iz mine/ if you find a critic dead/ remember what I said/ who killed a critic?/ guess the crew did it." Although many boasts of violence in hip-hop lie at the level of metaphor, this song was made more disturbing by its accompanying music video, which featured the crew delivering a serious beat down to what is presumed to be an unlucky critic.

In 1994, two members of the Wu-Tang Clan smacked a writer for an insulting illustration he did not draw—one incident among many involving violent confrontations between hip-hop artists and hip-hop journalists (Gordon 1998). Perhaps the most notorious and well-publicized artist-journalist confrontation was between Fugees member and solo artist Wyclef Jean and Jesse Washington. In an editorial by Washington in *Blaze*'s premier issue, the editor-in-chief writes: "I'm sitting in a conference room at the Hit Factory studios, sunk deep into a leather swivel chair. A nine-millimeter pistol is pointed at my chest. At the trigger end of the gun barrel stands platinum artist Wyclef, tipsy off the vodka. He's heated because *Blaze* is about to give Canibus's new LP, *Can-I-Bus?*, a negative review in our premiere issue. . . . At the end of our two hour meeting, one of his associates—who had mentioned earlier that he had never killed anyone who didn't deserve it—warned me not to breathe a word of what had just taken place" (Washington 1998, 8).

Washington proceeded to explain that Wyclef claimed that the version *Blaze* intended to review was unfinished and that the rapper would later provide them with a final copy. "Unfortunately," Washington writes, "Clef didn't deliver a finished version before we had to go to press, so we chose not to run the review. But we did decide to let readers know why we couldn't cover one of the year's most-anticipated albums" (1998, 8).

These accusations were covered outside the hip-hop world; for instance, the incident was sensationally reported on television networks such as ESPN, CNN, and FOX (Gordon 1998). In hip-hop publishing circles, it provoked a frenzy of controversy and heated opinion, with *Rap Pages* executive editor Allen S. Gordon devoting a full-page editorial to the situation. Gordon criticized Washington for using the incident to promote the launch of his new magazine. In the editorial, Gordon reveals that in a private meeting with Wyclef, he did not deny the gun incident took place. Although the editor argued that "if any artist threatens the life of or does bodily harm to a writer, they are to be banned from coverage," Gordon felt that the way Washington publicized the event was unethical and exploited a serious situation: "Mr. Washington's editorial devoted about three lines to the Clef incident, while the remainder of the space boasted about how revolutionary this new magazine is in respects to the competition (meaning us). *Blaze*, revolutionary? There is nothing revolutionary about your shit. Revolutionary would have been calling Wyclef a hypocrite for publicly promoting Hip-Hop unity and then turning around and pointing a gun at your chest" (12).

During his brief tenure as editor-in-chief at *Blaze* (before he was fired for unspecified reasons), Washington courted controversy that resulted in a more violent run-in with a hip-hop artist. "The Mad Rapper" was a fictional persona created by Puff Daddy associate Deric "D-Dot" Angelettie, and his real identity had been concealed from the public until *Blaze* published a postage stamp–sized picture of Angelettie and fingered him as the Mad Rapper. Angelettie and his associate Anthony Hubbard reportedly entered Washington's office and beat him with a chair, resulting in lacerations to the editor's face and fractures to his skull (Van Horn 1998).

In rock music, there has always been tension between critics and artists, with some verbal barbs being thrown at critics. I have received a handful of nasty emails from pop and rock artists who did not like my assessment of their CDs (such as Brad Smith, a member of alt-rock has-beens Blind Melon, and later a founding member of alt-rock never-weres Unified Theory). In rock, these tensions typically manifest themselves in an artist's lyrics or an interview, but in the hip-hop world they have also manifested themselves in violent attacks against critics and journalists.

Many have argued (e.g., Fernando 1994; George 1998; Rose 1994) that a kind of code of the streets has been brought along by hip-hop artists from their local communities—places where actions that are perceived as disrespectful can merit a physical confrontation. "That's where hip-hop and journalism collide," said Marcus Reeves, the music editor at the *Source* in 1998. "A lot of these rappers are trying to make a living, trying to sell records, and trying to feed a persona that we all want. And here we are as journalists out there, trying to get the information for our audience. When those two things conflict, you can get some heavy sparks flowing" (Van Horn 1998).

Peace Out!

In an attempt to maintain control of the so-called hip-hop nation and protect it from misrepresentation or erasure by mainstream acceptance, hip-hop community members have gone to great lengths to draw borders around their culture, a culture they feel is under attack. Hip-hop magazines emerged during the late 1980s and early 1990s, and as hip-hop became even more successful in the past decade, so did many of the magazines, which pulled in greater advertising revenues and, conversely, created more dependence on advertisers and corporate funding.

Although some hip-hop magazines have folded, the hip-hop industry continues to thrive, and the remaining magazines have been pulled even further into the web of corporate ownership. This success makes it still more difficult for community members to differentiate clearly between what is authentic hip-hop and what is not. It is a tension played out in the discourse of hip-hop artists and fans, as well as in the pages of hip-hop magazines that embody all the contradictions of hip-hop's current place in mainstream U.S. culture.

References

Allen, H. (2000). Hello, Harry. Letter to the editor. *Spin,* April, 154.

Bomb Digi. (1998). Which hip-hop publications are good?/wack? Letter to the editor. *Davey D's Hip-Hop Corner.* http://daveyd.com/medialetters.html.

Farley, J. (1999). Hip-hop nation. *Time,* 8 February, 54–64.

Fernando, S. H. (1994). *The new beats: Exploring the music, culture, and attitudes of hip-hop.* New York: Anchor Books.

George, N. (1998). *Hip-hop America.* New York: Viking.

Gordon, A. S. (1998). That's all I can stands, I can't stands no more. Editorial. *Rap Pages,* November, 12.

KRS-One, Method Man, Prodigy & KAM. (1998). Bulworth. From *Bulworth: The soundtrack.* CD. Los Angeles: Interscope.

Lester, S. (1996). Five years . . . and counting. *Rap Pages,* October, 6.

Louissaint, R. (2000). Press Release, 24 July.

McLeod, K. (1999). Authenticity within hip-hop and other cultures threatened with assimilation, *Journal of Communication* 49 (autumn): 4.

Rawsthorn, A. (1994). PolyGram kicks into rap groove with RAL/Def Jam move. *Financial Times,* 17 November, 28.

Rose, T. (1994). *Black noise: Rap music and black culture in contemporary America.* Hanover, Conn.: Wesleyan University Press.

Samuels, D. (1995). The rap on rap: The "black music" that isn't either. In *Rap on rap: Straight-up talk on hip-hop culture,* ed. Adam Sexton, 39–42. New York: Delta.

Simpson, J. C. (1992). The impresario of hip-hop. *Time,* 7 May, 69.

Soulflower, Elucid. (1998). Which hip-hop publications are good?/wack? Letter to the editor. *Davey D's Hip-Hop Corner.* http://daveyd.com/medialetters.html.

Staples, B. (1996). How long can rap survive? *New York Times,* 22 September, D4.

Stephens, G. (2000). Rap pages returns. *SOHH.* http://www.sohh.com. Accessed 22 May.

Trapp, R. (1994). PolyGram raps up hip-hop label in $33 million deal. *Independent,* 17 November, 36.

Van Horn, Teri. (1998). Trying to make sense of alleged Mad Rapper attack. *Sonicnet.* http://sonicnet.com. Accessed 25 November.

Washington, J. (1998). Editorial, *Blaze.* September: 8.

CASE STUDIES

10

Jewel Case

Pop Stars, Poets, and the Press

Thomas Swiss

Jewel's book for me shows true poetic meaning, the type that comes from right inside you, igniting your deeper fires, and bringing forward your source of words—your soul.
—Reader's review on Amazon.com

Her poetry seems childish and a little silly.
—Stephen Thomas Erlewine on Sonicnet.com

Introduction

n 1998, recording artist Jewel (Kilcher) released a book of poems, *a night without armor*, through HarperCollins, whose roster includes such well-known U.S. poets as Carolyn Forché, Robert Bly, Sylvia Plath, and Allen Ginsberg. The same week Jewel's book of poems was published, the online music magazine *addicted to noise* ran a story about the book and news of a poetry contest sponsored by her publisher. As a poet, I was intrigued. Titled "Jewel Box," the site included instructions for entering the contest, "an entrancing collection of photos" of the singer, and a number of her poems (http://www.tvgen.com/jewel). Here is one of them:

> *I Miss Your Touch*
> I miss your touch
> all taciturn

like the slow migration of birds
nesting momentarily
upon my breast
then lifting
silver and quick—
sabotaging the landscape
with their absence

my skin silent without
their song
a thirsty pool of patient flesh

The contest called for an online entry no longer than twenty lines
(Jewel's own poems tend to be brief) for a shot at a grand prize of five
hundred dollars. Ten runners-up would receive a signed copy of Jewel's
book and a copy of the companion CD, a "spoken-word" version of the
poems. Entries would be judged, the rules explained, "on originality, vision, how well they evoke their subject matter, creative use of language
and degree of imagination" (http://www.tvgen.com/jewel, accessed 3
March 1998). With a laundry list of criteria like that, entering was hard
to resist. Taking a few abandoned lines from my notebook (Jewel, too, I
learned later, often writes her poems in notebooks—usually while on the
road), I tried adding a few more to give the poem a semblance of narrative. Into the boxed field provided on the web page, I typed what seemed
to me a "Jewel-like" poem and clicked it on its way.

Nineteen Eighty-Six

And so we find my father,

one bored summer.
One summer
installing an intercom . . .

Room to room, the whole
house webbed—
wires half-tacked to floors

and baseboards, all
of them leading
to the kitchen where my

mother stands pumping

the red call-button.
Space-age! my sister
declared. Just like

the Jetsons

But all I heard was
the white noise, the bad
connections,

and the voices of my parents
like static from the moon.

What was I thinking? I am not quite sure. I know I had lately been reading press accounts about the future of pop music in a digital age, especially in light of the developing power of the web for both the distribution of music and commentary on it. I was wondering how the web would change poetry—which, too, had found new avenues for circulation and critique. I know I had also been thinking about spoken-word performances and poetry slams—although they seemed, in their theatricality, loosely "rock and roll," my middle-class white literary sensibilities could not quite read them as "poetry." Yet the press in the last few years had been hailing the cultural "return of poetry," largely because of these events and the sizeable audiences they drew. These thoughts, in turn, raised more personal questions about "popular" poetry versus what is usually referred to as "academic" poetry—who was Jewel, anyway, to be publishing with HarperCollins when most of us academics were having a hard time finding publishers at all? Well, it might be nice, I thought, to win Jewel's autograph—my kids would enjoy it. On the other hand, what if I won and my colleagues found out where I was now publishing my poems? On the Jewel Box web site!

Jewel Rules

Jewel's eighty-seven-poem collection eventually became one of the best-selling books of the year, selling more than 432,000 copies. Not surprisingly, it is the only book of poems on the *Publishers Weekly* list, coming in at number twenty-two for the year, with sales figures similar to books by popular fiction writers such as Anne Rice, Judy Blume, and Ken Follett. What are we to make of such an event, a best-selling book of poems by a twenty-four-year-old rock star whose first album, a few years earlier, sold a startling ten million copies? And what might it say about poetry, pop music, and the press? Taking a cue from the title of that album, *Pieces of You,* this chapter is composed of fragments or "pieces" that link a number of discursive strands. The strands are connected to the ways Jewel has been constructed as a "poet" by the press. Since the web is in the process of redefining what we mean by "the press" (as well as many other institutions and practices), I will particularly attend to the role the web has played as both a shaper of and vehicle for the popular reception of her poems.

Like many other chapters in this collection, this one is intended to be exploratory, a first foray into a subject that has been neglected by popular-music studies. Why explore poetry in a book about popular music and the press? First, publication of *a night without armor* would not have occurred, as Jewel herself has said, without her current status as a star in the music business. The press, of course, continues to have a hand in creating her celebrity and that of others, like Suzanne Vega, who have—inspired by Jewel's success—now published their own volumes of writing. Second, pop as a musical genre and poetry as a literary genre have long engaged each other as they have evolved. The lyrics of Bob Dylan, for example, or the psychedelic musings of Jim Morrison and the punk-lyric innovations of Patti Smith were all influenced, as each has noted, by the French poet Arthur Rimbaud. Morrison's and Smith's poems have been published, collected, and reviewed, and Dylan's lyrics have been published many times in "poemlike" fashion, as well as talked about in literary terms by the press. So has work by Nick Cave and Joni Mitchell. And then there is Lou Reed, who studied with the U.S. poet Delmore Schwartz, and Leonard Cohen, who wrote and published poems even before he recorded his first album in 1968. How had the press treated poems by some of these musicians, and on what basis were value judgments made?

Finally, as I have said, concurrent with the publication of Jewel's poems, her publisher released what it called a "spoken-word audio" of Jewel reading her poems on CD. While it is not clear how this CD represents a spoken-word performance and not simply a poetry reading, this categorization itself is of interest—even if her publisher intends it only as a marketing tool. Rock and performed poetry have a complex history involving the cultural status of both, as evidenced by coverage and reviews over the years of Patti Smith's early rock/poetry, Allen Ginsberg's tour with Dylan's Rolling Thunder Review in the 1970s, and, more recently, spoken-word performances both on MTV and at Lolapalooza. Allen Ginsberg, Bob Dylan, Patti Smith: founding figures in the worlds of poetry and pop music. Yet none of these artists has had a best-selling rock recording, *and* a spoken-word CD, *and* a best-selling book. That distinction belongs to Jewel.

Pressing Jewel

While the publication of *a night without armor* did not generate the amount of press Jewel's album had in 1995 and 1996, it nevertheless occasioned a good number of reviews—far more, and in sites with larger readerships, than the usual book of poems. In addition to appearing in such mainstream print magazines and newspapers as *Entertainment Weekly* and the *New York Post,* many of the reviews and stories about the book's publication were online on such sites as Amazon.com, CNN.com, Sonicnet.com, and Feedmag.com. I will focus on those.

The paperless web, as has often been noted, allows far more "coverage" of any subject. Since most corporate web sites are still seen as experiments for locating new audiences and advertising dollars, there is a pressure for major web sites to remain fresh—adding new content every few hours in some cases. Thus there were many more reviews of, comments on, and stories about *a night without armor* on the web than elsewhere. The reviews, at least those by "professional" critics, were decidedly mixed. Tim Appelo found that "Jewel's book of poetry is solid by celeb-poet standards, and a fair bit of it is actually sort of readable in its own right" (http://www.amazon.com, accessed 1 January 2000). Meanwhile, the reviewer of the CD for Sonicnet.com wrote that "the album is an audio companion to her poetry book by the same title, and both suffer from the same problem—Jewel is not a very good poet" (Earlwine 1999).

What I am interested in here is what kinds of knowledge and assumptions lie behind these different judgments, typical of those made by reviewers of Jewel's poems. Said another way, regardless of their differing "insights," what makes these opinions matter? Not much, as it turns out. And there are at least two reasons why. The first reason, as Marjorie Perloff argues in her essay "What We Don't Talk About When We Talk About Poetry," is that most "discourse about contemporary poetry is largely impressionistic, uninformed, and philistine" (1998, 173). In the case at hand, for example, what are readers to make of comments such as "a fair bit of it is actually sort of readable in its own right" or this simple and ungrounded dismissal: "Jewel is not a very good poet." As Perloff notes, these kinds of off-hand comments are all too common in poetry reviews, while reviews of books in related humanistic disciplines—art or architecture, for example—tend to be reasonably sophisticated and well-informed, helpful to one's understanding of what is going on in a particular field.

While Perloff's comments pertain to her reading of several years' worth of poetry reviews in the *Times Literary Supplement* and the *New York Times Book Review,* her criticism is no less (though—perhaps surprisingly —no more) true when applied beyond leading newspapers to the reviewing of poetry on the web. That is, most press accounts of Jewel's book of poems simply served the purpose of legitimating the reviewer's tastes in poetry—idiosyncratic, ahistorical, and largely unexplained tastes by reviewers who seem to have no special qualifications for the job.

Another reason it is difficult to take these commentaries seriously is that a good number of reviews simply downloaded the language the press had already employed in shaping Jewel's star persona as a musician. That is, many reviews of her book import the ideas, opinions, and critical takes from the reviews of her first album, as if *a night without armor* were not a book of poems, but rather a CD sequel to *Pieces of You.* In this way, then, the ideology and practices of journalistic rock criticism meet and shape the ideology and practices of journalistic literary criticism.

Poetry Criticism and Rock Values

In her essay, Perloff notes that most poetry reviews are still dominated by "a regressively romantic concept of the poet as a man speaking to men (or woman speaking to women—the principle is the same), by the notion that poetry is emotion recollected in tranquillity, the poet speaking for all of us—only more sensitively, perceptively, and expertly" (1998, 182). That is certainly true in Jewel's case—both her songs and her poems, for example, have been repeatedly judged by the press on criteria that include "honesty" and "sincerity." The following is a typical review—of the favorable variety—of her first album, from the February 1996 *CMJ New Music Report* on CDnow.com: "This soft and stirring debut from Alaskan-born Jewel reflects all of the peaceful serenity and splendor of her native state. With little more than acoustic guitar, there is nothing keeping Jewel's visual, and wonderfully simplistic, handcrafted songs on *Pieces of You* from reaching a high level of integrity, with a spirit that is simply enrapturing (accessed 1 January 2000).

As this passage suggests, critics' notions of "sincerity" and "honesty" are often tied to notions (much critiqued by pop scholars, but not journalists) about "authenticity." Reviews of this sort, for example, romanticize (or chastise) Jewel based on the assumption that both her poems and her song lyrics are necessarily autobiographical. Here is more criticism from the web, part of a much longer passage by Andrew Fraker that supposedly demonstrates—melodramatically and in the language of psychobiography—Jewel's authenticity as a suffering, sensitive poet: "Her parents divorced when she was eight years old, and writing became not only recreation but also an escape mechanism for Jewel. She wrote poetry to cope with the trauma of the divorce and the realization that she was an outcast among her peers" (1998, RollingStone.com, accessed 1 January 2000). In another review of her book, critic Tim Appelo praises Jewel's poems by ignoring her parents' divorce while still focusing on her upbringing: "Maybe it's not a bad idea to raise your kids on an 80-acre Alaskan farm with plenty of chores and no TV, as Mr. Kilcher did. Unlike most young people, let alone overnight stars, Jewel has led a life of some intrinsic interest" (July 1998, Amazon.com, accessed 1 January 2000).

It would be unfair to suggest that these accounts are not related to, and in some cases even based on, Jewel's self-presentation as a musician-poet. Because she is a celebrity, however, any account of Jewel's self-representation—as Richard Dyer (1986) first pointed out in his book on film stars and society—is complicated by the fact that Jewel's image is in part controlled by an army of photographers, label publicists, book publishers, designers, and so on. That said, it is no doubt true that Jewel has at least some say over how she is presented, and we should note the photos of a pensive Jewel adorning both the front and back covers of her book; the handwritten words on the cover, pointing to their supposed unmediated authenticity; and, most importantly, Jewel's many statements on poetry—in her preface to the book as well as to the print press and on talk shows like *Charlie Rose* and *Oprah.* "Poetry for me," says Jewel in a typical interview, "is the most honest expression I can find. It's the most immediate expression. I've always been the most frank, the most raw in my poetry writing" (CNN.com/books, accessed 23 December 1999).

Even as some critics praise "honesty" and "sincerity" in Jewel's poems, however, other critics dismiss or devalue those same traits in distressingly gendered ways. Brian Longhurst notes in his book *Popular Music and Society*: "Pop music has often been seen as 'immature' or superficial because of its implied audience of young women" (1995, 188). One could easily say the same about popular poetry—at least in Jewel's case. As Kembrew McLeod writes in an essay on rocker Liz Phair, "There is no room in rock critic discourse for what are perceived as inauthentic modes"—modes "that, for instance, are popular with teenage female or gay audiences" (1998, 10).

Indeed there is no room for Jewel's poems by the standards of the following critics, who stereotype, mischaracterize, or exclude certain kinds of (female) expression from what counts as "poetic": "Part of the charm of Jewel's debut album *Pieces of You* was her sweet, girlish naivete. Charm can quickly turn into an irritant if not tempered with wit and style, and that's part of the problem with *a night without armor: Poems by Jewel*" (Erlewine 1999). And here are three additional passages—the first a continuation of this review, a critical evaluation that writes off Jewel's poems and the writings of all teen girls as immature and superficial: "It's true that a few poems show promise, but it's hard to erase the impression that you're reading the awkward musings in your little sister's diary." Mark Rose reviewed the book on Feedmag.com under the title "Silver Jewels"; after describing Jewel as "catty," he focuses on her body as a way of supposedly talking about her poems: "Jewel occasionally puts her anger to good use, becoming a concerned, if somewhat catty, social critic. Jewel's own buxom physique is well documented in her videos, and it pops up frequently here, too. . . . Like her music, Jewel's poetry projects a kind of voluptuous, suspended girlhood, and its alluring confessions aren't terribly revealing" (accessed 10 December 1999). This final passage suggests it is not her talent but her good looks, market savvy, and choice of producer that has brought Jewel success: "Alaskan Jewel (hippy parents alert) Kilcher has plenty going for her. She's uncommonly attractive, has spotted the gap in the market for a less squawky Tori Amos and has sufficient songwriterly cachet to entice Ben Keith, who produced *Harvest, Harvest Moon* and Patsy Cline, to do the same on this debut" (Aizlewood 1996).

Other Pop Poets and the Press

How has the press treated poems by pop musicians whose books appeared before Jewel's? Were things better in the preweb world? The short answer to that second question is: Not really. In fact, as I will note later, the state of this brand of criticism was worse in the popular press—the web at least allows for extensive fan commentary and critiques. In addition, because of its expansiveness—and, as I have already remarked, the press's need to be continuously adding content to its sites—the web allows for other kinds of journalistic discourse that may more fully contextualize a book's critical reception.

Have other musician-writers received less arbitrary criticism than has Jewel? Reviews from a variety of venues, some of them now archived on various web sites, suggest that value judgments made about other pop poets' work is generally no less impressionistic and empty—if sometimes more generous. Critical contradictions abound; confusion and incoherence are the result. Here is a sampling of reviews of poems by Leonard Cohen, Lou Reed, and Patti Smith. From a review in *Publishers Weekly,* 8 November 1993, by Donna Seaman: "Cohen is direct and precise, a no-fuss-no-muss sort of poet who gets the maximum meaning out of homey words and an invigorating jolt out of clashing images" (111). "Reed writes lyrics that just don't make sense," reported *Booklist* on 1 October 1991. "They are better than most American poetry being written these days" (14). And in October 1994, in the *Academic Library Book Review:* "Patti Smith's stream-of-consciousness style permits superficial stabs at mystical vision, but beneath the sex, drugs, and four-letter words, she reveals a romantic sensibility" (9).

Leonard Cohen is a "no-fuss-no-muss sort of poet"? Deploying the language of advertising makes the poet sound like a home cleaning product. Lou Reed doesn't make sense? "Take a walk on the wild side" made good sense to many of us in the 1970s. Patti Smith's (womanly) "romantic sensibility" lies just beneath the subject matter of her lyrics? Is not her subject matter itself—according to this critic, "sex, drugs, and four-letter words"—romanticized in the poems? Why are we worrying about what lies "beneath" the poems?

Answering that question brings us back to the critiques I referenced earlier, and, in particular, two issues that continue to haunt both the reviewing of poetry and the reviewing of music in the press.

Locating Jewel

First, poetry, like music, has often been treated as a special case, not susceptible to ordinary critical treatment because of what is seen as its forbiddingly "abstract" character. While this treatment was at one time standard in both journalistic *and* scholarly prose, in the last fifteen years there has been a widening division between popular criticism and academic criticism. That is, features earlier critics attributed to and often praised in both song lyrics and lyric poetry—autonomy, univocality, transcendence, and so on—are features that have been deconstructed and mostly disregarded in the context-oriented materialist scholarship of contemporary cultural studies. For example, most academic critics would argue that poetic language is not a window to be seen through or a trapdoor readers need to get "beneath" in order to find meaning. As Perloff writes, poetic language is not "a transparent glass pointing to something outside it, but a system of signs" (1998, 191)—systems and signs mostly ignored in press accounts of Jewel's poetry as the critics continue to look for its roots in "authentic" experience and its supposed "deeper meaning," beyond language.

Second, academic critics have largely thrown over the long-standing critical tradition that has consistently situated lyric poetry (again, like music) outside its broader sociological and historical context. Critics argue that the former approach creates a false vision of poetry as a genre, as poetry does not exist independently of the social world. Simply to name something "poetry" or "music," in fact, is already to invoke someone's values—values that are in some part constructed culturally and dependent on who is doing the naming and *for* whom. There is no completely autonomous poetry, just as there is no autonomous music, but journalistic critics, especially those still in search of the "authentic," continue to critique as if there were.

What is missing from typical poetry reviews? Perloff argues it is a sense of history and a sense of theory—something you find in most other kinds of book reviews if the subject were architecture, for instance, or dance or design (1998, 182). Of all the journalistic reviews I read of Jewel's poems, however, only a few invoked either history or theory—even in passing. An exception is a piece on Sonicnet.com by Gil Kaufman with the heading " Jewel Scratches Surface with First Volume of Poems." Kaufman's article attempts to "place" Jewel's work by asking "published poets and experts in the field" what they think of it. Whatever its faults, the piece intends at least to locate Jewel's work and various judgments made about it within specific taste cultures and particular literary histories. Here is a typical passage: "Calling Jewel's poems less technically proficient than the contemporary verse of Jorie Graham and less political than that of Carolyn Forché, Share said that the singer's work "reads mostly like internal monologue worked up from diary entries. . . . Despite his assertion that people often turn to poetry and music for different reasons, Share said he was able to find a kinship between Jewel's poems and the work of established poets such as Ntozake Shange (*for colored girls who have considered suicide/ when the rainbow is enuf*) (accessed 10 November 1999).

As I noted earlier, the web is indeed remediating what we mean when we say "the press," incorporating, among many possible examples, extensive fan commentary and critiques. While we might consider this a refashioning of the standard "letters to the editor" section, in fact it feels somewhat different to me as a reader. For one thing, there is the sheer volume, in some cases, of readers' responses. The sites for Amazon.com and BarnesandNoble.com, for example, each contain a small handful of professional reviews of Jewel's book. But together the two sites also include more than three hundred responses from consumers. This clearly represents a "community" of readers and music lovers—each of whom is having her or his say and can speak to other commentators on the web page. Even though one will not find much in these comments beyond the kinds of impressionistic language I have been critiquing in this chapter, there are those, like the following from Amazon.com, that invoke the sociability of music and poetry: "I have read a few of Jewel's poems. She touches me and brightens up my day not only with her poems, but with her music. My brother and I don't really get along, but the one thing we can do is sing her songs together" (accessed 18 December 1999). And others challenge the credibility of Jewel's reviewers, as does another example from Amazon.com: "Jewel wrote a book of simple, straight-forward poems that seem to be getting a lot of bad reviews. I doubt that the so-called better writers that reviewed this book have lived a life half as remarkable as hers or have written anything half as insightful" (accessed 6 December 1999).

Fade Away

About six weeks after clicking in my poem on the Jewel site, I received an email marked "Urgent." "Congratulations," it began, "your poem has been chosen as one of the ten runners-up in the contest . . . Jewel herself selected your poem out of the thousands of entries that were submitted." The book and CD were on their way; my poem would appear with other winning poems at the site in about a week. Jewel herself had selected my poem! Out of a huge slush pile! My kids would be happy to have the autographed book. I went back to read the poem for the first time since I'd sent it.

Is it a "good" poem? I don't think so, although I have some allegiance to that last metaphor: the young narrator hearing his parents' voices as "static from the moon." But what the poem is lacking, for me at least, is both a sense of musicality—pasted together, as it literally was, it seems "clunky" to my ear—and a sense of tension in the story. That is, I think the speaker's point of view at the end of the poem is too easily and too quickly foretold. And what do Jewel's poems lack? In my opinion, something like what James Tate notes in his editor's introduction to *The Best American Poetry, 1977:* "What we want from poetry is to be moved, to be moved from where we now stand. We don't just want to have our ideas or emotions confirmed. Or if we do, then we turn to lesser poems, poems that tell you killing children is bad, chopping down the rainforest is bad, dying is sad" (1997, 7).

Jewel's poems strike me by this definition as "lesser poems": her relentless confessions, her less-than-fresh observations, and so on. And yet I have been (in her language) "touched" by Jewel's poems. Not because they are "universal" or "timeless" or "authentic," but because of their material involvement with what many poets distrust most: our highly mediated technological and commodity culture. Jewel's poems came to me, after all, via the web and involved me not simply as a consumer, but as a *producer* of writing—both in response to the contest and in the writing of this chapter. Apparently, if one reads the comments on various web sites, many of her fans, too, have found her poems to be starting points for their own writing.

Thanks to the Jewel phenomenon, I also had a chance to (in pop-marketing vernacular) "cross over." I had written a poem that had taken a different path and found a different audience than my other poems, which tend to appear in small-circulation literary magazines. It would be on a web site cosponsored by HarperCollins and *TV Guide,* thus read by thousands—or at least more readers than I have when I publish a poem in, say, the *Iowa Review* or *Ploughshares.* Unfortunately, that circumstance raises the issue I alluded to in the introduction to this chapter—debated widely these days in university tenure review committees—of what "counts" as published. At one time, being a "published poet" was a particular kind of credential—or people agreed that it was. These days, of course, one can "publish" anything to a web site. Moreover, as I found out, things can also be unpublished. When I went to the URL for the "Jewel Box" as I began writing this chapter, not only was my poem gone, but the entire site had vanished. In its place, in cyberspace, just this ghostly language: *Error. This page has either moved or been removed*—itself, I suppose, a kind of poem or else an extremely harsh critique.

References

Aizlewood, J. (1996). Review of *Pieces of You.* http://www.amazon.com. Accessed January 2000.

Dyer, Richard. (1986). *Heavenly bodies: Film stars and society.* New York: St. Martin's Press.

Erlewine, Thomas. (1998). Review of *A night without armor: Poems by Jewel.* http://www.sonicnet.com. Accessed December 1999.

Longhurst, Brian. (1995). *Popular music and society.* Cambridge: Polity Press.

McLeod, Kembrew. (1998). Exile in criticville: Liz Phair, rock criticism, and the construction of a "do me" feminist icon. Typescript.

Perloff, Marjorie. (1998). What we don't talk about when we talk about poetry. *Poetry on and off the page.* Evanston, Ill.: Northwestern University Press.

Tate, James. (1977). *The Best American Poetry, 1997.* New York: Scribner.

11

Taking Country
Music Seriously
Coverage of the 1990s Boom

Joli Jensen

n the 1990s, coverage of country music went through an interesting, and revealing, series of transformations. The overall story was about the "boom" in country music.[1] But in the early 1990s, most of the stories were about "why"—why a country music boom now? By mid-decade, explanations of "why" were becoming evaluations of consequences—what did the boom "mean" for country music? Journalists began offering gloomy pronouncements about the risks of commercial success to the content, diversity, creativity, and overall quality of "new" country music.

By the late 1990s, the mainstream coverage of country music had become an explicit morality tale about the dire consequences of economic success for country music's authenticity. By the end of the decade, the story of country music's boom had become a cautionary tale about the consequences of succumbing to the logic of commerce.

Why would country music reportage describe a still successful portion of the music industry as suffering for its success? Why would journalists start to predict, then write, about an "end of the boom," showing how country music must pay the price for its popularity? Why would early 1990s coverage celebrate the "new" country music as being *more* authentic, traditional, and adult-oriented than other forms of pop music, and late 1990s coverage tell mournful tales of how country music had lost touch with its tradition, its roots, and its "living legends"?

In this essay, I explore how and why mainstream journalism tells the country music story in the ways that it does, through an analysis and interpretation of 1990s boom coverage.[2] Journalism offers readers particular kinds of stories about media, culture, and society; through this case study, I explore the landscape that we are being anchored in when journalists tell us stories about country music. My goal is to help us recognize the possibilities and limits of the stories we are being told, not just about country music, but also about the roles of media and commerce in modern life.

Characterizing the Coverage

Country music reportage in the 1990s tells the tale of commercial boom and potential bust with sweeping, confident pronouncements about "us" and "music," and about "then" and "now." Mainstream journalists tell the history of country music in the knowing, neutral-but-supportive voice that characterizes much contemporary feature writing. Music critics who review concerts, performances, or new CDs are more explicitly evaluative in their articles, writing with taken-for-granted claims about a particular performer or performance in relation to what is good and bad about country music's current state. They mix statistics and quotes with descriptive accounts, so that performers and industry spokespersons validate their claims about what country music used to be, how it is being changed, and what those changes mean.

Assumptions about genre and generic boundaries are the unspoken frame for all the coverage. It is assumed that music comes in different styles, that country is a distinct, historically defined style, and that the country music that is popular in the 1990s is successful because it either is, or is not, like the country music that came before. The past is always present in country music coverage.

The Problem of Country Identity

Country music's generic boundaries have been a concern for as long as country music was a category, whether it was called old-time, folk, hillbilly, or country and western. The center of country music's identity is its authenticity—country must remain more "real" and more "traditional" than other forms of music if it is to "stay country." This generic identity is institutionalized in charts based on record sales, in radio station formats, in recording-company "arms," and in performance venues. It is connected to particular musical sounds, clothing styles, performance practices; the identification of a sound and style as "really country" still matters to performers and fans, and it is the central theme of country music criticism (Jensen 1988).

The tension in commercial country music has always been about staying "real" while still being commercially successful. Because of country's generic identity as traditional, rural, and noncommercial music, that identity is at risk every time country moves toward a more contemporary sound or a less rural orientation, or finds commercial success. Coverage of the 1990s country music boom addresses the issue of country music identity in ways that strongly resemble the coverage during earlier periods of financial success.

Country music worries more than any other musical genre about maintaining loyalty to the past while somehow "staying current" in the present. This tension is ever present in the coverage: from the 1950s to the 1990s, a key theme in journalistic accounts is whether the currently popular style of country music is "really" country. Yes, say those who argue that its popularity is based on its "heartfelt" content, and they cite examples of the "authenticity" of lyrics and the sincerity of performers. No, say those who argue that its popularity is based on stylistic compromises made for commercial success, and they contrast the presumably authentic, sincere music and performance of the past with examples of the presumably formulaic lyrics and calculated performance in the present.

Over time, of course, the commercial can become the traditional. Patsy Cline and Eddy Arnold, as well as Willie Nelson and Waylon Jennings, are now certified country legends, even though they were previously vilified as either "too pop" (Cline and Arnold) or "too rock" (Nelson and Jennings). In these and other cases, performers now defined as the essence of traditional or classic country were disdained, dismissed as "not really country" (see Jensen 1998).

Whenever country music changes in recognizable ways, those who care about the music address the consequences of commercial success. I argue in this essay that country music coverage (like music criticism in general) allows journalists and their readers to confront, and try to make sense of, the relationship between culture and commerce in modern life. It does so in ways that both limit and enable understanding.

Country music coverage valorizes and stigmatizes, idealizes and sentimentalizes. Country music reportage draws from, and offers readers, a psychic and aesthetic discourse that is fundamentally evaluative—What is good and bad country? This discourse fosters a morality play—What happens when good country goes bad, when it sells out and loses its soul? From questions about the consequences of commercial mediation for cultural quality, we get a story about the price of success that is simplistic, circular, and usually historically inaccurate.

Journalistic coverage of country music ends up telling us that good country is real and traditional; bad country is formulaic and commercial. But the same music can be demonized as formulaic and commercial (as was the Nashville Sound of the late 1950s and early 1960s) and later be valorized as real and traditional. And since real and traditional country music was also formulaic and commercial, what is going on?

Explanations of the Boom

How did journalists explain the so-called stunning success of country music in the 1990s? In a 23 August 1992 *Minneapolis Tribune* article, "The Real Country Music Top Ten: The Big Reasons Country Popularity Keeps Growing," staff writer Jon Bream summarizes a host of possible factors that included changing audience demographics (country is attracting a younger audience); baby-boomer disenchantment with rap and heavy metal; the appeal of "hunks in hats" like Billy Ray Cyrus, Clint Black, Alan Jackson; the appeal of "post-feminist" singers like Trisha Yearwood; the success of Garth Brooks; *Billboard*'s use of SoundScan to document record sales; increasing numbers of all-country radio formats; the rise of country music videos; the popularity of line dancing in clubs; and rock concert elements in live performances.

Obviously, these factors are not all equally causal, and they are interrelated in complicated ways. But Bream lists the most common claims I found in early 1990s "boom explanation" articles. Journalists use quotes to document and explain the boom, mixing cause and effect and often contradictory explanations to write their story. An example is a front-page article entitled "Country Music Making Hay in the City," by Boo Browning, staff writer for the August 2, 1991 issue of the *San Diego Union-Tribune.*

Browning begins with an image of country music as a "cosmic soundtrack" emanating from "every car radio, every roadside dive, every lumbering semi in sight." He describes "fans of all ages and attitudes snapping up the hits; . . . cash registers jingle to the tunes of savvy newcomers, neo-purists and veterans alike, and suddenly country music can be found in the unlikeliest of places." One such unlikely place is "non-rural, non-blue-collar, non-truckin' San Diego," where country station KSON has become the most listened-to station.

Browning's core explanation of country music's commercial success is content and audience oriented—"the disillusion of baby boomers with computerized dance-pop, heavy metal, rap and the fragmented state of pop in general." He allows Music City representatives to explain how the 1990s boom is a *real* boom, in contrast to the previous "Urban Cowboy" success. The "fluff" of the post–Urban Cowboy country music is now being salvaged by a more traditional, ballad-based country music, he and they argue. He quotes Nashville songwriter Rick Giles on why people like 1990s country music—"people just naturally gravitate to what's honest and what makes them feel."

This explanation presumes that the country music boom is based on the early 1990s state of popular music in general; there is a presumed connection between audience taste and content characteristics. An audience/content argument presumes that a genre's success is based on content that repels or appeals to new, wider, or growing audiences. But Browning ends the article with two alternative explanations for the boom —*Billboard*'s new use of SoundScan, and the rise of the Nashville Network and Country Music Television.

"The trend owes a respectable chunk of its success to a technicality," Browning writes, and he explains how SoundScan (the bar-code tracking of record sales, which *Billboard* began using in August 1991) made it undeniably clear that country music was *already* selling far better than had been previously recognized. Finally, Browning quotes Ralph Emery, who argues that country music videos shown on TNN offer a new and better way to introduce new country artists.

Explanations for the boom evolve and recombine as the decade continues, moving away from these technological explanations *and* away from content/audience explanations. The seminal SoundScan shift virtually disappears, even though it clearly caused the music industry, and the press, to take country music seriously. Only early 1990s articles mention that the new use of SoundScan gives country music respectability, or "full citizenship," in the music business.[3]

By the mid 1990s, technological explanations like the rise of TNN and the rise in the number of all-country radio stations become ways to *criticize* the contemporary country music scene, rather than to offer additional explanations of country music's success. Early in the decade, performers like Garth Brooks were lauded as evidence of country music's new vitality, interest, and appeal, but by the mid-1990s the popularity of performers like Brooks and Shania Twain are being seen as detrimental to the music, and as hastening its predicted downfall.

Real Music for New Audiences

In the early 1990s, much was made about how country music appealed to a suburban, middle-aged audience disaffected from other forms of music like rap, metal, and rock. In the October 1991 issue of *Newsweek*, country is favorably compared with problematic pop music forms. "Most country songs are solidly carpentered, and many tell what teen rock fans don't want to hear (or know too well): that people marry, have kids and still trash their lives. But country music also wins hearts by default. Rock and roll has splintered into the high-tech barbarism of heavy metal, the arch self-regard of 'alternative' bands, the postmodern cacophony of rap and the toothless complacency of the mainstream. It gets down to country music or one more boxed set from the '60s" (Gates, Peyser, and Mason 1991, 62).

In a 1992 *Time* cover story, Priscilla Painton and Georgia Harbison write about the "strange musical journey" that baby boomers have gone through, from a common rock language to "such abstruse and sharply subdivided categories as Christian Rap, Acid Jazz and Grunge Rock" created by new technology, "almost untouched by human hands." The "two major currents" of pop music do not connect with the seventy-six million baby boomers—"heavy metal speaks to priapic barbarism, and rap is so belligerent that for some it verges on anti-music" (62).

So where have these disaffected boomers supposedly turned? To the likes of Garth Brooks, who Painton and Harbison describe as "a balding Oklahoma country singer . . . who prances across stage like a cross between Mick Jagger and Ferris Bueller, swinging from rope ladders and smashing his guitar, and who brings 40-year-olds to tears with his existential hymns about accepting life's incidental malice" (1992, 62).

In this early 1990s article, Nashville's boom is described as determined by boomer demographics, where "country radio is trumping Top 40, and Nashville is churning out new stars so fast that Randy Travis' six years in the limelight qualify him as an elder statesman" (Painton and Harbison 1992, 62). The writers quote Bill Ivey, then director of the Country Music Foundation—"country music is definitely music for grownups," and "a connection is really being made between the audience and the music." Ivey contrasts the current 1990s climate with the adolescent excesses of the 1970s and 1980s—now people realize that "we have to live like grownups" in a weak economy, with little job security.

The argument is that country music addresses the concerns of middle age, rather than of youth. Jimmy Bowen of Liberty Records says that "20-year-olds are having their first romance, and we're talking about the third divorce over here" (Painton and Harbison 1992, 62). The story ends with a typically sweeping statement: "For many of the nation's still growing ranks of country fans, the songs are precious musical absolutions, forgiving them for the vanities they cherished and lost, and gently nudging them toward middle age."

Journalist Bruce Feiler is convinced that the move to the suburbs by baby boomers is the best explanation of country music's new popularity. He contrasts his analysis of country music as "the CNN of the suburbs" with what he calls the "conventional" explanations like changes in the music industry, the use of Soundscan, and changes in the pop music genres. He finds a "moral consensus" in 1990s country music, a consensus that is fairly status quo and conventional. Country music songs are about "anguished relationships" or "youthful folly," content that parallels the "self-referential talk show boom" on television (1996, 216). He argues that the audience's beliefs and experiences have moved closer to country music's essential landscape, as boomers age and move to suburbia.

These explanations all imply that country music is a meaningful, evolving, valuable genre that mirrors the needs and tastes of an ever-changing audience. Even if there is some undercurrent of disdain for middle age, talk shows, and suburbia in these accounts, they seem to be merely reporting on cultural trends. The early 1990s coverage reads the tea leaves of country's documented commercial success and argues that its popularity reflects and responds to what a large portion of the audience needs, wants, and finds meaningful.

Hunks in Hats and Postfeminism

But the emerging critiques of the boom focus not on the audience, but on the look and technology of contemporary country. The main themes of mid-1990s coverage are the dominance of "hunks with hats," along with the alleged stranglehold of radio formatting and a new "video-conscious" Nashville. These explanations suggest that the boom is becoming the enemy of the genre itself—country music is now being shaped *not* by audience desires, but by commercial processes.

The thrust of this coverage is summarized in the title of a 1996 *GQ* article by Billy Altman, described as a "music critic and historian" who "liked country when country wasn't cool." "And the Bland Played On" is subtitled "Hats, hunks, and hardbodies dominate the country-music charts and airwaves now, leaving classic old voices and original new ones out in the cold." This Manichean vision of flash-in-the-pan "hat acts" closing the door on country legends and creative newcomers dominates the later coverage.

"All that audience pleasing is coming at an artistic price," Altman argues, and then quotes Ken Levitan: "You turn on CMT, and everybody looks the same and sounds the same. The music's become almost like wallpaper; the individuality seems to have disappeared" (1996, 124). Altman contrasts this 1990s homogeneity with late 1980s authenticity, allegedly found in (Levitan-guided) acts like Nanci Griffith, Lyle Lovett, Guy Clark, and John Hiatt.

Garth Brooks and Shania Twain become emblems of what has gone wrong with country. They dominate record sales and country radio, they spawn imitators, and they and their minions (somehow) shut out the classic "legends," as well as prevent the inclusion of innovative newcomers. By the mid-boom coverage, these two performers, because of their commercial success, come to represent most of what is going wrong, rather than what is going right, with country music.

But the glib assurance with which the male "hat acts" are disparaged is more conflicted when female performers are considered. Gender is awkwardly addressed in the coverage: That 70 percent of the country radio audience is female is used to explain *both* the success of "hunks in hats" and the new success of women country singers. But it is *not* invoked as a reason for the "exclusion" of country "legends" like George Jones, Merle Haggard, and Charley Pride, even though a case for this could be made.[4]

In a 25 September 1998 front-page article in the *Atlanta Constitution,* "The Lady Is a Vamp," Steve Dollar compares "country babe" Shania Twain, "an edgy woman with attitude," to Garth Brooks, "a huggable cowboy with a hat." The notion of "attitude" allows writers like Feiler to find connections between Twain and what he defines as "strong female acts" like Kitty Wells, Patsy Cline, Loretta Lynn, and (in the early 1990s) Mary Chapin Carpenter, Wynonna, and Reba McIntire. "Female artists, long dismissed as 'girl singers' in Nashville, have begun to reinvent and dominate what had been one of the most sexist corners of American popular music. Led by a platoon of artists more interested in being current than bowing to tradition, women in Nashville have been consistently producing the genre's most original music, mixing old-fashioned values and country instrumentation with frank sexuality and a blending of outside forms" (1996, 216).

Here we can see the complexity of 1990s critical evaluation. If "real" old-fashioned country music was sexist, then it should be good that it is changing. But if country music is being "reinvented," then it is also good, if it is being changed in ways that make it "original" and current, just as long as it still includes at least some "old-fashioned values" so it is not *too* untraditional and therefore not country.

Pop music critic Dave Tianen shows the problem when he struggles to place Shania Twain as "country" in a 9 November 1997 piece in the *Milwaukee Journal Sentinel,* "Shania Won't Be the Death of Country." Tianen finds a "high-gloss, commercially astute but synthetic sensibility" in Twain's music but argues, like Feiler, that she is still somehow linked to "her forebears," like Loretta Lynn, Dolly Parton, and Tammy Wynette. "Even though extended family, Jesus and hard times don't appear" in her music, her themes of sexual rights, empowerment, vocational angst, and candor somehow connect her to Lynn, Parton, and Wynette. Yet even if she is thematically similar, Tianen argues, the "feel" of her work is "like a well-crafted pop album with country flourishes," and vocally she is "detached from country, . . . more derivative of Belinda Carlisle or Cyndi Lauper than . . . Patti Loveless."

So—is Shania really country? Yes, because she can be connected, somehow, to a few earlier female country performers, but no, because she does not sound or look country. Is she "original" or "synthetic"? Tianen ends his account with an interesting claim: "If country radio plays Shania Twain records and a new generation of country music fans buy them in droves, there's a basic sense in which Shania Twain is a country musician. Nothing Marty Stuart or anybody else says is likely to change that."

And that summarizes the dilemma facing journalists and critics in the mid-1990s. Marty Stuart, among many others, argues for the vital role of country music history and tradition and finds 1990s country music to be much too pop sounding and uncreative. Yet there is a vast country music industry—radio, records, venues, tours, theme parks—dependent both on keeping the distinction between country and other forms of pop music, *and* on shifting the boundaries to follow mainstream taste. Can good country music be commercially successful, and creative or original, but also untraditional, at least in part, at least when done by women, but still thematically or stylistically country? How?

Simply applying categories of "good" and "bad" country, as many 1990s country music critics did, avoids exploring how including women's experience might challenge traditional categories, or how innovation and creativity are necessary, valued, but always threatening to country music's identity. This double-edgedness of "tradition" is particularly evident when journalists talk about Nashville as a recording center, and the Opry as an institution.

How Authentic Is Nashville?
How Commercial Is the Opry?

In 1992, Nashville strikes *New York Times* reporter Karen Schoemer as a place where "trendiness was never much of a commodity," where MCA's Tony Brown, "arguably the most important record company executive in the country music industry" "lacks a high-powered air." In her 5 January article, "Pop Music: Turning Pickup Trucks and Broken Hearts into Pure Platinum," she says that "unlike rock or pop, country music is defined by its traditions; . . . one need only walk around Nashville to realize how much these traditions are still a part of the country music industry." She talks of how a "small-town atmosphere clings to Nashville," and how independently the town's country music operates from "their parent companies in Los Angeles or New York."[5]

This early 1990s coverage of Nashville as a cozy, homey alternative to commercial centers like New York or L.A. is uncomfortably combined with an image of Nashville as greedily churning out formulaic product that clogs the airwaves and excludes old-timers and newcomers. The Grand Ole Opry, in contrast, represents that which is most real and authentic about Nashville, but also, sadly, that which is no longer commercial. It *too* is exclusionary, but acceptably so, because the exclusion is being done in the name of tradition, not commerce.

Schoemer calls it "the Grand Ole Opry Time Machine" and describes how the Opry has "never abandoned its roots." The Opry's authenticity also gets contrasted with Music Row's corporate greed in Miriam Longino's account in the *Atlanta Constitution,* 10 January 1999, "Opry Faces Its Future": "In the 90s, some corporate powers on Music Row have shown signs of dollar-induced amnesia when it comes to the Grand Ole Opry. As country music has boomed . . . the stakes and competition have gotten higher. New acts come and go on Music Row like couriers, delivering one hit song and then disappearing forever. The country music culture isn't exclusively controlled by Nashville-based acts anymore, as free agents such as Twain and LeAnn Rimes sell millions in spite of not being in 'the club.'"

Longino confronts the central issue facing the Opry, which is the same dilemma faced by country music as a genre: What makes it traditional is also what limits its popularity and commercial success. The very thing that so endears the institution to country fans—its history and tradition—includes the "twang" and "hick image" that inhibit its commercial expansion. Destigmatizing the Opry, or country music, by making it less twangy, less rural, less hokey, would also dilute its identity.

The Opry, like small towns, social clubs, and ethnic enclaves, maintains its identity through exclusion and refusal to change; that refusal can guarantee that it becomes an anachronism. "The tightknit Opry family can be notoriously resistant to change," Longino notes.

So what are the Opry and country music to do? Longino quotes Porter Wagoner, who calls the Opry "a very important cog in country music"; like others, he defines it as "the mother church" and "the cornerstone of the industry." This is why Steve Buchanan, president of the Grand Ole Opry Group, whom Longino also quotes, can think of the Opry's having "a tremendous marketing value" because it "provides you with an association with people like Hank Williams and Patsy Cline."

So if tradition is merely a marketing value in country music, is it still authentic? As Longino says, there is a striking contrast between the "younger, slicker" artists and Porter Wagoner and his Hall of Fame friends. "They are the savvy, uptown acts that have turned the once homespun country music business into a global industry." So, then, *should* the Opry change? Opry star Bill Anderson is quoted as saying, "This is almost the year 2000, and things change. I think maybe we got to start meeting folks halfway."

But if the Opry changes to "meet folks halfway" and becomes "younger, slicker," and "more uptown," it stops being able to offer country music a "mother church." Tradition (like the sound of the steel guitar) has marketing value because it authenticates and defines the genre. The Opry (like the "living legends of country music" and those who've already joined "hillbilly heaven") authenticates contemporary country music performers through concepts like loyalty, tradition, home, and, most important, roots.[6]

In the early 1990s, singers like Garth Brooks, Alan Jackson, and Vince Gill were lauded as having allegiances to country tradition; country music is said to have left its "middle of the road" doldrums of the 1980s for a neotraditionalist sound. By the mid- and late 1990s, these performers and the imitators they supposedly spawned are being condemned for changing the music, and for preventing the popularity and success of those living legends and of alternative country performers. Country performers who explicitly and self-consciously ally themselves with an even older look, sound, and style are hailed as maintaining the "roots" of country music needed for the genre to survive its "onslaught" of popularity and commercial success. So, is the neotraditionalist, or the alternative country artist, an example of imitation, irony, creativity, innovation, authenticity, formula, pandering, increasing market value, or exploiting a niche? Some combination of these? And why does it matter?

Nashville and the Price of Success

Why tell the 1990s country music story this way? Why begin with a celebration of country music's "new" popularity, ascribe it to audience tastes and the quality of the lyrics and sound, and then begin to bemoan its popularity and commercial success and predict its downfall? Why blame success for harming the music, and for excluding those who either were the sound of the commercially successful formulas of the past or are postmodern references to them?

Country Music Foundation director Ed Benson argues that country music cycles are actually "surges, plateaus and then no significant downturn" (Feiler 1996, 216). In spite of the obvious self-interest in this statement, let us presume, for now, that country music's past—since the 1920s—is best understood as a continuing effort to increase its share of the market while undergoing stylistic evolution and changes, as well as industrial ones. Surges, plateaus, and even downturns can be explained in relation to taste, style, industry shifts—all in the interest of commercial success.

But for journalists, fans, and music critics, "good" country music is always at risk of becoming "bad" based on criteria that have to do with generic boundaries, based on lyrics and sound and presumed performer loyalty to tradition. Altman's *GQ* article typifies the coverage of boom consequences. He claims that the 1980s "groundbreakers" like George Strait, Roseanne Cash, Randy Travis, and Mary Chapin Carpenter "all emerged from very discernible folk, blues and honky-tonk traditions that lie at the heart of country music. That this type of music managed to cross over to the pop market was an unexpected blessing" (1996, 124).

Unexpected blessing? This is a romantic rewriting of the recent past. An analysis of 1980s coverage will, I am certain, show that these figures were often criticized for being either not country enough (Carpenter, Cash) or too Nashville (Strait, Travis).

Altman then contrasts these allegedly more authentic (because more roots-connected) performers with the postboom generation of "hats, hunks and hardbodies," "performers whose identities seem to have sprung up out of corporate marketing concerns rather than musical ones." As Altman sees it: "In Nashville's money-chasing haste to be hip and happening, country music has begun accelerating down a slick, homogeneous highway. The contrived music now being churned out is not only causing an unprecedented breach between the genre's past and its future, but is also starting to foster the same kind of identity crisis that ultimately caused previous booms (like the Kenny Rogers-led countrypolitan movement of the late 70s) to go bust" (1996, 124).

The "boom-bust" saga is told with the same themes, but different dates, by Brian Mansfield in *USA Today,* 29 December 1998, in "Country Pumps Up the Sales Volume." In his analysis, while the "surface" looks good, "behind the positive notes, lie sour chords that make Nashville nervous." The "spark and sass" of the Dixie Chicks are offered as "a sharp contrast to much of the genre, which seems afflicted by the homogeneity that crops up every few years when Nashville's powerbrokers think they've figured out what sells—or when they know they haven't got a clue." Mansfield claims that "such cyclical sameness is usually broken by one or two artists who redefine the genre"—Randy Travis and Dwight Yoakam in 1986, Garth Brooks and Clint Black in 1989, Shania Twain in 1993—but "a new savior has yet to emerge." So he finds it "ominous" that there is a planned Broadway production of *Urban Cowboy,* whose crossover success and backlash "nearly wiped out the country industry in the early 80s."

The threat of generic extinction is a narrative that dominated coverage (and subsequent histories) of country music in the 1950s and early

1960s, though back then it was rock and roll (not format radio or the rise of a teen audience) that was blamed for "almost killing" country music. In the 1990s boom, the danger is not another form of music, but the very processes through which "Nashville power brokers" operate. *Commercialization* is the danger, the narrative asserts. What can "save" the music from extinction is the restoration of authenticity. The "realness" of the music is at risk, the narrative says, because of Nashville's "money chasing haste."

Explaining the Coverage

The early explanations of the boom are about how and why cultural genres are popular; the later coverage is about commercial success and its attendant risks. Each reflects a very different understanding of the role of media in society. The first, more cultural, perspective imagines the media as distribution systems, ways to locate and respond, at least in general, to diverse and evolving audience tastes and desires. The second, more critical, perspective imagines the media as commercial enterprises designed to deliver cultural products to markets that they themselves construct and define.

In the terms of the mass culture debates of the 1950s (terms that still operate, at least implicitly, in contemporary cultural criticism), the first tradition imagines country music as popular culture distributed by the mass media, the second imagines country music as potential folk culture that is being turned into homogenized mass culture.[7]

Country music reportage drew on the first tradition when initially reporting on the boom, and on the second when predicting and explaining its supposed consequences. The question is, Why? Why tell the story of country music success as evidence of its value and worth, then begin predicting its downfall, and then blame Nashville and commercial forces for ruining the music? The early 1990s music was as commercially created as the late 1990s music; country music has been commercially created in the 1980s, 1970s, 1960s, and 1950s, and in the 1940s, 1930s, and 1920s. Why do journalists keep offering stories about country music losing its soul?

To figure out why the coverage is the way it is, we need to recognize that music journalism is a form of cultural and of *social* criticism. When we talk and think about music, we are talking and thinking about modern culture in general, about modern life. The "loss of soul" theme is a core dilemma of modernity—it is the concern that implicitly and explicitly shapes most accounts of modern life.

In music criticism, as in cultural criticism and in social criticism, the story is of a lost Eden. Once upon a time there was a "before time," when things were more genuine, sincere, spontaneous, communal, trustworthy, honest, authentic. Industrialization, urbanization, and (in current cultural criticism) commodification have allegedly cut us off from the "really real" that was so much more abundant "back then." In the terms of postmodern thought, we are now awash in simulacra, in artifice and spectacle.

In the terms of music journalism, we therefore need, and should respond to, the "reality" of roots music, be it country, rock, jazz, or blues. We should, in genres like jazz and some forms of rock, also revere the experimental and aesthetically new and adventurous, the "artness" of popular music. When audiences do not, this can be blamed on "the industry" or on the domination of particular performers or sounds—they "shut out" the really real. In this way, the complex story of the mass mediation of culture becomes a more compelling—and self-serving—story about how "real music" is being squelched by corporate greed.

The dilemma of social, cultural, and music criticism in general, and of country music criticism in particular, is how to understand, and evaluate, the commodification of culture. The music we enjoy is simultaneously meaning and product, just as we are simultaneously audience and market. Rather than explore this conflation directly, journalists draw on romantic images of country music's popular appeal and write morality plays about authenticity at risk in the media marketplace.

What this narrative does *not* allow us to understand is that country music has always been commercially constructed, and that some styles of country music are not *inherently* more authentic than other styles (see Peterson 1997). The "legends" of country music were commercially produced and disseminated; the "traditional" sound of country music is a sound designed to *seem* authentic. But country music is no more (or less) "real" than pop or rock or jazz or blues or folk.

Country music coverage avoids exploring a central conflation in modern American life, which is also (not surprisingly) a central unresolved conflict in media studies—what does it mean to commodify culture? Commodification means variety, fashion cycles, and responsive diverse markets, if we imagine the media as innovation-oriented cultural distribution systems. But commodification means repetitive, formulaic product if we assume that the media are hegemonic forces designed to maintain the status quo. If we believe the media respond to autonomous individuals whose taste is organized demographically, then commercial success is a measure of what a certain number of people are pleased by and will buy. If we assume that the media *create* markets for their products, then commercial success is evidence of the public's being duped and cheated.

Added to this basic contradiction in perspectives on media and audiences is another story about "natural" versus "constructed" culture. Unlike obviously collaborative, staged, and "produced" forms of culture like television, film, theater, and dance, commercial music is imagined and admired for being somehow spontaneous in its origins. Country music from the hills, hip-hop from street corners in the 'hood, blues and jazz from smoky dives, churches, the fields, and Africa—American pop music allegedly depends on regular infusions of these more "natural" well-springs. In country music in particular, the historical origins of country music are imagined to be hills and hollers and hoedowns. But these are indeed imaginary origins—as Peterson (1997) documents so effectively, country music consciously references those origins in more or less intense ways, cyclically.[8]

But music has not, and does not, emerge like trees and flowers from "natural" environments. Music since the twentieth century is made in and through commercial venues, from clubs to concerts to radio stations to music videos to record stores to the Internet. Yet music criticism in general, and country music criticism in particular, usually ends up telling us stories about how "the industry" hampers, rather than enhances, popular music.

Yet we could argue that, thanks to commercial mediation, we are now awash in an unprecedented, extraordinary variety of musics—innovative, synergistic, multiple, mutating. We could notice that we live in a time of musical richness and democratization that is utterly unprecedented, thanks to "the commercial music industry." So why do we keep telling stories about how the industry is a greed-based creator of homogeneity, a relentless squelcher of innovation? Why not write stories that describe the commodification of culture as, say, a crucible of innovation and responsiveness?

Who Benefits? The Possibilities and Limits of the Country Music Story

Coverage of the 1990s country music boom offers us a story about the consequences of cultural mediation. Music critics and journalists *could* have explored how cultural material is shaped by a complex array of forces, including demographics, tastes, sentiment, creativity, distribution, media outlets and interdependencies, measuring technologies, and, most important, its own storytelling habits and practices. These traits of the early coverage were exchanged for the more compelling tale of corporate greed overrunning tradition and innovation.

Music reportage *could* explore the contradictory roles of the mass media as attempts to address and capitalize on tastes and trends; it *could* consider how fashion cycles promote both innovation and imitation. It could also acknowledge and question the assumed dichotomies between authentic and commercial, natural and constructed, traditional and innovative.

Instead, the 1990s country music coverage keeps telling the same story, over and over. What is gained from yet another version of how "commercial forces" challenge the integrity of country music? Who benefits from continuous warnings that the genre itself is in peril? Why write about how "true" or "good" country music cannot survive the evil forces of the marketplace?

Who benefits? Well, almost everyone. Journalists get a dramatic story, easy to understand, and one that implicitly puts them in the role of record-keeper and defender of what is being threatened. Readers get to imagine themselves as more savvy in their tastes than that vast market of people who love formulaic crud. They also get to root for the authenticity underdog, the beleaguered "creativity" or "roots" that are allegedly always at risk.

With this story, country music performers have virtuous reasons to explain why they seem to "sell out" (the system made them do it) or why they do not sell enough (the system shuts them down). Producers can ally themselves with the more creative, innovative, or authentic types against the formulaic others of Nashville, who are relentlessly working to exclude them. Or they can define what they are doing as "fighting the system" or as "being creative" or as "staying true" to the music, no matter *what* their work sounds like.

And finally, the genre itself benefits from this narrative. Country music, as the common ground for all the worry, threats, rebirths, and soul-protecting, maintains its identity through a recurring, sentimental tale of struggle. Country never ever *fully* sells out, because it is country music, which cares about home, family, staying loyal and true. Country music explicitly tells its own story about loyalty to the Opry, the fans, the traditions, the sound. For fans, performers, and even country music scholars, the music is a way to identify and connect with notions of the good, the true, the authentic, the valuable, the ever-receding, and the always at risk. A self-identified "us" gets to be on the side of the real, the true, the meaningful, against an ever-present "them" who represents the commercial, the false, the hollow.

Even though I too can succumb to this story, I believe it is simplistic and self-serving. But so are most social, cultural, and personal stories. The nature of narratives is to offer reassurance, to anchor us in a symbolic landscape where we feel comfortable, even a little smug. But in the case of media and culture, I would like to encourage us to seek, and generate, more complex, thoughtful, and respectful alternatives.

When we tell various versions of how the Forces of Commerce threaten the Forces of Authenticity, we miss the chance to figure out why we so eagerly dance with the devil, every day. We disdain the mass media while participating in them, even if it is the "alternative" or "authentic" sound or music or venue or media that we so cherish. Mainstream and alternative, commercial and authentic, require each other because they construct each other. Neither is inherently more virtuous or "real," but they have become ways for us to talk about notions of virtue, and of reality.

I have noticed, too, that the criticism of the music industry by avid music listeners and fans sounds uncomfortably like the criticism of academia by tenured radicals. They/we can find endless fault with a system we benefit from, every day. Rather than recognize the moral complexity of our own position, we simply tell stories that allow us to feel superior. These stories let us feel better than those unfortunate "others" who are, we presume, dupes and sellouts. Such stories do not help us understand the complexity of what is really going on, with us or with them.

Music criticism and music journalism are sites that offer rich opportunities to question the ways we tell stories about modern life. But they remain stubbornly self-righteous and nonreflexive sites, places where the music is imagined as some kind of natural taste formation that is always being threatened, compromised, or corrupted by the forces of commerce. My hope is that we can reexamine the categories with which we think, so that we can find better stories to live by. There are many ways to tell stories. Can music journalism offer new, more complex ways to tell the media/culture story, or will we continue to circulate, and congratulate ourselves with, the same self-serving one?

Notes

1. My focus here is on the mainstream press, including *Time, Newsweek,* the *New York Times,* and the *Washington Post.* The 1990s saw a concomitant rise in country music criticism in local and national newspapers and magazines. This essay deals mostly with boom coverage in mainstream reportage, although aspects of that coverage also appeared in country music performance criticism.

2. A Lexis-Nexis keyword search brought up well over five hundred mainstream press articles that combined terms like "country music" "boom, " "popularity," "authentic, " "Nashville, " and so on. From these articles, I selected nearly a hundred for their focus either on general claims about "country music in the 1990s" or on specific performers/performances as they connected with "country music in the 1990s." I then interpretively analyzed and indexed the articles for their key claims and themes. My thanks to Craig Walter for gathering the initial collection for me.

3. For examples of initial SoundScan coverage, see Michael Goldberg, "Biz Blasts New LP Chart," *Rolling Stone,* 11 July 1991, 17; Robert G. Woletz, "Pop Music: Technology Gives the Charts a Fresh Spin," *New York Times,* 26 January 1992, Arts and Leisure sec., 26.

4. None of the coverage I found directly confronted the content consequences of a women-dominated radio audience for the record industry. My listening to late 1990s mainstream country radio suggests that songwriters and performers are succeeding by offering songs (sung by men) about how the woman
is (secretly, silently, or after the divorce) adored, appreciated, and right, as well
as songs (sung by women) about how unappreciated, unadored, and right they
also are. In contrast, fifties, sixties, and seventies honkytonk-themed songs (seen
by many as "real" country) are a male vision of success, failure, and relationships,
with the woman perceived, by the man, as social climber, honkytonk angel, or
suffering saint at home. So, is the symbolic world of the honkytonk more real/
country than the symbolic world of the appreciated/unappreciated woman?
Why? Could they just be demographically distinct?

5. This style of coverage is very similar to the ways in which early 1960s
Nashville was portrayed; see, for example, Richard Marek, "Country Music Nashville Style," *McCall's*, April 1961, 160–170.

6. The notion of "living legend" is particularly intense in country music reportage and is now becoming part of mainstream coverage. See, for example,
the photo essay in *Rolling Stone*, December 1996, "Legends of Country Music,"
which also gives biographical sketches of Johnny Cash, Buck Owens, Tammy
Wynette, Earl Scruggs, Willie Nelson, Merle Haggard, Loretta Lynn, George
Jones, Charlie Louvin, Kitty Wells, and Johnny Wright. For more on death and
fame in country music, see my "Posthumous Patsy Clines: Constructions of Identity in Hillbilly Heaven," *Afterlife/AfterImage*, edited by Steve Jones and Joli Jensen,
New York: Peter Lang, forthcoming.

7. For a detailed analysis of how the mass culture debates continue to shape
our commentary on media, culture, and society, see my *Redeeming Modernity: Contradictions in Media Criticism* (Thousand Oaks, Calif.: Sage, 1990) and *Is Art Good
for Us? High Culture and the Public in American Thought* (Lanham, Md.: Rowman
and Littlefield, 2002).

8. Peterson (1997) shows how country music goes through alternating cycles
of what he calls hardcore (more twangy, rural, roots-oriented music, in today's
terms) and softshell (more smooth, pop-sounding, less twangy and intensely
"country"). This is one way to cope with the problem of simultaneously retaining
generic identity while shifting the boundaries to incorporate a wider audience.

References

Altman, B. (1996). And the band played on: Hats, hunks, and hardbodies dominate the country-music charts now, leaving classic old voices and original new
ones out in the cold. *GQ*, March, 124.

Feiler, B. (1996). Gone country. *Cosmopolitan*, August, 216.

Gates, D., with Marc Peyser and Michael Mason. (1991). New kids on the range.
Newsweek, 7 October, 62.

Jensen, J. (1988). Genre and recalcitrance: Country music's move uptown. *Tracking: Popular Music Studies* 1, 1: 30–41.

———. (1998). *The Nashville sound: Authenticity, commercialization, and country
music.* Nashville: Vanderbilt University Press.

————. (2002). *Is art good for us? Beliefs about high culture in American life.* Lanham, Md.: Rowman and Littlefield.

Painton, P., with Georgia Harbison. (1992). Country rocks the boomers. *Time*, 30 March, 62.

Peterson, Richard. (1997). *Creating country music: Fabricating authenticity.* Chicago: University of Chicago Press.

12

Sweet Nothings

Presentation of Women Musicians in Pop Journalism

Brenda Johnson-Grau

**Rock 'n' roll is for men. Real rock 'n' roll is a man's job. . . .
I don't want to see no chick's tit banging against a bass.**

—Patti Smith

ven though Patti Smith's own career in rock brought her critical acclaim soon after she made the rather uncharitable remark quoted in the epigraph, it shows us that women in rock have had some trouble gaining—or holding onto—respect.[1] The history of rock 'n' roll shows us that the presence of women has been continual and constant, yet the pop press routinely eliminates or underplays the contributions of women musicians. Their presence on the charts or in the clubs is deemed unusual because rock 'n' roll has come to be routinely defined as a naturally male-dominated art form. When female artists' success makes their presence undeniable, their achievements are undermined by reference to their sexual attractiveness and home life or to their (tawdry or passive) means of gaining success. The representation of women musicians continues to focus on their gender.

202

History of Women in Rock

Here is a list by decade of female artists and groups with female members. Many had careers that spanned several decades; others had one big hit. All these women had a presence in the national media at one time or another.

1950s: Big Mama Thornton, LaVern Baker, Ruth Brown, Etta James, Janis Martin, Georgia Gibbs, Wanda Jackson, Mickey & Sylvia, Chordettes, Estelle Phillips, Shirley and Lee, Teddy Bears, Dodie Stevens, Cordell Jackson, Dee Clark, Annette, Mary Ford, Platters.

1960s: Brenda Lee, Chantels, Little Peggy March, Shangri-Las, Carla Thomas, Mary Wells, Dee Dee Sharp, Marcie Blaine, Doris Troy, Ruby & the Romantics, Barbara Lewis, Angels, Inez Foxx, New Christy Minstrels, Brenda Holloway, Cilla Black, Dixie Cups, We Five, Fontella Bass, Barbara Mason, Shirley Ellis, the Jaynetts, Velvet Underground.

1970s: Carpenters, Freda Payne, Melanie, Delaney & Bonnie & Friends, New Seekers, Honey Cone, Heart, Staples Singers, Betty Wright, Dawn, Climax, Pointer Sisters, Gladys Knight & the Pips, Girlschool, Donna Summer, the Runaways, Deneice Williams, Joan Armatrading, Brides of Funkenstein, X-Ray Spex.

1980s: Jody Watley, the Au Pairs, Area, the Divinyls, Deee-Lite, Eurythmics, Tiffany, Donna Summer, Delta 5, Sheila E., Bow Wow Wow, Siouxsie and the Banshees, Whitney Houston, Grace Jones, Suzanne Vega, Lita Ford, Sheena Easton, Tanita Tikaram, Salt-n-Pepa, Roxanne Shanté, Indigo Girls, Rosie Flores, Sonic Youth, Victoria Williams, Lydia Lunch, Aimee Mann, Sally Timms.

1990s: Amy Grant, the Lunachicks, Vanessa Williams, Elastica, Babes in Toyland, Me'shell Ndege'ocello, Björk, Sheryl Crow, Brandy, L7, Shawn Colvin, Erykah Badu, Meredith Brooks, Monica, Sleater-Kinney, Fiona Apple, the Muffs, Liz Phair, Queen Latifah, Roxanne Shanté, MC Lyte, Yo Yo, Lauryn Hill, Foxy Brown, Da Brat.

2000s: Alicia Keys, Jessica Simpson, Jennifer Lopez, Fluffy, Eve, Poe, Republica, Britney Spears, Sneaker Pimps, Nobby, Three Hour Tour, the Donnas, Dolores O'Riordan, Mystic, Pink, Dido.

By no means exhaustive, the list simply indicates a pattern. During the rock era, there have been lots of women making music and selling lots of records (Dickerson 1998). Women musicians are not an anomaly or a fluke. They are part of the picture. In most histories of rock and pop, however, they get short shrift. Rock critics and historians of pop music have a tendency to forget things that they dislike or that do not fit their peculiar version of rock 'n' roll authenticity. In a typical example of rewritten history, selective amnesia, and idiosyncratic taste making, *Rock & Roll: An*

Unruly History presents itself as authoritative but finds little room for women. Longtime rock critic and author Robert Palmer has the decency when narrating the early history of rock to mention women, including Janis Martin, LaVern Baker, and Sylvia (of Mickey and). The Supremes, however, do not rate even a picture (the Temptations get six pictures and a heck of a lot more respect) or any copy. The "girl groups" are given a couple of pages but only as an expression of the triumphs of Phil Spector. Pictured with Bill Graham, Janis Joplin is rapidly dismissed: "The media soon singled out [Big Brother and the Holding Company's] vocalist, Janis Joplin, for praise, with predictable results: band splits, chanteuse goes out on her own. As has often been the case throughout rock's history, several less-hyped 'second tier' San Francisco bands have proved especially influential" (1995, 169). (Ask Robert Plant or Ellen Willis about the importance of Janis Joplin and you will get another version of the story.)

While no one would deny the influence and artistry of the Muscle Shoals musicians, Palmer manages to imply, in a brief list of her hits, that Aretha Franklin's own musicianship was negligible in her success. Because Palmer's is a "boy's life with guitar" version of rock history, Patti Smith is lionized, but Linda Ronstadt doesn't even appear (although the Eagles do). Rather than continue this litany of petty offenses, I will just assert that such a history distorts the record by substituting boosterism for scholarship. In such histories, the parameters of rock are frequently redefined—after the fact—to exclude the achievements of women musicians.

Articles from the 1960s in such magazines as *Ebony, Look,* and *Time* document the success of such musicians as the Ronettes, Martha and the Vandellas, and the Supremes. In the June 1965 issue of *Ebony,* an article titled "Supremes Make It Big" describes the Supremes in this way: "Sweet-sounding Detroiters push to top as new rulers of 'rock'; first girl vocal trio to make million-seller record list with three consecutive hits" (80). In another article from *Ebony,* "Ronettes" (November 1966), the success of the Ronettes is celebrated with "Rock 'n' roll girls trio teams up with the Beatles on a whirlwind, 14-city, U.S. entertainment tour" (184). The aspirations of women in rock 'n' roll were also touted in other articles in national magazines. In a *Look* magazine article, "Luvs Story," 2 May 1967, for example, an all-female band called the Luvs is profiled in this way: "Two summers ago, in a car bursting with radio rock, four Greenwich, Conn., high-school juniors decided to get into the band bag. The same decision, with different names and settings but always the same background music, has been made by thousands of teen-agers since the Beatles first plugged into American current" (M14).

Girls and women have always had rock 'n' roll aspirations and rock 'n' roll success. Yet, "of 122 total [Rock and Roll] Hall of Fame members, just 14 are women or groups that include female members. Similarly, just over 10 percent of the Hall of Fame's list of the 500 most influential rock songs feature women or bands that include women" (Deggans 1996). Why? The answer seems to lie in a curious mythological history that has developed parallel to actual events in the history of rock.

History of the History of Women in Rock

In the late 1960s, as the first generation of rockers saw their children reach the age of consent, "rock 'n' roll" was redefined as "rock" to accommodate a new generation's need to trash the past and define itself. In the process, many successful and influential female artists were derided and marginalized as "girl groups" or simply expunged from the record. Much was made of groupies and the prowess of rock guitarists, and women were excised from the mix. Trouble is, women were continually present—both as aspirants and as successful artists. In the mythology being created, however, they did not belong. Over the years, "women in rock" articles have relentlessly pigeonholed all the many aspiring and successful female musicians (see table 12.1).

In "The Queen Bees," an article in *Newsweek*'s 15 January 1968 issue, no fewer than ten women are listed as singers in current rock bands. Although some of the names will be unfamiliar to even the most knowledgeable archivist, the article establishes that women were a presence in the rock arena. "In the beginning, the rock world was all Adams and no Eves. The Beatles, Rolling Stones, Animals, Dave Clark Five, all as exclusively male as the Viennese Choir Boys. But, today, all that has changed. Ever since that volcano of sound named Mama Cass Elliot erupted, an extraordinary collection of hot and cool contraltos has poured onto the rock stage until, now, the typical rock group resembles a beehive, three or four drones humming about a queen bee" (77). Just eighteen months later, we get this version of rock history in the same magazine:

> Largely, [rock music] has been a world of male groups, of pounding, thunderous music that drowns out the words, which are rarely of moment.
> It needed the feminine touch and now it has got it. Lately, spawned in the river of folk and rock music, there has surfaced a new school of talented female troubadours, who not only sing but write their own songs. (Saal 1969, 68)

This article and one entitled "Female Rock" from 1971 repeat the myth that rock has been somehow inhospitable to women:

> Until lately, notable female rock groups have been about as numerous as girl goalies in the National Hockey League.

Table 12.1   Articles/Books on Women in Rock, 1968–1999

Date	Publisher	Title	Artists Included
15 Jan. 1968	*Newsweek*	Queen bees	Cass Elliot, Janis Joplin, Spanky McFarlane. Grace Slick, Linda Ronstadt, Sandi Robinson, Mama Cowsill
14 July 1969	*Newsweek*	The girls—letting go	Joni Mitchell, Lotti Golden, Laura Nyro, Melanie, Elyse Weinberg
12 April 1971	*Time*	Female rock	Joy of Cooking, Pride of Women, Goldflower, Fanny
12 July 1971	*Time*	King as queen?	Carole King, Linda Ronstadt, Rita Coolidge, Carly Simon
1974	Nash Publishing	*Rock 'n roll woman*	Nicole Barclay, Toni Brown, Terry Garthwaite, Claudia Lennear, Maria Muldaur, Bonnie Raitt, Linda Ronstadt, Carly Simon, Grace Slick, Alice Stuart, Wendy Waldman
1978	Tempo Books	*Superwomen of rock*	Debby Boone, Rita Coolidge, Olivia Newton-John, Linda Ronstadt, Stevie Nicks, Carly Simon
21 Jan. 1980	*Time*	Chick singers need not apply	Pat Benatar, Carolyne Mas, Ellen Foley, Ellen Shipley
29 March 1980	*New Musical Express*	Women in rock: Cute, cute, cutesy goodbye	The Passions, the Raincoats, Au Pairs, the Slits
15 April 1982	*Washington Post*	New roles in rock: Girl groups are back & they've got the beat	Go-Go's, Joan Jett, the Waitresses, Girlschool, Angels, Dynettes
1 June 1982	*Mother Jones*	Girls! Live! On stage!	Go-Go's, Siouxsie Sioux, Chrissie Hynde, Patti Smith, Marianne Grace Slick, Debora Iyall, Leslie Woods, Pat Benatar, Joan Armatrading, Viv Albertine, Stevie Nicks, Deborah Harry, Yoko Ono, and others
15 April 1982	*Washington Post*	New roles in rock	Go-Go's
1982	Putnam Press	New women in rock	68 musicians, including Gaye Advert, Pauline Black, Carlene Carter, Sheena Easton, Ellen Foley, Grace Jones, Lene Lovich, Kirsty MacColl, the Raincoats, Wendy Wu
4 March 1985	*Time*	These big girls don't cry	Madonna, Cyndi Lauper

Table 12.1 (continued)

Date	Publisher	Title	Artists Included
4 March 1985	*Newsweek*	Rock and roll: Woman power	Cyndi Lauper, Madonna, Tina Turner, Chrissie Hynde, Sheila E, Joan Jett, Caka Khan, Pointer Sisters, Pat Benatar, Go-Go's, Annie Lennox
28 Aug. 1988	*Los Angeles Times*	Popline	Sam Phillips, Toni Childs, Betsy
April 1988	*Musician*	Anima rising	Toni Childs, Tracy Chapman, Sinéad O'Connor, Michelle Shocked
21 Sep. 1989	*Rolling Stone*	The women's movement	Natalie Merchant, Tracy Chapman, Björk Gudmundsdottir, Edie Brickell, Neneh Cherry, Sinéad O'Connor, Michelle Shocked, Margo Timmins, Paula Abdul, Mica Paris
17 May 1992	*Calgary Herald*	Women rockers do it all	L7, Hole, Babes in Toyland.
Oct. 1992	Seal Press Feminist	*She's a rebel: The history of women in rock & roll*	Willie Mae "Big Mama" Thornton, the Supremes, Joan Baez, Chris Williamson, the Runaways, Go-Go's, Pat Benatar, 10,000 Maniacs, Natalie Merchant, Tracy Chapman
10 Dec. 1993	CNN	Women rockers on a roll	Juliana Hatfield, Bangles, Go-Go's, L7, P. J. Harvey, Luscious Jackson, Babes in Toyland
10 April 1994	*Los Angeles Times*	Women rockers —the sound and the fury	Breeders, PJ Harvey, Luscious Jackson, 7 Year Bitch, Hole, Stereolab, Liz Phair, and others
9 Oct. 1994	*New York Times*	When women venture forth	Liz Phair, Me'Shell Ngegéocello, Breeders, Hole, Belly, Veruca Salt, Echobelly, and others
16 July 1995	*Calgary Herald*	Rewriting the rock rule: Power is the new word for women in rock	Melissa Etheridge, Veruca Salt, PJ Harvey, Elastica, Belly, L7, and others
28 Jan. 1996	*New York Times*	The angry young woman: The labels take notice	Tracy Bonham, Poe, Alanis Morrissette
14 Jan. 1996	*USA Weekend*	Angry young women	Alanis Morrissette, Ani Difranco, Liz Phair

(continued on next page)

Table 12.1 (continued)

Date	Publisher	Title	Artists Included
14 Jan. 1996	*New York Times*	Three women and their journeys in song: Too feminine for rock? Or is rock too macho?	Joni Mitchell, Carly Simon, Linda Ronstadt
May 1996	Juno Books	*Angry women in rock*	Joan Jett,, Kathleen Hanna (Bikini Kill), Valerie Agnew (7 Year Bitch), Lois Maffeo, Naomi Yang (Galaxie 500), Kendra Smith, Phranc, Candice Pederson (K Records), Bettina Richards, Chrissie Hynde, June Millington (Fanny)
Feb. 1996	St. Martin's	*Grrrls: Viva rock divas*	Courtney Love, Liz Phair, Kim Gordon, Pam Hogg, Sonya Aurora
21 July 1997	*Time*	Galapalooza!	Lilith Fair, Cassandra Wilson, Tracy Chapman, Fiona Apple, Paula Cole, Jewel, Sarah McLachlan
13 Nov. 1997	*Rolling Stone*	Women of rock	Madonna, Ruth Brown, Tori Amos, Chrissie Hynde, Sheryl Crow, Liz Phair, Bette Midler, Yoko Ono, Tina Turner, Queen Latifah, Fiona Apple, Sinéad O'Connor, k. d. lang, Diana Ross, Natalie Merchant, Shirley Manson, Ronnie Spector, Kim Gordon, Joan Jett, Mary J. Blige, Ani DiFranco, Etta James, Joan Baez, Bonnie Raitt, Melissa Etheridge, Me'Shell Ndegéocello, Jewel, Courtney Love
Nov. 1997	*Spin*	The girl issue	Sarah McLachlan, Alanis Morissette, Liz Phair, Spice Girls, and others
5 July 1998	*London Times*	Are sisters really doing it for themselves?	Spice Girls, Honeys, Juice, Soap, Made in London, and others
10 Jan. 1999	*Milwaukee Journal*	Singers embody both strength and sexuality	Sinéad O'Connor, Tori Amos, Ani DiFranco, Shirley Manson
18 Feb. 1999	*Boston Herald*	Whine of the times	Alanis Morissette, Fiona Apple, Sheryl Crow, Meredith Brooks, Tori Amos, Shawn Colvin, Paula Cole, Liz Phair
19 Feb. 1999	*Gannett News Service*	Women rock music world	Lauryn Hill, Sheryl Crow, Alanis Morissette, Shania Twain, Spice Girls, Jewel, Celine Dion

Which is understandable. . . . There is nothing particularly feminine about strumming a deafening electric guitar, flailing with feet and hands at an electric keyboard, or stomping the stage shouting overamplified sex lyrics. (Female rock 1971, 68)

Reasons—mainly "women's lib"—are given for the "recent" entry of women into the rock arena. Pride of Women is "leggy but irate girls." Fanny and Goldflower are not good enough to compete with "top-level" male bands, but Joy of Cooking is. With "pretty" Toni Brown and "tough" Terry Garthwaite, the band produces "a reasonably rich mixture of blues, wailing gospel and riffs of pure country, folk and hard rock, all curiously overlaid with Latin conga rhythms."

In the 21 January 1980 issue of *Time* magazine, Jay Cocks writes about a new group of "women rockers" in "Chick Singers Need Not Apply." Pat Benatar, Ellen Foley, Ellen Shipley, and Carolyne Mas are all applauded for their "mainline, rock-bottom rock 'n' roll." As usual there is a problem: "Rock is still a kind of music—a life-style—in which women are frequently called 'chicks' and are, as performers or presences, expected to behave accordingly." Cocks champions the talent and style of these artists as powerful but notes that "the rock business will not let you forget how you look" (81). In 1980, Deanne Pearson of the *New Musical Express* gets together a group of women musicians to discuss the new role of women in rock: "For the last 25 years men have dominated and controlled rock music. . . . Until recently rock 'n' roll has been a male domain. . . . With the emergence of punk three years ago, there was a sudden influx of women into rock." The article specifically downgrades the achievements of some women artists in this way: "Not that there has ever been a shortage of women in music. The image of the coy, pretty but brainless sweet-girl vocalist is well known; a decorative visual in front of the real grafters" (1980, 27).

In *Mother Jones* in 1982, Ariel Swartley invites you to "meet the women who are reviving rock & roll." *Newsweek* touts "Rock and Roll: Woman Power" in 1985; *Musician* tells us "Why the Best New Artists of 1988 Are Women" (Flanagan 1988), and so on. These stories, seemingly magnanimous (and inevitably self-congratulatory) in their tributes to female rock 'n' rollers, rob women of their historical presence in rock 'n' roll. Each female musician, in effect, must start from scratch. Each generation (girls and boys) believes that women in rock are somehow "new." As a hegemonizing action, it works well. Women artists get defined more by their gender and less by their music. Therefore, they (as well as their music and their ideas) are continually marginalized.

Time asks: "Madonna and Cyndi Lauper are the hottest women in rock. Why?" Cyndi Lauper is presented as an artist with a goofy sense of style. Madonna's style is "sluttish"; her "voice has the whispered assurance of one of those phone-for-sex girls (These big girls 1985, 72)." In a

Newsweek cover story that appeared the same day, Lauper and Madonna are said to be "reinventing pop's feminine mystique with hot videos and wild styles" (Rock 1985, 48).

And the articles continue as the decades roll on. In 1992, it is riot grrls and women's punk rock: "Women Rockers Do It All," headlines J. Farber's article in the *Calgary Herald* on 17 May 1992. In 1996, it is a whole different set of "angry young women" (Esselman 1996). "Galapalooza" is 1997's model (Farley and Thigpen 1997). In 1999, "women rock [the] music world" (Puckett 1999). The lineups change but the song remains the same. "Today's *female* rocker resists labels," according to P. Howell in "Rewriting the Rock Rule" in the *Calgary Herald* on 16 July 1995 (my emphasis), but they cannot escape one. "It's ghetto-izing," says L7's Jennifer Finch; "we want to be seen as bands first, not just women who play," Farber reports. For applause or excoriation, the adjective "female" is always primary.

Girls Together Only

Not only portrayed as unusual and antipathetic to rock and roll's essence, women musicians who do make it to the front of the stage are undermined and made extraordinary by being compared only to other women, as if the history of rock and pop has been played out in different rooms with all participants wearing gender-specific headphones. Natalie Imbruglia is the "pretty girl [who] comes out of nowhere with radio-friendly, professionally administered beats, and a face that knows it way around a camera. . . . And a new video queen is crowned. From Lisa Loeb to Jewel, from Alanis to Fiona, even from the Spice Girls to All Saints" (France 1998). The lineage is always and only other females. In a review of a PJ Harvey performance, for example, under the head "PJ Harvey Tells Her 'Stories' with a Therapeutic Conviction," Robert Hilburn in the 22 September 2001 *Los Angeles Times* writes:

> Pop observers have spent decades trying to find artists worthy of the new Bob Dylan tag, but few have sought to proclaim a new Joni Mitchell, another landmark artist whose music examines social and sexual politics with uncommon literary flair and depth.
> While Patti Smith and Sinéad O'Connor have examined the human condition with enough originality and insight to be considered the Joni Mitchells of their generations, no one has deserved the comparison as fully as Harvey.

While ostensibly laudatory to both artists, such a statement is essentially insulting to both—and to Bob Dylan as well.

In assessing the putative ancestry of Destiny's Child, Ann Powers writes in "Destiny's Child" in the *New York Times,* 29 April 2001:

> As America's reigning girl group, Destiny's Child is in the thick of this post-feminine revolution. From the Shirelles to TLC, girl groups have helped women hash out the differences between good and bad, liberation and entrapment, love and dependency. Since hip-hop's rise, girl groups have grown even tougher. En Vogue's lethal deployment of old-fashioned dazzle and TLC's forceful reimagining of the streetwise, regular girl made the space for Beyoncé Knowles and her lieutenants in Destiny's Child, Kelly Rowland and Michelle Williams, to take on the predicaments of womanhood with the determination of warriors.

In a column called "The Pop Life" from the *New York Times,* 7 April 1982, Steve Holden links the Go-Go's with Joan Jett and suggests: "The success of the Go-Go's and Joan Jett signals not only a generational turnover in rock, but the strengthening of women's role in rock. Olivia Newton-John, Stevie Nicks, and the woman-led sextet Quarterflash, from Portland, Ore., also have albums high on the charts." He then goes on to favorably contrast their style and that of Joan Jett with the "glamorous, pampered regality" of Joni Mitchell and Linda Ronstadt. "Both the Go-Go's and Joan Jett make simple, aggressive rock-and-roll that doesn't go out of its way to imitate the macho posturing of most male hard-rock acts. But in no way could their music be described as passive."

As the first—depending on how you define it—all-female rock group to have a number one album on the *Billboard* pop charts, the Go-Go's gained a range of accolades and opportunities. In a *Rolling Stone* cover story, they are acknowledged in this way: "The group's hit music is conceived, written, arranged, and performed almost entirely by women; peer behind the full skirts and teased hairdos, and you will not see the lurking presence of a guru like Phil Spector or Kim Fowley, or even a Mike Chapman, Peter Asher, or Chris Stein. Look directly at those skirts and hairdos and you won't see them flaunting their sexiness à la the Runaways or ignoring it like Fanny did; they're simply comfortable being female and playing the rock & roll songs they write" (Pond 1982, 13).

Such a passage, while laudatory, adds some baggage to the trip up the rock ladder. In addition to being a band, the Go-Go's are expected to vindicate their gender. It is not about artistry. It is about what kind of woman the musician is. Frank Chickens are "ninja-girls. That means they're too stroppy to be geishas" (Quantick 1984). In *Newsweek,* Madonna is accused of taking the low road, while other women have taken the high road:

> What bothers Madonna's detractors, though, isn't that the singer deals with sex—it's that she exploits her own sexuality in a way that's trite. Fortu-

nately, there are female singers who don't take the easy way out. In "Beat of the Heart," Scandal's Patty Smyth projects an aura of smarts and savvy—of a woman who controls her sexuality and not vice versa. And Pat Benatar has gone so far as to explicitly reject the theme of male domination: playing a street waif, she stands up to a vicious pimp in the "Love is a Battlefield" clip, a piece that ends with a jubilant street ballet celebrating sisterhood. (Rock 1985, 54)

(Hey, wasn't Benatar the bad girl who degraded all women with her song "Hit Me with Your Best Shot"? Oh, how the worm turns.)

In *Time*, the relative merits of the two artists are debated, and Cyndi Lauper wins. "Cyndi is more of an artist than Madonna," Irving Azoff is quoted as saying. "Madonna will be out of the business in six months" (These big girls 1985, 74). In *Newsweek* (Rock 1985), the virgin/whore dichotomy is employed to suggest that women like the good Cyndi Lauper (who "has successfully used the resources of rock to project the image of 'a new woman'") need to be encouraged and women like the bad Madonna (who "has managed to make shattered taboos into new foundations for old stereotypes") need to be stoned, um, discarded.

More recently, longtime rock critic Robert Hilburn, in "Jackson's 'All for You' Concert Misses the Beat" in the 1 October 2001 *Los Angeles Times,* uses comparisons with Madonna to critique Janet Jackson: "Jackson's limitations were magnified by another piece of bad timing: Her tour arrives on the heels of the far more satisfying and forward-thinking Madonna tour." In a review of Macy Gray in the *Los Angeles Times* (14 September 1999) titled "Second Chance at a Dream," Hilburn writes that "[Gray] also sings about sexual matters, in such tunes as 'Sex-o-matic Venus Freak,' with an aggression that is rare for a woman in pop." What a ridiculous remark! If you want to play the gender card, let's pull out LaBelle, Donna Summer, Wendy O Williams, and Madonna. Or, we can play the person card and note that Gray cites Prince among her influences. One way or another, it is uninformed and inappropriate to define an artist's choices and decisions by her gender.[2]

Dream Dates

"I've been really lucky. . . . No one has ever yelled 'Take off your top!' while I've been onstage," Margo Timmins told *Rolling Stone* for an article titled "The Women's Movement" (21 September 1989, 73). Timmins may have been spared such a special moment from fans, but reviews of the Cowboy Junkies still find space for discussions of her "maidenhood" (?!?), as in M. Boehm's "Waking Up Isn't Hard to Do for Cowboy Junkies" in the *Los Angeles Times* (8 May 1992): "There's no way that Timmins will ever be a stage-bounding, eardrum-blasting, eye-riveting firebrand like Maria McKee. But maybe she has it in her to evolve from too-fragile maidenhood toward the wistful but nevertheless sturdy presence and vocal bearing of an Emmylou Harris."

Evaluating the attractiveness of female musicians is another way that pop journalism deflects attention away from their artistry. The sexual meaning of rock 'n' roll becomes defined by the sexual preferences of the rock critic. In a cover article on Jewel for *Rolling Stone*, Neil Strauss writes: "All interviews are a seduction process, on both sides, but this one is really working. . . . I am nervous, as if meeting a girlfriend's parents for the first time" (1999, 39). He cannot mask his glee when he is invited to spend a [chaste] night in bed with the singer/songwriter. (We cannot possibly hope, I suppose, that he will soon be organizing a slumber party with the members of Korn or Wu-Tang Clan.) In *The Observer* (December 1978), a writer had this to say about Kate Bush: "She is like some extravagantly exotic orchid . . . she has a face which houses giant eyes, and pouting lips which like to smile but can just as easily make a theatrical snarl. The hair is an auburn mane. She has a small, lithe body, dancer's legs, and a suggestion of fullness of breast" (Steward and Garratt 1984, 59). Bush's body type is apparently more interesting and important than the instrumentation of her compositions.

In 1966, a *Time* article titled "The New Troubadours" (28 October 93) profiles several groups: the Mamas and the Papas, the Lovin' Spoonful, and Simon and Garfunkel. Strange to say, however, only Cass Elliot ("a Big Bertha") and Michelle Philips ("a beauty") are described in terms of their looks and weight: "Phillips's wife Michelle is a willowy ex-model," and "anchor girl is rotund (200 lbs.) Cass Elliot." In a 28 June 1968 *Time* cover story, "Aretha Franklin," Franklin is described as "chunky" (62). *Newsweek*'s "Queen Bees" article describes Janis Joplin as having "earthy good looks" and provides the weight and height of Spanky McFarlane of Spanky and Our Gang (77). The Supremes are "attractive" in *Ebony*'s 1965 article (81). Natalie Merchant is "ravishing," according to the *Los Angeles Times*'s Chris Willman in "10,000 Maniacs Visit Southland" (15 August 1989). Britney Spears is a "teen dream" (Daly 1999, 60).

In a cover story on Edie Brickell and The New Bohemians in *Spin* magazine, Michael Corcoran writes, "The Edie who looks back from the pictures is pert and irresistible, a conspiracy of long, flowing brown hair, tight, faded jeans, and a white cotton t-shirt that conforms to the kind of smallish breasts that women fret over but men just accept as part of God's universe" (1989, 33). Smallish breasts?!? The woman is wearing jeans and a t-shirt, for goodness' sake.

In an otherwise straightforward story on the history of the Pretenders and their recent album, writer Scott Cohen of *Spin* finds it necessary to inject this Victoria's Secret–level insight: "Chrissie prefers stockings to panty hose because she doesn't like to wear panties" (Cohen 1986, 50). A writer connects Gwen Stefani to the "easy" (read "sluttish") Madonna in an 11 May 1997 *Montreal Gazette* review titled "Bouncy Blonde; No Doubt Boils Down the Madonna Message ("Do Me") for a New Generation." For the *LA Weekly* of 1 September 1988, under the head "Sweethearts of the Radio," Kim Fowley writes about his version of the Bangles: "Susanna Hoffs is a tiny goddess, Debbi Peterson is the Blond Amazon Glacier Queen. . . . We men and boys who watch MTV and buy records, cassettes, and CDs are tired of hearing about crack, poverty, loneliness, boredom, lifestyles of the numb and dumb. Samantha Fox is too trashy; Kylie Minogue, too silly; Madonna, too conniving. The Bangles are the real thing: wife-candidates you can lust after, the women in the airplane who wear matching uniforms and sweet hellos" (15). A review of articles on Staind, Pearl Jam, Michael Jackson, Bruce Springsteen, REO Speedwagon, Duran Duran, and Gorillaz reveals no similar assessments.

Who's Your Boyfriend?

Once her physical appearance has been dissected, her home life (boyfriends or parents or both) is frequently the next topic for the profile of a female artist. The Supremes—but not the Four Tops or the Standells—had to contend with reporters asking about their boyfriends and their parents. So did the Go-Go's, reports R. Harrington in "The Go-Gos Go Get 'Em," in the 19 September 1982 *Washington Post*: "And then there's 'How do your parents feel?'" Carlisle adds, petulantly. "How would your parents feel? How would anybody's parents feel? They never ask the boys!" So do Britney Spears and Jewel and Monica and Brandy. Maybe part of the anger in Alanis Morissette's "Jagged Little Pill" was a response to that worldview. What does my boyfriend think, what does my ex think? Well, here is what I think . . .

Writer Karen Schoemer in her article/interview with Linda Ronstadt in *Trouble Girls: The* Rolling Stone *Book of Women in Rock* seems a tad more interested in finding out about Ronstadt's love life than in discussing her long and varied musical career (O'Dair 1997). When her first single was a success, Natalie Imbruglia was constantly asked about her putative dalliance with David Schwimmer (France 1998). In the September 1999 issue of *Select*, a timeline of Courtney Love's life includes details of her virginity loss and various boyfriends along with a sidebar of pictures and a few prime quotes from the disaffected (and the affected, for balance). Shirley Manson and Gwen Stefani—but not Tom DeLonge and Gary Grice—have to deal continually with the issue of current and past boyfriends.

An obsession with tracking boyfriends and lovers and husbands frequently leads to imputations of undue influence. Courtney Love has to contend with persistent rumors that her husband, Kurt Cobain, was responsible for the success of *Pretty on the Inside* and that ex-boyfriend Billy Corgan helped along *Celebrity Skin*. On the *Rolling Stone* web site, the entry for Hole includes this disparaging comment: "What finally broke Hole, however, was not their album or their live shows, but rather Courtney Love's relationship with Kurt Cobain, the enigmatic, disaffected frontman of Nirvana, who briefly became the most popular, influential rock band in the U.S. with the release of the 1991 album Nevermind. As Cobain became a rock star, Love tagged along, earning media attention thanks to her stormy relationship with Cobain" (Hindin 1999, 1). *Rolling Stone* also spent most of its first cover story on Madonna detailing the men she had used to get to the top.

Rapacious vampires sleeping their way to success are matched by passive automatons following their master's voice. When Janet Jackson's album *Control* arrived in 1986, it was a huge hit. Her musical career was in her own hands, according to the lyrics of the song: "I'm in control and I love it." For *Spin*, though, the issue in their cover article, "Damn It, Janet: The Battle for Control of Janet Jackson," was all about what man—her father or John McClain of A&M Records—would ultimately control her career (Stevenson 1987). Twelve years and a huge record contract with Virgin later, it turns out, it was Ms. Jackson herself. In 1999, Shania Twain had to deal with the same issue: Is her husband Mutt Lange her Svengali? She has to defend her own integrity: "The reality is, it's just all me. . . . I pick everything I wear, everything I do, every move I make. I am directing myself artistically, period, no ifs, ands or buts about it" (Shania 1998, 57). In an interview from 1978, Linda Ronstadt is faced with this statement: "People often assume that [producer/manager] Peter Asher picks all your songs, the musicians come in and tell you what to do, and you just get up there and sing." Her response: "I pick the tunes . . . I chose the band" (Herbst 1978, 57). No male artist of Ronstadt's stature would have to defend his musical integrity.

Can the Burden Be Lightened?

"I don't really think a lot of guys know what a burden it is to be a girl sometimes," Gwen Stefani once told a reporter (*Buffalo News*, 15 April 1997).

Spin magazine's second-anniversary issue featured Madonna on the cover with the tagline "Sex as a weapon: What did she start?" The point of the accompanying article is that "video made the video star. It made most of them female. Sex is their calling card, but will it also be their downfall?" (Janowitz 1987). So, too, the success of Lilith Fair had opened the women to charges of exclusivity and anti-male bias. As all these examples have, I expect, shown, however, the armalite rifle of sex is being wielded at, not by, women musicians. Are things getting any better? Maybe. Certainly, women musicians are more likely to expect equity now and are more likely to be vocally peeved at not getting it: "Every interview I've done in America, I've been asked about the . . . political implications of the fact that I happen to be a girl," complained Justine Frischmann of Elastica. "They're asking me to marginalize myself. I've always been brought up to expect absolute equity. . . . It shouldn't even be something that particularly is talked about" (O'Dair 1997, 524).

Neneh Cherry says, "I suppose [sexism]'s there [in the music industry], but I'm going to step over anyone who tries that with me" (Rogers 1989, 73). Certainly, more women musicians are on the scene and selling records (witness their continued success at the Grammys). Concert and record reviews are less likely to focus specifically on gender issues. The rock 'n' roll establishment, as epitomized by *Rolling Stone, Spin,* and the Rock and Roll Hall of Fame (Deggans 1996), however, has not changed much, as S. Holden reports in "Three Women and Their Journeys in Song" in the *New York Times,* 14 January 1996:

> How else to explain the dearth of women on the Rock-and-Roll Hall of Fame's recently published list of the 500 most influential songs? This bogus canon, selected by James Henke, the Hall of Fame's chief curator, with input from other rock critics and writers, does a conscientious job of recognizing early blues, rhythm-and-blues and country-music influences. But the short shrift it gives to the contributions of women is an embarrassment to the institution that promotes it.
>
> While the list recognizes minor British Invasion acts like Gerry and the Pacemakers and Peter and Gordon, artists who changed the way women expressed themselves in music are overlooked. Influential hits like Carly Simon's "You're So Vain," Rickie Lee Jones's "Chuck E.'s in Love" and Tracy Chapman's "Fast Car" are excluded. Linda Ronstadt, the queen of Los Angeles rock in the 1970's, is nowhere to be found. Nor are Laura Nyro (a significant formal innovator), Joan Baez, Judy Collins, Joan Armatrading, Rickie Lee Jones, Suzanne Vega, Heart and the solo Stevie Nicks. Even in the pop-soul area, the list is ungenerous to women. Dionne Warwick and the solo Tina Turner go unacknowledged.

In 1999, VH-1, the cable music channel, compiled a list of the "100 Greatest Women of Rock and Roll," featuring twenty influential musicians for each of five nights. Covered by S. Rodman in a *Boston Herald* article titled "These Women Rock" (26 July 1999), the series included video clips and interviews along with dozens of testimonials from people ranging from

Roberta Flack (no. 45) and Sheryl Crow (no. 44) to Elvis Costello (unlisted) and John Mellencamp (also unlisted), and from Kim Gordon (no. 91) of Sonic Youth to President and Mrs. Clinton. Wait for the punch line: "When asked, producer Lauren Zalaznick points out that doing a similar list exclusively for men would be redundant. She said less than 10 percent of the '100 Greatest Artists of Rock and Roll' list comprises women." Gender determines importance to rock orthodoxy; so, many important artists simply fail to rate a ticket to ride on the magic bus.

What then can we expect from the coming years? Women musicians will make records (some great, some good, some bad) and sell them (lots, some, not many), but the chalk line defining the sacred body of rock will be redrawn to exclude their contributions. Maybe things will suddenly change on some road to Cleveland—after all, Joni Mitchell made it into the Rock and Roll Hall of Fame in 1997—or maybe they will not. Magnanimity of spirit may be more than we can expect from journalists and critics, but so, unfortunately, is historical accuracy.

Notes

Acknowledgments: I thank Glenn Johnson-Grau for invaluable help in researching this essay. As this article was going to press, *We Gotta Get out of This Place: The True, Tough Story of Women in Rock* (Hirshey 2001) appeared. Its version of women's place in rock history may or may not help set the record straight.

1. The epigraph is from Janowitz 1987 (60).

2. The subtext of all these extracts is equally interesting: Joni Mitchell (or Madonna or Pat Benatar or . . .) is bad in one decade and good in another, as the permutations of reputations play out over time. Nonetheless, it is always woman against woman. Sisterhood is powerful, isn't it?

References

Cohen, S. (1986). Chrissie Hynde. *Spin,* December, 49–52.

Corcoran, M. (1989). Edie Brickell. *Spin,* March, 32–36.

Daly, S. (1999). Britney Spears: Inside the mind and heart (and bedroom) of America's new teen queen. *Rolling Stone,* 15 April, 60–65, 129–130.

Deggans, E. (1996), Have women arrived in music industry? Don't be so sure. *St. Petersburg Times,* 19 January.

Dickerson, J. (1998). *Women on top.* New York: Billboard Books.

Esselman, M. (1996). Angry young women. *USA Weekend,* 14 January, 14.

Farley, C. J., and D. E. Thigpen (1997). Galapalooza! *Time,* 21 July, 60.

Female rock. (1971). *Time,* 12 April, 68–69.

Flanagan, B. (1988). Anima rising. *Musician,* April, 37–38, 121.

France, K. (1998). Natalie Imbruglia: The "torn" bird. *Spin,* June, 74–80.

Gaar, G. G., and Y. Ono. (1992). *She's a rebel: The history of women in rock & roll.* Seal Press Feminist.

Harrington, R. (1982). New roles in rock: Girl groups are back and they've got the beat. *Washington Post,* 15 April.

Herbst, P. (1978). The *Rolling Stone* interview: Linda Ronstadt. *Rolling Stone,* 19 October, 50–59.

Hindin, S. (1999). Hole. http://rollingstone.tunes.com/sections/artists. Accessed 4 October 1999.

Hirshey, G. (2001). *We gotta get out of this place: The true, tough story of women in rock.* New York: Atlantic Monthly Press.

Janowitz, T. (1987). Sex as a weapon. *Spin,* April, 54–62.

Juno, A. (1996) *Angry women in rock.* Juno.

Katz, S. (1978). *Superwomen of rock.* New York: Tempo Books.

King as queen? (1971). *Time,* 12 July, 52.

New women in rock (1982). New York: Delilah/Putnam/Omnibus.

O'Brien, L. (1999). Singers embody both strength and sexuality. *Milwaukee Journal Sentinel,* 10 January, Lifestyle sec.

O'Dair, B., ed. (1997). *Trouble girls: The* Rolling Stone *book of women in rock.* New York: Random House.

Orloff, K. (1974). *Rock 'n roll woman.* Los Angeles: Nash.

Palmer, R. (1995). *Rock and roll: an unruly history.* New York: Harmony Books.

Pareles, J. (1996). The angry young woman: The labels take notice. *New York Times,* 28 January, sec. 2.

Pearson, D. (1980). Cute, cute, cutesy goodbye. *New Musical Express,* 29 March, 27–29, 31.

Pond, S. (1982). The Go-Go's. *Rolling Stone,* 5 August, 13–16.

Powers, A. (1994). When women venture forth. *New York Times,* 9 October, sec. 2.

Puckett, J. L. (1999). Women rock music world. *Gannett News Service,* 19 February, ARC.

Quantick, D. (1984). Enter the ninja. *New Musical Express,* 31 March, 13.

Raphael, A. (1996). *Grrrls: Viva Rock Divas.* New York: St. Martin's.

Rock and roll: Woman power. (1985). *Newsweek,* 4 March, 48–57.

Rogers, S. (1989). The women's movement. *Rolling Stone,* 21 September, 73.

Saal, H. (1969). The girls—letting go. *Newsweek,* 14 July, 68–69.

Scheerer, M. (1993). Women rockers on a roll. CNN, *Showbiz Today,* 10 December.

Schorow, S. (1999). Whine of the times—Why are Alanis and other '90s girl rockers so bitter? Dylan oughta know. *Boston Herald,* 18 February.

Sex rock. (1975). *Time,* 29 December, 39.

Shania Twain. (1998). *Rolling Stone,* 3 September, 56–60.

Smith, A. (1998). Are sisters really doing it for themselves? *Sunday Times* (London), 5 July, Features sec.

Stevenson, J. C. (1987). Damn it, Janet. *Spin,* January, 44–51.

Steward, S., and C. Garratt. (1984). *Signed, sealed, and delivered: True life stories of women in pop.* Boston : South End Press.

Strauss, N. (1999). Jewel. *Rolling Stone,* 24 December, 36–42.

Swartley, A. (1982). Girls! Live! On stage! *Mother Jones,* June, 25–31.

These big girls don't cry. (1985). *Time,* 4 March, 74–75.

13

"The Day the Music Died"— Again

Newspaper Coverage of the Deaths of Popular Musicians

Sharon R. Mazzarella and Timothy M. Matyjewicz

Iconography is very much a postmortem affair.

—Mark Kingwell

On 8 December 1980, John Lennon was murdered by Mark David Chapman, a Lennon fan, in New York City. The former Beatle and solo artist was forty years old. Nearly a decade and half later, on 8 April 1995, Kurt Cobain's body was found at his home in Seattle. Cobain, lead singer/songwriter for the grunge band Nirvana, shot himself at the age of twenty-seven. Just over a year later, on 9 August 1995, fifty-three-year-old Grateful Dead frontman Jerry Garcia was found dead in a drug treatment center in California. Yet another year later, rapper/actor twenty-five-year-old Tupac Shakur died on 13 September 1996 of wounds suffered in a 7 September drive-by shooting in Las Vegas. All four deaths generated extensive media coverage that, for the most part, attempted to make sense of them. Informed by frame theory, this chapter analyzes the *New York Times* and the *Washington Post* coverage of these four deaths during the month immediately following each to understand the role of newspapers in creating "myth and memory" (Kitch 1999, 1).[1]

219

Popular Musicians as Postmortem Icons

The *New York Times* and the *Washington Post* played a major role in myth-ologizing these men, in some cases turning them into icons. Writers used the "icon" frame (discussing the musician's role as a generational spokesperson, symbol, or role model) in their coverage of the deaths of Lennon, Cobain, and Garcia, less often in the coverage of Shakur. Specifically, Lennon was framed as an icon for the sixties, Cobain for Generation X, Garcia for the counterculture of the sixties. Some articles credited the artist with being a catalyst for social upheaval: "'I Wanna Hold Your Hand' marked the first shot of a social and cultural revolution that was to brand the '60s as a decade of rapid, chaotic change" (Kornheiser and Zito 1980). Similarly, headlines informed us that Lennon was the "Leader of a Rock Group That Helped Define a Generation" (Rockwell 1980). Often, the framing of Lennon as a generational icon pointed out the aging of that generation: "John Lennon . . . personified the ideals of a generation now hovering on the brink of middle age" (Walters 1980). The *New York Times*'s Frank Rich declared: "The murder of John Lennon this week was the most personal kind of loss. When the news broke Monday night, ex-Beatlemaniacs, now poised on the brink of middle-age, raced to their phones to console each other, to sob, to remember. And the more we talked about those memories, the more we realized that our childhoods would have been empty without the Beatles. And that the Beatles would have been nothing without John Lennon" (1980) A *New York Times* article quoted a fan, Sheryl Lester: "'We lost more than John Lennon,' she said. 'We lost our adolescence'" (Haberman 1980).

Jerry Garcia was referred to as "defining the '60s." "He seemed the ge-nial embodiment of a positive ethos forged in the '60s" (Harrington 1995). According to *New York Times* music critic Jon Pareles, "Mr. Garcia's smiling, bearded face became an icon of a utopian 1960's spirit," with the result that he "had come to represent the survival of 1960's idealism" (1995b). He was, according to the *New York Times*'s J. Peder Zane, "the man whose life and music symbolized the exuberance and excesses of the 1960's" (1995).

Unlike their generally positive use of the icon frame for Lennon and Garcia, writers who employed it for Cobain—whose death the *Washington Post* christened "the suicide that spoke to a generation" (Blumenfeld 1994)—often added a negative spin on both the artist and the generation who supposedly identified with him. A *Washington Post* article informed us that "Cobain, 27, was presumed to speak for a youth subculture whose fatalistic outlook was forged by the dissolution of family, lowered expectations in the job market, and endemic drug abuse and violence." The article continued: "More than any current rock performer, he bore the burden of being anointed by the media as a spokesman for the angst-ridden twentysomething generation" (Harrington and Leiby 1994). "Kurt Cobain's jagged visceral lyrics embody their despair," another *Washington Post* article announced. "Cobain was an icon of their alienation" (Blumenfeld 1994). Similar sentiments were echoed by articles in the *New York Times.* "Mr. Cobain's lyrics, often contradictory and full of angst, spoke to a generation overshadowed by the enormous baby boom and coming of age when jobs were shrinking" (Egan 1994).

Shakur was more likely to be framed as an architect of gangsta rap than an icon, although that frame did appear occasionally. He was, according to Esther Iverem of the *Washington Post* (1996a), "arguably the most visible media creation of ghetto-gangsta-as-authentic-black . . . selling young people a lifestyle leading to an early grave." She went on to label him "black America's James Dean for the '90's." Another *Washington Post* writer said that Shakur's "bitter, explosive and often cruel music shocked critics but struck home to a generation of rap fans already hardened by life" (Constable 1996).

The greatest contrast in the application of this frame lies in the coverage of Lennon's murder and Cobain's suicide. One subtle way in which journalists told us we should perceive Lennon as a more important icon and his death as a greater tragedy than Cobain's lay in their choice of other famous deaths to use as points of comparison. They often compared Cobain's death to those of Jim Morrison, Janis Joplin, and Jimi Hendrix—all young rock 'n' rollers who suffered drug-induced deaths for which they were held partly responsible (see Harrington and Leiby 1994). On the other hand, Lennon's death was often compared to the assassinations of prominent and beloved political figures—notably Martin Luther King Jr. and John F. Kennedy—the implication being that Lennon was more than just a musician. Certainly, the fact that Lennon was murdered, as were King and Kennedy, is a factor in this comparison, but it also appears to be something more. For example, an article in the *Washington Post* proclaimed: "What [Lennon's murderer] had done was stop the music, the way a predecessor had ended Camelot, the way a prototype had stopped Martin Luther King Jr.'s dream, the way dreams were ending in too many places lately" (Prochnau 1980). When Lennon was compared to popular-culture figures, they were more likely to be classical musicians (McLellan et al. 1980) and Shakespeare (Crowds of Lennon 1980) than self-destructive rockers.

Interestingly, Shakur, who also was murdered, was rarely compared to assassinated leaders or even to other media personalities (once to Cobain and a couple of times to poets). More often, he was framed as yet another African American man killed by the violence of the streets—part of a larger societal problem. One article quoted the Nation of Islam's Conrad Muhammad: "'We're not honoring a gangsta rapper today. . . . We're honoring a young black who was a child of God who was murdered—and who should not have been murdered'" (Iverem 1996b). Shakur was not an icon, he was a statistic.

Some writers, while making icons of some of these men, referred to their reluctance to be designated as icons and role models. Cobain, we were told, "was utterly disdainful of his own role as the 'voice of a generation,' and central to his message was rejection of what he saw as the crude, commercial motive of labeling any age group" (Freedland 1994). Similarly, Garcia "always made it clear that he abhorred the idea of himself as a leader or shaper of lives" (Mortensen 1995).

At other times, typically in letters to the editor, we were told these men were unacceptable icons, inappropriate role models.[2] While few, these letters were often vitriolic, such as one from a parent, Mildred Jeffrey (1980): "I am appalled by the tributes paid to [John Lennon] by people presumably as commonsensical as Governor Carey (flags lowered!) and many journalists and newscasters." Jeffrey's criticism was rooted in her perception of Lennon as an unacceptable role model who led legions of "brainwashed" young people to reject a mainstream lifestyle. Similarly, a reader took issue with Iverem's (1996b) labeling Shakur "black America's James Dean for the '90's": "It was a tragic death, but it was his choice to live the lifestyle he did and to ignite the hatred of those who finally did him in. Tupac was no James Dean, no role model for African American youth" (Fuller 1996). This sentiment was echoed in an editorial in the *New York Times:* "The last thing young people need is someone advising them to shoot first and talk later" (Staples 1996).

Likewise, Garcia's place as a role model/icon was attacked by *Washington Post* columnist Colman McCarthy, who pointed out that Garcia "fueled himself on LSD and touted the drug for others," then went on: "Whatever musical gifts Garcia had—and there's debate about that—he gave no social message to his audiences other than relax, trip a bit, do whatever feels good" (1995). Further, the *Washington Post* ran an article that attacked Cobain's authenticity: "His roomy house here, complete with skylights and a gray shingle exterior, is a case in point. Xers are meant to be the slacker generation, yet here was the slacker-in-chief living the yuppie dream: married, padding around a $1.1 million luxury mansion with a garden for his baby daughter to play in, with Microsoft and Boeing executives for neighbors" (Freedland 1994).

It appears that a large factor in framing these men as icons was generational. Fred Fogo's analysis of press coverage of John Lennon's murder found a major recurring theme: The sixties had died along with Lennon. Furthermore, Fogo's analysis indicated that "Lennon's death opened a mass-mediated space where a generational segment talked to itself about its identity and 'place' in the social order through a ritual grieving process that implicitly strove for unity and consensus" (1994, xi).[3]

Similarly, Mazzarella found that the press coverage of the suicide of Kurt Cobain linked him to the so-called Generation X—young people born from about 1964 through 1979. This was accomplished, in part, by designating Cobain's fan base as Generation X and identifying his personal problems as problems that allegedly also plagued that generation. "In attempting to make sense of Cobain's suicide," writes Mazzarella, "the media additionally were attempting to make further sense of an entire generation" (1995, 64).

Because one's taste in popular music is often a function of one's generation, it could follow that coverage of the deaths of musicians would play up the generation angle. But in his analysis of our relationship with "media friends" (i.e., celebrities), Joshua Meyrowitz argues this is a function not of music, but rather of media: "Unlike traditional societies with relatively unchanging cultural heritages, each generation has its own media experiences and special media friends" (1994, 78). In fact, in her analysis of four decades of U.S. newsmagazine coverage of celebrity deaths (including nonmusicians such as Jacqueline Kennedy Onassis), Carolyn Kitch identified "generational significance" as one narrative element used to create "myth and memory" (1999, 16, 1). She points out that such coverage "conflate[s] celebrities . . . with the generations in which . . . people find their identities" (19). Such general biases seem to play a role here.

Specifically, according to Gamson and Modigliani, when covering stories, journalists "contribute their own frames and invent their own clever catchphrases, drawing on a popular culture that they share with their audience" (1989, 3). This supports research by Mazzarella (1995), who postulates that journalists covered Lennon and Cobain's deaths differently because those who wrote about Lennon's death shared with their audience a personal link with him that did not exist in the case of Cobain. Lennon was the baby boomers' idol, their role model. A comparison of Frank Rich's *New York Times* columns written fourteen years apart supports this notion. In response to John Lennon's death, Rich reminisced about "my own experiences with the Beatles" (1980). By 1994, Rich was not writing of his experiences with Kurt Cobain, but instead asked his sons, "both rabid Nirvana fans" (1994), to explain to him the importance of Cobain's music and death. Although Rich's column on Cobain was sympathetic, many others were not.

Carolyn Kitch suggests that in covering celebrity deaths, "journalists cease to be reporters and become mourners along with the audience" (1999, 24). For instance, they may cease writing in the third person and use the communal "we" in describing the significance of the death—a characteristic of the 1980 Rich article, as well as of numerous other articles on John Lennon (see Fogo 1994; Kitch 1999). In coverage of the death of Tupac Shakur, this shift never happened, and it happened so rarely in coverage of Kurt Cobain that when it did occur, it seemed strange. For example, in a *Washington Post* article, Douglas Coupland (often erroneously given credit for coining the phrase Generation X) recalled his own reaction to Cobain's March 1994 drug overdose in Italy and his April 1994 suicide. The article, written in the form of a letter to Cobain and titled "Letter from a Fan," concluded: "And this is what I felt: I felt I had never asked you to make me care about you, but it happened—against the hype, against the odds—and now you are in my imagination forever" (1994). Similarly, in a *New York Times* article headlined "Kurt Cobain Screamed Out Our Angst," music critic Lorraine Ali wrote: "Cobain's death hurts" (1994).

A generation gap was apparent in articles on Shakur's death. In a *Washington Post* column, Courtland Milloy expressed bewilderment over his eighteen-year-old daughter's reaction to Shakur's shooting—she was ready to rush to Las Vegas to be with him. Milloy, on the other hand, related to Shakur's mother, former 1960s Black Panther Afeni Shakur: "My daughter longed for the return of Tupac the rapper. And I found myself hoping that the son of the Black Panther would survive" (1996). Milloy was not the only journalist to fondly recall 1960s African American revolutionaries in the context of modern-day rappers. Esther Iverem of the *Washington Post* lamented: "While 1960s revolutionaries taught the importance of being willing to die for beliefs, it is a totally different matter to die in senseless gang violence or over a high stakes game of 'Yo Mama,' proving your 'realness' by how much you can bluff, how many bullets you can take, how many times you can cheat death" (1996a).

Perhaps the view of Jerry Garcia as an icon of the sixties made him a more sympathetic figure to these journalists than were Cobain and Shakur. His death, although framed as somewhat self-inflicted, was presented less negatively than Cobain's and Shakur's. However, journalists did not appear to feel Garcia's death as personally as they did Lennon's. In mourning Lennon's death journalists also mourned their own lost youth, but they saw Garcia not as the embodiment of their youth and dreams, but as an older relative—"rock's kindly uncle" (Pareles 1995a), a "father figure to hordes of nomadic fans" (Grateful 1995). While they might have mourned Garcia's as a death in the family, it was not the same as mourning their lost youth.

Mourning

This mourning, both on the part of journalists and the audience, was the most frequently employed frame in the coverage of the deaths of Lennon, Cobain, and Garcia and all but absent in the coverage of the death of Shakur, which rarely mentioned mourning fans, assorted memorials, or the author's own mourning. The exceptions were a couple of articles on the Nation of Islam's "Hip Hop Day of Atonement" in Harlem, and even that was described as "less a memorial and more a lesson in the futility of 'gangsta' values and to the street violence that recently ended the 25-year-old rapper's life" (Marriott 1996). Mourning fans were mentioned only in Shakur's *Washington Post* obituary, which reported that he was "mourned by rap fans across the country, many of whom identified with the angry, despairing outlook he projected" (Constable 1996).

In the cases of Lennon, Cobain, and Garcia, nearly every article that employed the mourning frame also used one or more others, notably the icon frame. For example, in covering the death of John Lennon, the *Washington Post* reported that "several hundred people, many with tears in their eyes, gathered outside the [Dakota] building" (Lennon's home). The article credited Lennon (and the Beatles) with "creating the music that indelibly marked the generation" (Weil et al. 1980). While the link with the icon frame provided a justification of sorts for the public's mourning, it also told readers that there was more to mourn than the death of a person. For example, numerous articles on John Lennon's death also declared it to be the death of the sixties or of sixties values. "If there were any illusions left at all for children of the 60's," wrote Frank Rich, "they too died on Monday night" (1980). According to Fogo, coverage of Lennon's death focused on "what has been lost, not what might have been" (1994, 51). A *New York Times* article on Jerry Garcia included both frames in the same sentence: "Garcia, whose death on August 9 led to spontaneous tearful vigils across the United States, never strove to be a rock icon" (Pareles 1995a). In the case of Kurt Cobain's suicide, however, the death-as-warning frame accompanied the icon and mourning frames, especially as they related to Cobain's young fans. The *Washington Post*, for example, quoted a twenty-five-year-old fan: "He killed himself for the same reason I'd kill myself. . . . We lack something. We have no core" (Blumenfeld 1994).

The extensive use of the mourning frame is not surprising, for, as Joshua Meyrowitz argues, "the media that gave birth to the relationship [with media friends] also provide the most ritualized channels for mourning a media friend's death" (1994, 76). According to Carolyn Kitch, the ritual of media mourning enables journalists to "mediate a larger cultural process" that "draws audiences together in a common understanding. . . . Commemoration provides consolation—and, as the word itself suggests, creates collective memory" (1999, 3). Following Kitch, that this frame was not employed in the death of Shakur suggests that he was being framed not as a figure who drew "audiences together in a common understanding," but rather as a divisive figure who "had a gift for making enemies" (Pareles 1996a). Indeed, articles presented him in this manner in three ways. First, many journalists rehashed the debates over the merits of gangsta rap. Certainly, Shakur's music divided many, including many within the African American community. Activists like C. Dolores Tucker of the National Political Congress of Black Women had denounced Shakur and gangsta rap (Lipsitz 1998), while others celebrated him as an authentic voice from the streets and praised him for "keeping it real." These debates were replayed over and over in the articles on his death.

Second, Shakur was presented as a central figure in the alleged feud between East Coast and West Coast rappers and their labels, which was becoming more and more violent (see Wartofsky 1996). Shakur, we were told, had been "born in the Bronx but [was] working in California" and had been a "West Coast loyalist" in a world where hip-hop "musicians and their entourages, or posses, too often act like rival gangs, picking fistfights or worse" (Pareles 1996a). Multiple articles publicized the theories that his highly visible role in this feud caused his death.

Third, articles often talked about the two contradictory sides of Shakur's personality, both captured in a *Washington Post* column by Kenneth Carroll, who likened Shakur to a poet but bemoaned his use of violence and degradation in his songs. "His death was a lamentable loss of a gifted, misguided, young poet who spoke with insight and energy to his hip-hop world, but who committed the unpardonable sin of using his immense poetic talents to degrade and debase the very people who needed his positive words most—his fans" (1996). Indeed the *Washington Post*'s Alona Wartofsky began one article by noting that "Tupac Shakur's alarmingly short life was characterized by contradictions" (1996), while the *New York Times*'s Jon Pareles (1996b) describes Shakur as "a complex and sometimes contradictory figure." Pareles continued: "He was an intelligent, vivid writer who had studied acting at the High School of Performing Arts in Baltimore; he was an accomplished rapper with a husky baritone and crisp enunciation. He was also a convicted sex offender, and the words 'Thug Life' and 'Outlaw' were tattooed on his body." Finally, an article in the *Washington Post* declared that Shakur did not "completely fit the 'gangsta' mold" and called him a "thoughtful man" with a "sensitive side"—the implication being that it was all an act, a pose (Constable 1996). Yet it was an act that, according to many, got him killed, something that articles felt compelled to point out.

Identifying Villains

When covering celebrity deaths, media typically identify "villains," according to Kitch, who suggests that the "mourners' need to assign blame underlies journalistic coverage" of celebrity deaths (1999, 20). The articles analyzed here identified villains in a variety of ways, notably through the frames death-as-warning, lifestyle, and tortured artist.

The death-as-warning frame shows up frequently in coverage of all four deaths, but articles on Lennon's death differed markedly from coverage of the other three. The warnings delivered as a result of Cobain's death pointed to heroin use or suicide, in particular the potential for teens and other members of Generation X to imitate his actions (see Anders 1994; Harper 1994; Mazzarella 1995). Articles about the death of Jerry Garcia focused on the ramifications of a lifestyle characterized by risky health behaviors, notably substance abuse: "Captain Trips smoked three packs of cigarettes a day, lived off junk food, took all kinds of drugs and became a heroin addict dying ignominiously in a rehab center where he was being treated for a relapse. President Clinton warned: young people should say: 'I'm not going to die that way'" (Trafford 1995). In both cases, the implication was that these men were responsible for their own deaths.

Moreover, the death-as-warning frame was used extensively in the coverage of Shakur's death. Warnings were issued about the dangers of living the "gangsta" lifestyle in particular and of "the larger problems of African American males in this society" in general (Stephney 1996). Headlines warned: "Tupac's Squandered Gift" (Carroll 1996), "Rap Star's Death Highlights Harsher Reality" (Stephney 1996), and "In One Death, Mirrors of Our Times" (Pareles 1996a). On the other hand, most of the articles that employed this frame for Lennon's murder advocated gun control. In fact, according to the *Washington Post,* "John Lennon's death appears to have done more to center attention on handguns than any recent event" (Gold 1980). Interestingly, no calls for gun control ensued as a result of Shakur's death, although numerous calls went out to end the celebration of the "gangsta" lifestyle, again implicating Shakur as in part responsible for his own death—it was not easy access to guns that killed Shakur, but the lifestyle *he* chose to lead. With such headlines as "A Death As Real As It Gets; Tupac Shakur's Gangsta Image Was the Rapper's Fatal Flaw" (Iverem 1996a) and "Tupac Shakur, 25, Rap Performer Who Personified Violence, Dies" (Pareles 1996b), article after article rehashed

Shakur's rap sheet, "his various run-ins with the law" (Wartofsky 1996), including weapons charges, probation violations, assault and batteries, police officer shootings, and eleven months in prison for sexual assault (Shakur himself had been shot five times in 1994). Moreover, while Lennon's murder was the result of the actions of a deranged stalker/fan, Shakur's was framed as part of a "gang war," the East/West Cost feud (Staples 1996).

In fact, many articles focused on the lifestyle frame, with references to an excessive lifestyle that included drinking, drug use, crime, and other "unhealthy" behaviors, implying that such a lifestyle was the "villain" responsible for the death. This frame shows up often for Shakur, Cobain, and Garcia, but in only one Lennon article: "The Beatles not only said they smoked pot, which made it immediately okay with their followers, but said they dropped acid" (Kornheiser and Zito 1980). Ought we to conclude that John Lennon did not lead a hedonistic or otherwise self-destructive lifestyle, while the others did? Perhaps it was not the men's lifestyles that led to differences in use of this frame, but rather the role of that lifestyle in contributing, or not contributing, to their deaths— Shakur's criminal record and violent past, Cobain's suicide, and Garcia's poor health (typically attributed to his excessive lifestyle) versus Lennon's murder by a stalker.

An additional frame in these articles, the tortured artist, was completely missing from articles on Jerry Garcia, scarce in the Lennon and Shakur articles, but abundant in the Cobain coverage. That nearly half of the Cobain articles used this frame is likely due to his having killed himself. Speculation on his psychological condition could offer answers as to why he would take his own life. "Cobain himself had acknowledged using drugs to find relief fr_m the pressures of fame and the depression that plagued him" (Kurt 1994). Still other articles described Cobain's childhood and his parents' divorce when he was eight years old. He was "a shy teenager" whose "father had forced him to pawn his guitar and join the Navy" (Harrington and Leiby 1994). In the few references to John Lennon's troubled past, "the unresolved personal problems of his childhood" were often mentioned, as was the notion that his albums "included songs that attempted to exorcise his childhood traumas" (Palmer 1980).

Although used less frequently, the frames of lifestyle and tortured artist also identified villains. These are crucial frames for our purposes, in that they appear to be directly related to the manner in which the musician died—neither was used extensively to cover John Lennon's murder, something over which he had no control. However, Cobain, Garcia, and Shakur were presented as having some control over their own deaths, which we were told resulted in part from an excessive lifestyle (e.g., drug use, violence) or, in Cobain's case, a decision made to escape a "tortured" life.

Journalistic Practice

While there were some notable similarities in the coverage of the deaths of Lennon, Cobain, Shakur, and Garcia, the differences appear to be in part related to the way each man died and in part rooted in journalistic practices, generational identity, and genre. In the case of John Lennon, journalists seem to have abandoned tenets of objectivity and mourned along with their audience—they too had lost their idol, and together they mourned their lost youth. On the other hand, most journalists felt no personal loss at the death of Kurt Cobain and Tupac Shakur, and so they were more critical (although not necessarily more objective) in their coverage of their deaths—a criticism that transferred to Generation X and gangsta rap respectively. For example, in a *New York Times* editorial, Brent Staples said, "It has become clear that gangsta rap and its trappings are culturally poisonous and that the companies that exploit them are bloodsuckers" (1996).

A letter to the editor responding to Cobain's death accurately sums up what appears to be the pervading theme of newspaper coverage of his death versus Lennon's: "Lennon's death was a tragedy, whereas Cobain's death was a sad, self-inflicted premature ending" (Mackie 1994). On the other hand, the coverage of Garcia's death took a middle ground—perhaps the respectful mourning that would accompany the death of a family member. Thus, both the cause of death and the journalists' personal feelings (or lack of feelings) about the musician and his music genre contributed to the frames they chose.

Our analysis is not without its shortcomings. A fuller picture of how the print media framed these celebrity deaths would need to include newspapers from around the country as well as magazines, in particular music publications such as *Rolling Stone*. Furthermore, journalists' race, class, and gender almost certainly inform their coverage of events and people, and future studies of this topic could address such demographics. Such a comprehensive picture would contribute to a more in-depth understanding of the links between journalistic practice, popular music, and loss.

Notes

1. One way the news media construct "myth and memory" is through the creation and application of frames—"central organizing idea[s] for making sense of relevant events and suggesting what is at issue" (Gamson 1989, 157). Accord-

ing to Gamson, frames consist of "metaphors, catch-phrases, appeals to principle, and the like" (1988, 165). One way in which journalists successfully construct frames is through referent images—images, ideas, and beliefs that the public already holds (Binder 1993). Referent images can be conjured through written words or pictures to strengthen the impact of media frames; they are what allow the reader to associate the content of an article with the intended perspective. Given that media frames "organize the world both for journalists who report it and, in some important degree, for us who rely on their reports" (Gitlin 1980, 7), frame theory is ideal for analyzing media coverage of celebrity deaths, notably the creation of "myth and memory."

We wanted to use the same database for all three deaths, the Lexis-Nexis Academic Universe, which includes full text citations only from the *Washington Post* and the *New York Times* for the time of John Lennon's death. These two newspapers are among the "Big Four" that determine the agenda for other newspapers (Johnson 1985).

2. Although letters to the editor are not written by newspaper staffers, newspapers decide which letters get published. They write headlines for letters and, at times, edit them. Such letters contribute to the general narrative constructed in these newspapers and are what Kitch (1999, 22) calls "the final voice to speak at the memorial service."

3. Fogo's eight-year study analyzed editorials, commentaries, features, and letters to the editor. Although he did not analyze "straight news" reports of Lennon's murder, his work provides a useful comparison.

References

Ali, L. (1994). Kurt Cobain screamed out our angst. *New York Times,* 17 April.

Anders, G. (1994). "This is what not to do." *Washington Post,* 9 April, sec. B.

Binder, A. (1993). Constructing racial rhetoric: Media depictions of harm in heavy metal and rap music. *American Sociological Review* 58: 753–67.

Blumenfeld, L. (1994). The suicide that spoke to a generation. *Washington Post,* 9 April, sec. B.

Carroll, K. (1996). Tupac's squandered gift. *Washington Post,* 22 September, sec. C.

Constable, P. (1996). Rapper dies of wounds from shooting. *Washington Post,* 14 September, sec. A.

Coupland, D. (1994). Letter from a fan. *Washington Post,* 9 April, sec. B.

Crowds of Lennon fans gather quickly at the Dakota and hospital. (1980). *New York Times,* 9 December, sec. B.

Egan, T. (1994). Kurt Cobain, hesitant poet of "grunge rock," dead at 27. *New York Times,* 9 April, sec.A.

Fogo, F. (1994). *I read the news today: The social drama of John Lennon's death.* Lanham, Md.: Rowman and Littlefield.

Freedland, J. (1994). Generation hex. *Washington Post,* 24 April, sec. G.

Fuller, R. P. (1996) Free for all. Letter to the editor. *Washington Post,* 21 September, sec. A.

Gamson, W. A. (1988). The 1987 distinguished lecture: A constructionist approach to mass media and public opinion. *Symbolic Interaction* 11, 2: 161–74.

———. (1989). News as framing: Comments on Graber. *American Behavioral Scientist* 33, 2: 157–61.

Gamson, W. A., and A. Modigliani. (1989). Media discourse and public opinion on nuclear power: A constructionist approach. *American Journal of Sociology* 95, 1: 1–37.

Gitlin, T. (1980). *The whole world is watching.* Berkeley: University of California Press.

Gold, B. (1980). What does "gun control" mean to you? *Washington Post,* 18 December, sec. E.

Grateful Dead canceling tour. (1995). *New York Times,* 16 August, sec. C.

Haberman, C. (1980). Silent tribute to Lennon's memory is observed throughout the world. *New York Times,* 15 December, sec. A.

Harper, M. (1994). Names and faces. *Washington Post,* 25 April, sec. G.

Harrington, R. (1995). Dead end. *Washington Post,* 10 August, sec. C.

Harrington, R., and R. Leiby. (1994). Nirvana singer found dead. *Washington Post,* 9 April, sec. A.

Iverem, E. (1996a). A death as real as it gets. *Washington Post,* 14 September, sec. C.

———. (1996a). Verses of sorrow for Shakur. *Washington Post,* 23 September, sec. D.

Jeffrey, M. (1980). A forgotten legacy of John Lennon. Letter to the editor. *New York Times,* 29 December, sec. A.

Johnson, J. W. (1985). Some newspaper advice from Tom Winship. *Editor & Publisher,* 7 December, 26.

Kingwell, M. (1998). Ten steps to the creation of a modern media icon. http://www.adbusters.org/magazine/20/kingwell.html. Accessed 19 January 1999.

Kitch, C. L. (1999). Telling "everyone's story" through celebrities: Mourning, memorial, and meaning in American newsmagazines. Paper presented at the International Communication Association meeting, San Francisco, May.

Kornheiser, T., and T. Zito. (1980). Lennon: Always in front. *Washington Post,* 10 December, sec. A.

Kurt Cobain's jagged trip through depression. (1994). *Washington Post,* 14 April, sec. C.

Lipsitz, G. (1998). The hip hop hearings. In *Generations of youth: Youth cultures and history in twentieth-century America,* ed. J. Austin and M. N. Willard, 395–411. New York: New York University Press.

Mackie, C. (1994). Kurt Cobain: "Eternal sullenness." Letter to the editor. *New York Times,* 1 May, sec. 2.

Marriott, M. (1996). At a ceremony for Shakur, appeals for peace. *New York Times,* 23 September, sec. B.

Mazzarella, S. R. (1995). "The voice of a generation": Media coverage of the suicide of Kurt Cobain. *Popular Music and Society* 19, 2: 49–68.

McCarthy, C. (1995). '60s spirit goes beyond dead values. *Washington Post,* 22 August, sec. C.

McLellan, J., R. Harrington, J. LeMoyne, and J. A. Miller. (1980). John Lennon 1940–1980. *Washington Post,* 10 December, sec. D.

Meyrowitz, J. (1994). The life and death of media friends: New genres of intimacy and mourning. In *American heroes in a media age,* ed. S. J. Drucker and R. S. Cathcart, 62–81. Cresskill, N.J.: Hampton Press.

Milloy, C. (1996). At a loss over Shakur's two faces. *Washington Post,* 15 September, sec. B.

Mortensen, C. A. (1995). Jerry Garcia didn't inspire us to use drugs. Letter to the editor. *New York Times,* 21 August, sec. A.

Palmer, R. (1980). Lennon known both as author and composer. *New York Times,* 9 December, sec. B.

Pareles, J. (1995a). He let his music do the talking. *New York Times,* 20 August, sec. 2.

———. (1995b). Jerry Garcia of Grateful Dead, icon of 60's spirit, dies at 53. *New York Times,* 10 August, sec. A.

———. (1996a). In one death, mirrors of our times . . . *New York Times,* 22 September, sec. 2.

———. (1996b). Tupac Shakur, 25, rap performer who personified violence, dies. *New York Times,* 14 September, sec. 1.

Prochnau, B. (1980). A strange young man who stopped the music. *Washington Post,* 10 December, sec. A.

Rich, F. (1980). Growing up with the Beatles. *New York Times,* 14 December, sec. 2.

———. (1994). Far from Nirvana. *New York Times,* 14 April, sec. A.

Rockwell, J. (1980). Leader of a rock group that helped define a generation. *New York Times,* 9 December, sec. B.

Staples, B. (1996). Editorial notebook: How long can rap survive? *New York Times,* 22 September, sec. 4.

Stephney, B. (1996). Rap star's death highlights harsher reality. Letter to the editor. *New York Times,* 18 September, sec. A.

Trafford, A. (1995). Advice for the anti-smokers: Take a message from Garcia. *Washington Post,* 15 August, sec. Z

Walters, R. (1980). Paperback talk. *New York Times,* 28 December, sec. 7.

Wartofsky, A. (1996). Gangsta life and death. *Washington Post,* 16 September, sec. D.

Weil, M., J. L. Rowe, J. Wadler, and M. Sager. (1980). Former Beatle John Lennon slain in N.Y. *Washington Post,* 9 December, sec. A.

Zane, J. P. (1995). A look into Jerry Garcia's future. *New York Times,* 13 August, sec. 4.

CODA

14

Fragments of a Sociology of Rock Criticism

Simon Frith

1

For most of the 1980s I was a quality rock critic. First on the London *Sunday Times* and then on the *Observer* I had weekly space on the arts pages to review concerts, monthly space to review records. I was the first person to be titled "*Sunday Times* rock critic." I displaced the paper's all-purpose music writer, Derek Jewell, who was now confined to pop reviews (Frank Sinatra, the easier listening end of jazz), and I had the power to decide where the pop/rock divide lay (Derek was welcome to Pink Floyd; I took Shirley Bassey). At the time, though, what interested me was not the problematic distinction between rock and pop but how my job compared to that of the paper's other critics. I remember getting a memo, sent to "all music critics," saying that as CDs were replacing vinyl records, the *Sunday Times* would supply us with CD players. When I called up for mine, I was told that the offer did not apply to me: A rock critic was not a music critic. Fair enough (and CDs were a classical norm well before they were commonplace in rock), but this did make me think about the way in which the *Sunday Times*'s critical hierarchy worked. When arts page space was squeezed by late ads, my words were usually the first to go, even though such ads were often for rock records—one reason why the paper had decided to use a specialist rock critic to begin with.

The critical map I then sketched looked something like the following.

235

Music/Art Critics

Critics of classical music and fine arts had more space assigned than I, rarely had copy cut, and were never chopped out altogether (as I might be). More interestingly (given my own experience of combining rock writing with a university career), their critical authority was essentially academic. Their reviews drew on the assumed knowledge and shared language of the classical/art worlds themselves. A professional artist or classical musician is someone who (unlike an "amateur" performer or "primitive" artist) has been trained, has graduated from a conservertoire or art school; professional artists and musicians work in and on an agreed account of musical tradition or art history; they subscribe to institutional principles of musical analysis or artistic technique. The critics subscribe to the same principles. They have mostly themselves been to music or art schools; they regard themselves as part of these worlds (compare the way in which rock critics routinely scoff at academic rock work). To make a living as a classical music or art critic means not just doing journalism, but writing program and catalogue notes, promoting concerts and curating exhibitions, serving on grant-giving committees, teaching part-time. For British music critics it means broadcasting on the BBC's classical radio station, Radio 3. The acerbic Hans Keller, one of Britain's most influential postwar music critics, was a BBC employee who wrote academic studies and weekly journalism; my classical colleague from the *Observer*, Nicholas Kenyon, edited an academic journal, went from the *Observer* to be head of Radio 3, and now runs the BBC Proms, the world's biggest festival of live classical music.

For these writers, critical authority is based on qualifications granted by the music/art worlds themselves. Their job is to explain that world to the lay public; they are on the artists' side. There are obvious curmudgeonly critics who take on the role of denouncing the new in the name of the old, but twentieth-century music and art criticism was a key feature of modernism, and even in postmodern times it is the critics' job to explain the inexplicable, whether work by Cornelius Cardew or Damien Hirst. No other critics work in quite this way except, perhaps, writers on dance. By the time I was a rock critic in the 1980s, jazz criticism had something of the same approach, but while some British jazz critics were players and teachers (like Graham Collier), the jazz world was not academic in the same way as the classical world.[1] And rock criticism had long marked out a different approach for itself—the early attempts by classical critics like the *Times*'s William Mann to apply their analytic terms to Beatles music were seen to miss the point. The most interesting question for me was not why classical music and fine-art critics worked in these ways, but why newspapers still employed them. Not for the advertising revenue they generated; not for the readership they attracted; rather, it seemed, for the prestige: The *Sunday Times* was thus associated with high culture even if most of its readers cared not a jot.[2]

Theatre Critics

There is no doubt that theatre critics have far more influence than other arts writers on the commercial success or failure of what they review. This is because of the peculiarities of the theatre itself—new stage plays cannot be sampled by readers for themselves like records, TV series, or books; their success depends on some sort of public response (unlike works of art, which need attract only one buyer). But it gives the theatre critic a kind of kudos, a public notoriety that other critics lack (the *New York Times* theatre critic always has some public name recognition, for example; his critical colleagues do not). When I was at the *Sunday Times,* the theatre critic was the poet and war reporter James Fenton, and he was clearly central to the paper's reputation for arts coverage. Fenton was an established literary figure, but he was not an academic, and, in general, theatre critics' expertise is as theatre buffs rather than theatre scholars. They do not come from the theatre world itself but identify with it. Britain's most famous postwar theatre critic, the *Observer*'s Kenneth Tynan, thus ended up working for Laurence Olivier at the National Theatre; Michael Billington, the *Guardian*'s long-serving theatre man, has written the definitive study of Harold Pinter.

Such critics are not academics, but their work is essential reading in academic theatre studies courses. Their authority comes from the sheer number of theatre productions that they have seen (in Britain, theatre critics have longer careers on a newspaper than have other arts writers) and from the passion of their commitment to a form that is continually under threat from new media. Theatre critics are read more than classical music or art critics, not because readers are very likely to go to the plays they cover, but because play reviewing is more like news reporting: An opening night in the West End or on Broadway remains more of an event than a new gallery exhibition or the London leg of a global rock tour.

As journalists, theatre critics are most like sportswriters: They come to the job as theatre/sports lovers, usually from a young age; they establish reputations, which grow with accumulated experience; they become intimates with the players (ghosting their biographies); they are moralists, doing their best to defend the true values of the theatre or the sport from the corrupting effects of commerce and television, charlatans, and cynics.

Book Critics

The expertise of book criticism is straightforward. Nonfiction books are reviewed either by academics (history, biography, science) or practitioners (politics, war); fiction is reviewed by novelists, poetry by poets. The issue here is not the reviewer but the reviewed. When I was at the *Observer* with Jon Savage, we tried, with no success, to get the books editor to cover cultural studies, pop studies, social theory, books of interest to rock fans. Like other newspapers, the *Observer* planned its book pages around publisher rather than reader interest. Books on the list of mainstream trade publishers were reviewed; those from academic or small presses were not. Literary editors' values have not changed much for a hundred years.[3]

Film Critics

Film critics were the first to develop the review as an uncluttered consumer guide. What film critics write is of little interest to filmmakers (few newspaper film critics know or care much about the film production process) or to film scholars. Film critics (unlike theatre critics) are not committed to a particular artistic practice or tradition. Their job is to answer a simple question: Should I go and see this film or not? Film critics watch new releases on behalf of their readers, and arts editors have two ideas about who might do this best: On the one hand, they choose critics as somehow representative of the readers themselves (young, middlebrow, female, or whatever); on the other hand, they choose film fanatics, people who would go to every movie anyway, whether they are being paid or not. The value of the latter is that they can place every new release, explain to readers how it relates to all the other films they might have seen. In Britain, then, film critics tend to be either smart young writers at an early moment of their career (which makes film criticism something like TV criticism) or aging film buffs whose tastes are trusted (which makes film criticism something like theatre criticism). At certain moments of film history (the Tarantino effect), the film buffs are thought to be out of touch with readers' tastes and are replaced.

In the 1990s, film was increasingly treated on arts pages as a young person's medium, and two aspects of film coverage became even more obvious. First, there is a clear contrast between film features (written under PR influence to plug a new release) and film reviews. It is now commonplace to read an article extolling a new film on one page and a review panning the same film on the next page. This is a trend that is obvious in rock criticism too. Second, there remains remarkably little exchange between academic film theory and newspaper film writing, even though film studies is by now a solidly established university subject. Film critics do not so much scoff at film theory as ignore it. Ideas filter through anyway (auteurism, film noir, etc.), but for all the efforts of the British Film Institute to promote a single British film culture, the worlds of filmmaking, film watching, and film studying remain quite separate.

TV Critics

There are two kinds of TV critic. In the upmarket press, TV critics are primarily entertainers, employed for their writing skills and using a TV column as a site on which to be funny, reflect on the state of the world, or both. Programs are not so much criticized as used as topics of conversation. In the downmarket press, the TV writer functions as a gossip (news of the soaps and the stars) and a man or woman of the people, recommending programs "the people" might like, scorning the highbrow and the pretentious. Not for nothing did the most successful such populist TV critic, the *Sun*'s Gary Bushell, start his reviewing life championing "oi" bands in *Sounds*. Most TV coverage in the press, in fact, is devoted to listings and previews, to capsule criticism in advance. TV critics make no claim to a superior understanding of television; they do not see anything we cannot. We read them because they make us laugh or describe a soap incident we missed. A good review in an upmarket paper can be a boost for program makers who have not otherwise much of a viewing audience to boast of. Extensive coverage in downmarket papers is part of the process through which people become TV personalities. But TV critics are not expected to know anything about TV production or TV policy or TV theory. They are interested only in what the viewer, like them, sees on the screen.[4]

Rock Critics

In the 1980s, newspapers employed rock critics to attract younger readers and generate advertising. I was approached by the *Sunday Times* as someone who clearly knew the rock scene (I had been part of the editorial collective of *Let It Rock*, a columnist on *Melody Maker*) and could make sense of it to outsiders (I wrote for the *New Statesman* and *New Society*). Britain's first pop critics in the 1960s (Nik Cohn in *Queen*, George Melly in the *Observer*, Colin MacInnes in *New Society*) were essentially sociological critics, reporting back from exotic teen scenes to a bemused adult readership, and there was still something left of this in the 1980s. But I was also expected to be a straight consumer guide (like the film critic) and to place performers in a musical/ideological tradition (like the theatre critic). I was not employed as a musicologist: Detailed analysis of what a rock musician actually did would have been cut by the subeditors as pretentious. And my academic interest in rock, in its political economy, seemed equally irrelevant to the immediate assessment of, say, Kirk Brandon's Spear of Destiny. In retrospect, it is not surprising that I felt quite apart from the *Sunday Times*'s other critics. What they did was not what I did. I occupied a quite different writing world.

2

Sometime in the mid-1970s I wrote an article with a friend, Kevin Buckley, for a reggae fanzine called *Pressure Drop*. It was a report on the reggae scene in Coventry, where I then lived, and described in somewhat breathless detail the musical network that was about to become the Specials, Selecter, and the Two Tone label. I have rarely written about a phenomenon before rather than after the event, and this is still one of my favorite pieces, if only for its naiveté.

Fanzines are central to the history of rock criticism both as places in which writers are freed from the commercial pressures of either the record or the publishing business and as the most effective way of putting together new taste and ideological musical communities. Paul Williams's *Crawdaddy!* was in effect a fanzine (Jann Wenner's *Rolling Stone* was not), and much of the most influential early rock writing (not least by Lester Bangs) appeared in Greg Shaw's *Who Put the Bomp*. But there are different kinds of do-it-yourself publishing.

Ideological Magazines

Ideological magazines champion a particular sort of music in terms of its supposed political or social meaning. Rock was first shaped ideologically by writers in the underground press—rock 'n' roll was part of a broader libertarian or socialist argument (there is a continuity here with Dave Marsh's *Rock 'n' Roll Confidential*). But subsequent musical movements have been defined by rock fanzines as such—Pete Frame's *Zig Zag* (which in the 1970s first put together the idea of alternative rock), Mark P's *Sniffin' Glue* (which defined British punk), *Boy's Own*, the magazine that constructed British dance-club culture in the late 1980s. Fanzine arguments feed into the mainstream of rock criticism either directly through the writers themselves (so that Simon Reynolds and David Stubbs of the high-theoretical 1980s fanzine, *Monitor*, went on to work for *Melody Maker*) or in what one might call semi-fanzines, commercially sold magazines with an uncommercial sensibility, like *New York Rocker*, the magazine for which I most enjoyed writing, or the *Wire*, the only music magazine I now still buy.

Collectors' Magazines

In Britain, collectors' magazines were the earliest forms of musical fanzine, part of Britain's jazz and blues scenes in the 1940s and 1950s. All musical genres have such magazines (the most flourishing British webzines are those devoted to 1970s progressive rock groups); unlike the ideological 'zines, collectors' mags are less concerned to create or critique a scene than to celebrate its history (see Atton 2001). Some collectors' magazines, at some times, have enough readers to be commercially available, from *Blues Unlimited* to *Straight No Chaser*. They are organized around information rather than polemic, but as their raison d'être is to make unknown acts or records well known, to rescue forgotten performers from oblivion, collectors' magazines do tend to write against the fashion-driven profit-taking logic of the mainstream music business. Their editors often also work as specialist deejays, radio broadcasters, shopkeepers, importers, label bosses.

Personal Magazines

While nearly all fanzines depend on the energy of a single individual, some articulate an individual sensibility exclusively—Jon Savage and Paul Morley, for example, published their own such titles before being employed by *Sounds* and *NME,* and these days my favorite reading is Frank Kogan's *Why Music Sucks,* which entirely reflects his concerns, even if through the responses of his various contributors. (*WMS* has become much more occasional since Kogan himself became a regular *Village Voice* rock writer.)

The joy of fanzines from a writer's point of view is that one does not have to answer to an editor's or record company's view of what matters: One does not have to sell a story. The problem is that one does not get paid. But the key to fanzine culture, what is common to all the various titles, is the assumption that there is no difference between reader and writer (this is what links rock fanzines to the original science fiction fanzines). In magazines like *Who Put the Bomp* and *Zig Zag,* letters and articles had just the same status; part of the attraction of collectors' magazines is the nuggets of information that come in from unlikely sources. Fanzines are a material realization of a rock critical utopia, a democratic conversation between music lovers, a social celebration of a particular kind of musical attention and commitment.

3

I was once employed (by a maverick and short-lived literary editor at the *Guardian*) to review novels. Rather to my shame, I discovered that I got a thrill at finding myself quoted on the back of paperbacks. I did not exactly write with an eye to a back-cover sound bite (I was not in the job long enough), but I certainly understood the temptation to do so. These days I chair the judges of Britain's annual Mercury Music Prize, which means being sent around 150 CDs every June. Many of these come with the equivalent of the book-cover blurb: labels stuck on the CD box with various endorsements. These quotes, though, are always credited to a magazine or newspaper, not to a critic or writer, and come with a star rating. Rock criticism is here subsumed to the sales process.

Wearing my academic hat, I have always known that rock critics were part of the rock business. There has always been a regular flow of music journalists into music PR, and while writer/PR relations can be fraught (we call them begging for a hot ticket/advance release; they call us begging for coverage of a new or failing act), both sides understand their mutual dependence. Indeed, one discovery I was surprised to make once I got on every record company's press list was how much rock coverage is lifted straight from the press release, how tightly PR departments control the arts-page rock agenda. When did you last read a rock-star feature that was not tied to an upcoming concert or new release?

I do not doubt that the routinization of the rock sales process in the last twenty years has meant among other things the increasingly efficient targeting of a record's likely market. What has perhaps been less obvious is the increasing use of rock coverage in newspapers' and magazines' own branding. When I was on the *Sunday Times,* I soon realized that a good press office was one that did not waste my time, that understood my tastes and readership and pitched me records and concert tickets accordingly. Just as record companies knew how to push teen acts to *Smash Hits,* metal acts to *Kerrang!,* guitar bands to *NME,* so they were now learning what might be a *Sunday Times* act, a *Time Out* record, a *Cosmo* star. Such matching of taste and publication soon resonated with the ways in which magazine and arts editors were themselves seeking an edge in an increasingly competitive market. Branding in this context meant associating a publication with a genre; what attracted readers was who was written about, not who was doing the writing. Nick Kent is probably the only remaining British rock writer to get a cover credit (for his occasional pieces for *Mojo*), and even such a one-time writer-friendly magazine as *NME* has now gone the way of *Smash Hits:* It no longer employs personality critics with scattershot opinions about everything, but rather edits every contributor into a house style expressing house opinions.[5] What matters for the editor of *NME* as for the editor of the *Guardian*'s Friday Review section is that rock coverage reinforces the *NME/Guardian* brand (and not coincidentally these two titles run Britain's most successful magazine/newspaper web sites).

From this perspective, the "corrupting" effect of commerce on criticism is not that bad reviews are pulled because they might affect advertising revenue or PR cooperation, but that they are written with reference not to what the music sounds like but to what it stands for. Once upon a time, this still meant an argument: The newspaper rock critic, at least, was an intermediary between a musical or subcultural world and a general readership. Now, though, the rock critic writes as an insider for insiders: It is this sense that they are part of the latest hip happening that newspapers want (which is one reason, I think, why there was virtually no good criticism of 1990s dance music).

4

When I was still writing for the *Village Voice,* back in the 1990s, I got into a spat with the feminist critic Evelyn McDonnell. She had written an article about the women writers left out of the rock critical pantheon.[6] I suggested that this was to accept the terms if not the membership of that pantheon and thus a particularly male view of rock criticism. Maybe the importance of women rock writers was not that they were just as good as the men, but that they were engaged in a different project.[7] When I wrote for *Creem* in the mid-1970s, for example, nearly all my dealings were with the women who effectively ran it (the then editor, Susan Whitall, was not mentioned in McDonnell's piece). I always thought this was the reason why *Creem*'s role in the making of mainstream U.S. hard rock was to both glamorize and laugh at it; *Creem* just did not take rock as seriously as did a boys' paper like *Rolling Stone*. The gender nature of the pop/rock divide has often been noted, but, in material terms, it is a false distinction. A&R departments (mostly male) may have tense dealings with marketing departments (mostly female), as Keith Negus has well shown, but a successful rock act depends on both of them, just as performers' visual images are as significant for their star quality as the sound of their recordings—rock photographers (often women) have a place in rock history alongside studio engineers (mostly men). And from a reader's perspective, the latent pomposity of rock critics needs the constant lancing of a pop sensibility. This is one reason why Julie Burchill had such an impact on *NME* in the 1970s and why *Smash Hits* was so refreshing in the post-punk era of New Romanticism. It has always been ironic that the rock critics who give voice to rock's anti-commercial ideology are, in fact, part of the promotion process.

McDonnell found this argument patronizing, an unsubtle way of saying that women should confine themselves to making the house look good while their men go out and do the real work, but I don't think she appreciated my real distaste for the self-importance of rock critics. I found the *Voice*'s annual Pazz & Jop poll deeply depressing, for example, both for its earnest consensus and for the tone of the critical quotes. Nearly every rock critic in the United States, it seemed, wrote with the same self-righteousness. This is, I suppose, an aspect of what it means to be a critic. It takes a certain arrogance to pass judgment on a record, a thickness of skin to proclaim one's views in print. But for rock writers, critical judgment is too often the same thing as the presentation of self. I have occasionally taught journalism student seminars on rock writing. To prepare for it, participants have to review a record I assign. I always choose something poppy: Cliff Richard, Robbie Williams, Melanie C. The students almost always slag these records off—not for what they sound like (there is often little evidence that the record has been played), but for what the artists represent: The review is written to show the writer's own rock credibility. This is to pose as a rock critic rather than to be one, and it is a pose one can find in student newspapers across the country. Writing about rock here means defining an in-group, keeping the wrong sorts of sounds/people out, rather than attempting to draw people in, to expand a record's reach.

The resulting macho prose draws on the fantasy rather than reality of rock criticism (most rock critics are in real life rather weedy), the fantasy that to write about rock is somehow to live its lifestyle. In practice, most critics are not paid well enough for hedonistic excess, and to survive as a freelance means organizing one's life efficiently enough to meet tight deadlines and turn out copy to order. Lester Bangs is rock's most celebrated writer because of his lifestyle, not his critical acumen (it is difficult to imagine someone writing a biography of Greil Marcus, Robert Christgau, or even Dave Marsh). The only British writer of comparable interest, Nick Kent, is admired for the same reason, his supposedly wasted habits and friendships with the stars.

What is at issue here is a sublimated version of the rock critic's envy of those stars, but the source of that envy is quite complex; it is not simply, as the cliché would have it, that people only start writing about music when they realize they cannot themselves make it. Most critics share with fans a yearning that rock live up to the demands first made on it in the late, liberatory sixties. Rock acts are judged against a kind of Platonic ideal, whether in terms of intention (and not selling out) or delivery (and the transcendent live rock moment). Even as I write this, I read a *Guardian* critic on Kathryn Williams, one of the year's Mercury nominees. The critic enjoys her performance but finds it, in the end, a little bland (a favorite critical term). Williams is not really "dangerous" like PJ Harvey. I read this, nod (I have undoubtedly written many similar reviews in my time), and then pause for thought. What does "dangerous" mean here? Does Polly Harvey sometimes harm her fans? "Dangerous" seems an excessive term to describe music that is, perhaps, emotionally unsettling or physically uncomfortable.

Such excess is a critical norm: Rock is treated as if it is—or should be —a constant source of upheaval, and if in reality the rock business is highly rational this only adds to the argument that good rock should somehow rage against the machine. The problem is to make this argument credibly—the critical business is pretty rational too—hence the importance of the myth of Lester Bangs. And there is a further critical difficulty here, another kind of contradiction. Rock criticism is rooted in populism, it necessarily celebrates popular taste, and there has always been a very thin line between populism and anti-intellectualism. How can one display one's anti-intellectual credentials in the very act of being an intellectual? If rock's appeal is taken to be essentially visceral, then so should writing about it be.

I have been a published rock critic for thirty years, and I have rarely been completely happy with what I have written. Looking back, there have been two writers I have envied, critics who have not just changed the way I have listened but also justified rock criticism as a way of illuminating much bigger cultural and social issues. Greil Marcus is sufficiently admired to need no further encomiums here. Britain's best rock critic, Richard Williams, is less well known (he is mentioned nowhere else in this book, for instance).[8] Both Marcus and Williams do something that is surprisingly rare in rock criticism: They listen to the music first and then try to describe and understand it; most everyday critics start from their assumptions of what a sound or group is all about and write about it accordingly. For Marcus, the best rock music illuminates the broad sweep of cultural dreams and self-deceptions; for Williams, it is made by particular people with particular histories in particular places. Either way, their starting point is that the only critical faculty that really matters is the ability to be surprised.

Notes

1. On most arts pages, world music is treated more like classical music than like rock. World-music writing rests on a similar sort of academic authority, and it is not coincidental that the BBC broadcasts world music on the classical Radio 3 rather than on the popular Radios 1 and 2. For further discussion of world music, critics, and the academy, see Frith 2000.

2. For an interesting discussion of arts-page policy fifteen years later, see Scott 1999.

3. On the cultural consequences of such a limited critical policy, see Curran 2000.

4. My remarks here are equally applicable to radio critics. See Garner 2000 and Garfield 1999, entertaining reportage that shows how the BBC now uses the tabloid press to market its deejays.

5. For this argument see Forde (2001, "From Polyglotism to Branding: On the Decline of Personality Journalism in the British Music Press," forthcoming in the new Sage journal, *Journalism Studies*.

6. The article summarized the introduction to Evelyn McDonnell and Ann Powers, eds., *Rock She Wrote: Women Write about Rock, Pop, and Rap* (New York, Delta 1995).

7. It is often noted too that the criticism of black music has been dominated by white critics, from jazz to rap and jungle. But, again, the issue here may not be how and why black writers are excluded from critical debate, but why black music flourishes without needing critics—compare the history of punk and house music.

8. Williams was a key figure in the development of British rock criticism in the pages of *Melody Maker* in the late 1960s. He went on to be *London Times* jazz critic, to edit *Time Out* (and pioneer a serious critical approach to disco), to work in A&R for Island, to write the definitive study of Phil Spector, to present the Old Grey Whistle Test, to return to *Melody Maker* in the late 1970s as editor. He is now chief sports writer for the *Guardian*. Some of his writings on music have been collected in Richard Williams, *Long Distance Call* (London: Aurum Press, 2000).

References

Atton, Chris. (2001). 'Living in the past'? Value discourses in progressive rock fanzines. *Popular Music* 20, 1: 29–46.

Curran, James. (2000). Literary editors, social networks, and cultural traditions. In *Media organizations in society*, ed. Curran, 215–39. London: Arnold.

Forde, E. (2001). From polyglottism to randing: On the decline of personality journalism in the British music press. *Journalism* 2, 1: 23–43.

Frith, Simon. (2000). The discourse of world music. In *Western music and its other*, ed. G. Born and D. Hesmondhalgh, 305–322. Berkeley and Los Angeles: University of California Press.

Garfield, Simon. (1999). *The nation's favorite: The true adventures of Radio 1*. London: Faber and Faber.

Garner, Ken. (2000). Between one medium and another: What the British press says about British radio. *Journal of Radio Studies* 7, 2: 392–409.

Scott, Robert Dawson. (1999). Bridging the cultural gap: How arts journalists decide what gets into the arts and entertainment pages. *Critical Quarterly* 41, 1: 46–55.

The Outro

Chris Nelson

s'pose it stumps none of us anymore, least of all pop culture scholars, when folks wind up everywhere but the places we expect. Of course their journeys, and in particular what they yield, are still fascinating. Take Lester Bangs, smelly rock scribe, proselytizer for Black Sabbath, and a man who aimed his prose not at the ivory tower but the Bowery gutter. The same Mr. Bangs is either the actual subject of, or spiritual informer behind, numerous essays right here in this very tome —which, you'll note by peering at its backside, is published not by a Bowery zine, but by the venerable institution of Temple University Press.

It just so happens that Temple is the very Philadelphia school whose hallowed halls I left before nabbing a master's degree in the early 1990s. Back then I wanted to be a rock scribe myself, I just didn't know it. Night after night, I would ditch Derrida (whose ideas actually seemed pretty punk rock) and head over to the dark confines of McGlinchey's on South Fifteenth, where the bar pushed ninety-cent Yuengling draft porters and the jukebox pumped the Stones' "Dead Flowers." Occasionally I'd carry in something like Nick Tosches's *Hellfire* or Jon Savage's *England's Dreaming,* but mostly I'd pore over Lester's posthumous anthology, *Psychotic Reactions and Carburetor Dung.* You can still see rings on an Iggy essay where my mug sweat onto the page. Some of the pieces—the title work, a draft of a review of Peter Guralnick's *Lost Highway*— have damn near every other sentence underlined, highlighted, bracketed, or scribbled beside, as different bits would boogaloo all over my brain during each read and reread and reread.

Lester ushered me into his psyche, for sure, as well as into and beyond the music. But he also helped me cut into my own core to look around at what was there. His fretting over whether to buy the Count Five's *Psychotic Reaction*—a disc he initially judged as mediocre but that ultimately became the emblem of his addiction for gonzo rock power—mirrored my own urge to discard James Joyce for Chuck Berry. It's not that I thought Joyce wasn't worth the time. Tromping through *Ulysses* and all its attendant handbooks has a certain kinship with poring over liner notes and record guides, so I fell right in. But I came to Joyce and all the others backassward: At the time, they were as close as I knew how to get to rock 'n' roll within the safe confines of academia. Then Lester made it plain for me: Joyce and Johnny B. Goode are equals. "Nothing more nor less than a record," he wrote, "a rock 'n' roll album of the approximate significance of *Psychotic Reaction* . . . could ever pulverize my lobes and turn my floor to wormwood" (*Psychotic Reactions and Carburetor Dung*, 11). What does Joyce do if not pulverize your lobes? Of course, rather than get me high on Joyce, that realization, courtesy of Lester, was a backdoor validation of my instinctual passion for Chuck Berry songs. The light bulb buzzed over my head. If *The Great Twenty-Eight* is just as significant as *Dubliners*, then I'd turn my attention to the *Twenty-Eight.*

Like none of us before and few of us since, Lester Bangs completed the circle of rock writing as triumphantly as Pete Townshend laying waste to his guitar, because Lester's work itself turned our floors to wormwood. Witness the most accurate and invigorating description ever penned of rock salvation, written while Lester was on a U.K. tour with the Clash in 1977:

The politics of rock 'n' roll, in England or America or anywhere else, is that a whole lot of kids want to be fried out of their skins by the most scalding propulsion they can find, for a night they can pretend is the rest of their lives, and whether the next day they go back to work in shops or boredom on the dole or American TV doldrums in Mom 'n' Daddy's living room nothing can cancel the reality of that night in the revivifying flames when for once if only then in your life you were blasted outside of yourself and the monotony which defines most life anywhere at any time, when you supped on lightning and nothing else in the realms of the living or dead mattered at all. (239).

Now couple that skill for distilling the very essence of rock with a lustily led life and you'll see why Lester himself—whose closest stab at the great rock bio was a quick cash history of Blondie—is the subject of Jim DeRogatis's thorough profile, *Let It Blurt: The Life and Times of Lester Bangs, America's Greatest Rock Critic.* Which brings us to the center of this here essay, for it was *Blurt* that drew me down to Chicago's Empty Bottle on 15 April 2000 to consider the state of rock criticism nigh on twenty

years after Lester's death. Bangs, as some folks know, was also a singer, re-
leasing two albums and the single for which DeRogatis's book is named.
DeRo is also a writer-musician, who, outside of his work for the *Chicago
Sun-Times,* is perhaps best known as drummer for the Ex-Lion Tamers, a
Wire cover outfit that opened for their inspirations on a 1987 U.S. tour.
Rather than celebrating the History of Lester with a Borders-boring
reading, DeRo assembled a band with the Mekons' Jon Langford at the
mic to play a set of Bangs's own work and his fave covers.

It seemed appropriate for me to revisit old rituals for the gig, so I
claimed a seat early at the Empty Bottle bar, intent on adding some new
sweat rings to the pages of *Psychotic Reactions and Carburetor Dung.* Soon I
was knee-deep in "The Clash," the same essay in which Lester birthed
the beautiful explanation of rock just quoted. There he was, going on
about righteousness, not sonic goodness, mind you, but a band quality
that's rare in the rock gene pool, and, I might add, in rock writing itself:
"Being righteous means you're more or less on the side of the angels,
waging Armageddon for the ultimate victory of the forces of Good over
the Kingdom of Death . . . working to enlighten others as to their own
possibilities rather than merely sprawling in the muck yodeling about
what a drag everything is" (226).

Amen.

Now, to my mind, rock writing should be utterly righteous. And by that
I mean it should wake us to possibilities, rather than moan about what a
drag things are. I'm not saying that anyone should impose a no-bad-rat-
ings edict—we all gotta call 'em like we see 'em, obviously. But there is
an aesthetic that runs through the best rock criticism that holds as a primary tenet the confident faith that somewhere out there, someone is
making great music. You may not know who it is, or where they are at the
moment they're creating their *Slanted and Enchanted,* and it may take you
a while to find it once they do. But you know that someone is tapping the
emotions that one day will lead to a new *Nevermind* or *It Takes a Nation of
Millions to Hold Us Back.* It's the essence of rock 'n' roll, after all, that anyone can land on the earth and one day create a Count Five or a Bikini
Kill. Beyond faith, just figure the numbers: There are too many Janes
and Joes out there making noise for all of them to be doing crap at once.

I hand you back to Lester, with tinkering: "The righteous [rock critic]
may be rife with lamentations and criticisms of the existing order, but
even if he doesn't have a coherent program for social change he is informed of hope" (226).

How accurately this applies to my vocation as a whole right now I
don't know, but my gut tells me not as much as I'd like. I know from conversations that folks like DeRo's buddy at the *Chicago Tribune,* Greg Kot,
is informed of hope, as are old-school deans like Greil Marcus and Dave

Marsh. But these days there're probably as many music writers as musicians out there, not just in *Rolling Stone, Spin,* the *Village Voice,* and a million other rags, but on a gazillion pro web sites that offer news and opinion without much analysis. That's not to mention living in the average fan, who in some ways is replacing the trusted critic. Armed with a web site, and more importantly, programs like Napster, she or he can witness to the power of the Memphis Goons, then pass around near-CD-quality MP3s to back up the claims. "Who do you trust?" Tom Petty used to ask his audiences. Well, who do you—the snotty scribe who packs reviews with oblique references, or the kid in the dorm room who's happy to let you and your cable modem have at his collection of music?

Maybe it's always been this way, but I get a sense that there are too many of us in the paid profession who pinball between "sprawling in the muck yodeling" and ironic defense. I'm not saying we shouldn't flip our minds around. Lester, for one, was a master of learning to love in hindsight. But these days it feels like many writers second-guess themselves right outta the gate. They may be quick to dump on the Backstreet Boys or Britney Spears, but then they're just as quick to gush with calculating hipsterism about this or that song by the same artists—perhaps for fear of seeming out of step with counterclockwise, uber-cool tastemakers or maybe simply of not having a sense of humor. I hate to echo conservative op-ed types, but the routine smacks of relativism. And unless there's a thoughtful argument behind it, it's mealy-mouthing that ultimately makes readers mistrustful. Or maybe it's fear of looking wrong twenty years down the line, something that Lester apparently never thought about, but that many of us consider now precisely because we all grew up with *Psychotic Reactions and Carburetor Dung.* Whatever the reason, it feels like there are too many Play-Doh opinions where there should be underlying aesthetics—what Lester ID'd in the Clash as "brutal conviction."

Brutal conviction is the lifeblood that charges our innards and shoots sparks in our brains. Without it, how can you proselytize? Because I do believe that proselytizing, preaching the gospel and spreading the good news of whatever your musical bag is, is ultimately what we rock writers are here for. When we really nail it, rock writing, just like the music, shows us part of ourselves, from shiny crowns to warty feet and aching heart between. But beyond the complex analysis, beyond the plain review, we do what we do because there's fire in our guts for schooling others and ourselves, and it burns every bit as hot as the ball that scorches oh so gloriously every time "Louie, Louie" or "Cretin Hop" or "Little Red Corvette" cascades into our ears.

It's really as simple as that. It's as simple as me needing to tell you—indeed it is a need, because I can't be satisfied until I've shared this goodness with someone—that when DeRogatis, Langford, and their cohorts closed out the night with the Velvet Underground's "Sister Ray," it was a glorious moment, bursting with victory, in which the guitars' groove and feedback danced wildly with the lusty grind of the Farfisa and finally DeRo's expert thud, thud, thud on the tom.

More transcendent still—and when I say transcendent I'm thinking of Ralph Ellison talking about the blues "fingering that jagged edge of pain" and somehow, inexplicably, rising above—was "Day of the Dead," Lester's recounting of the day that he learned while driving in a car with his mother that his beloved dad had just burned to death in another city, that's that, don't say a word, shed a tear, end of story, little Lester, go on and grow up now. DeRo draws an insightful picture of that afternoon in his book, but natch, nothing could be as knowing as Lester's own attempt to confront the horror: "Ooh mama, take me away / from that terrible, terrible day / A car of death and the cask enclosing / You've lost yourself and everyone knows it."

Despite the devastating subject, the music isn't mournful but urgent, both on Lester's *Jook Savages on the Brazos* and as DeRo & Co. played it at the Empty Bottle. Langford sang passionately from scribbled crib sheets, dashing each piece of paper to the ground in mock punk triumph, but triumph nonetheless. The guitar lines were bright, giving wind to young Lester's feet as he tries to flee the crushing pain before it defines him for life.

And DeRogatis, quite possibly the only person on the planet who knows all the words to this nearly lost bit of greatness, pushed Lester along on this night, shouting the lyrics while his hulking figure brought stick against kit with punishing blows. There on a tiny stool was a man who found a sense of completeness in not just limning the life of America's greatest rock critic, but who, for a single night, proselytized by example, with brutal conviction, about the fiery righteous music. And in doing so, gave us the hope that our rock writers, too, can be righteous.

About the Contributors

Jeff Chang is senior editor of *Politics* at 360hiphop.com. While backing into a so-called career as a hip-hop journalist, he was a community organizer, a public interest lobbyist, and an indie hip-hop un-mogul. Born and raised in Hawai'i, he is writing a book on the music and politics of the hip-hop generation.

Martin Cloonan is lecturer in adult and continuing education at the University of Glasgow. He has written widely on the politics of popular music in journals such as *Popular Music* and *Popular Music and Society*. His book *Banned! Censorship of Popular Music in Britain: 1967–1992* was published by Arena in 1996.

Kevin Featherly is an editor and correspondent for Newsbytes News Network, part of the Washington Post Company. He is the author of *Guide to Building a Newsroom Web Site* (1998), and has served as an adjunct professor of online journalism at the University of Minnesota.

Mark Fenster earned a Ph.D. from the University of Illinois and a J.D. from Yale Law School, and has taught in communications departments at Indiana University and Shenandoah University. He is the author of *Conspiracy Theories: Power and Secrecy in American Culture* (1999).

Simon Frith is professor of film and media at Stirling University. His most recent book is *Performing Rites: On the Value of Popular Music* (1998). His most recent job as a critic was "Rock Steady" columnist for the *Scotsman*. He chairs the judges of the Mercury Music Prize.

Gestur Gudmundsson holds a Ph.D. in sociology and was educated in Iceland and Denmark. His main research areas are youth culture, rock, and the sociology of education and work. His books include *Let's Rock This Town* (in Danish, 1984), *Rokksaga Islands* (the history of Icelandic rock, in Icelandic, 1990), and two books on the Nordic Model.

Michael Jarrett is professor of English at the Pennsylvania State University, York Campus. He is the series editor of *Sound Matters* (Temple University Press)

253

and the author of *Sound Tracks: A Musical ABC,* vols. 1–3 (Temple, 1998) and *Drifting on a Read: Jazz as a Model for Writing* (1999).

Joli Jensen is professor of communication at the University of Tulsa. Her books include *Redeeming Modernity: Contradictions in Media Criticism* (1990), *The Nashville Sound: Authenticity, Commercialization, and Country Music* (1998), and *Is Art Good for Us? Beliefs about High Culture in American Life* (2002).

Brenda Johnson-Grau is a senior editor at UCLA. She is a member of the editorial board of *Popular Music and Society.* From 1984 to 1990, she edited *Onetwothreefour,* a journal of popular-music studies.

Steve Jones is professor and head of the Department of Communications at the University of Illinois–Chicago. He has authored and edited several books, including *Doing Internet Research, CyberSociety,* and *Virtual Culture.* Jones's interests in technology and policy are evident in his book *Rock Formation: Technology, Music, and Mass Communication* (1992).

Holly Kruse earned a Ph.D. from the Institute of Communications Research at the University of Illinois. Her publications include several journal articles and book chapters about popular music. Currently, she is assistant professor of communication at the University of Tulsa and is working on a book about independent pop and rock music scenes.

Ulf Lindberg, Ph.D., is Swedish lecturer at the Department of Scandinavian Studies, Aarhus University, Denmark. His 1995 dissertation in comparative literature is *Rockens text. Ord, musik och mening* (The rock text: Words, music, and meaning). He is also coauthor of *In Garageland: Rock, Youth, and Modernity* (1995).

Timothy M. Matyjewicz earned a B.A. degree with a dual major in media studies and philosophy from Ithaca College in 1999. He also has an AAS degree in audio/radio production from Cayuga Community College. He began attending graduate school in fall 2000.

Sharon R. Mazzarella (Ph.D., University of Illinois) is associate professor in the Department of Television and Radio at Ithaca College, where she teaches courses in youth culture, media effects, and research methods. She is coeditor of *Growing Up Girls: Popular Culture and the Construction of Identity* (2000) and is writing a book on media framing of Generation X.

Kembrew McLeod is an assistant professor in the Department of Communication Studies at the University of Iowa. He received his Ph.D. in communication from the University of Massachusetts–Amherst. His book *Owning Culture: Authorship, Ownership, and Intellectual Property Law* was published in the Toby Miller–edited series "Popular Culture and Everyday Life" (2001).

Morten Michelsen is assistant professor in the Department of Musicology, University of Copenhagen, Denmark. He received his doctorate in 1998 with the thesis "Language and Sound in the Analysis of Rock Music" and has written in the field of popular music aesthetics and analysis.

Chris Nelson has written for Sonicnet.com since 1995. He is researching a book on the Riot Grrrl movement and writing "Campaign Shoutin'," Sonicnet's weekly rock column. He received the Scripps Howard National Journalism Award for Investigative Reporting on the Web for his series on Woodstock 2000.

Robert B. Ray is director of film and media studies at the University of Florida, where he is professor of English. He is the author of *A Certain Tendency of the Hollywood Cinema, 1930–1980, The Avant-Garde Finds Andy Hardy,* and *How a Film Theory Got Lost, and Other Mysteries in Cultural Studies.* He is also a member of the Vulgar Boatmen.

Thomas Swiss is Center for the Humanities Professor of English and director of the Web-Assisted Curriculum at Drake University. He is the author of two collections of poems, *Rough Cut* (1997) and *Measure* (1986). He is the coeditor of a number of books, including *Mapping the Beat: Cultural Theory and Popular Music* (1998) and *The World Wide Web and Contemporary Theory: Magic, Metaphor, and Power* (2000).

Hans Weisethaunet is associate professor of ethnomusicology at the Grieg Academy, University of Bergen, and earned his Ph.D. from the University of Oslo, Norway. His dissertation, *The Performance of Everyday Life: The Gaine of Nepal,* was published by Scandinavian University Press.

Index

257